Malaprop Jones

Alan Potter

Table of Contents

Chapter One

The young woman's distress was clear for all to see. She cried, and sobbed deeply and, in my view, was almost inconsolable. I knew she was in pain but couldn't figure out just how much, so I waited, watching her closely. I did not know whether a hug and a shoulder to cry on would fit the bill in this case. Would it even help? Would it be acceptable in this politically correct day and age?

I considered that it probably would not be sufficient to even scratch the surface of her distress. I was certain that I had no way to alleviate the grief that she must be experiencing now. After all, I had never lost someone so close to me as this poor thing. On balance, I decided that the hug would not help even if it were acceptable.

She sat alone on the settee, and her grief and subsequent distress became more and more animated. Her sobs grew louder, and between these audible signs of her grief, her voice began to vent her innermost feelings and her clear disbelief at its cause. The one question to which she demanded an answer was the one question to which I did not and could not have an answer. The police equally had been reluctant to say why he had died; neither would they even hint at the how. We all stood there dumbfounded, trying to come up with an answer to her question. Why had her beloved husband of just three years been snatched from her life? That question bothered me as Lyn's friend, so it was too painful to fathom what effect it was having on her.

I just had to do something to help Lyn come to terms with what had happened and deal with her grief at this terrible, terrible news. As her best friend, I had been asked by the police to sit with her, so it was down to me. They had started this whole process by informing her of the death of her husband, and now it was my turn. After all, there seemed little point in my being there if all I was going to do was sit and watch her express her grief and her distress increase. Doing nothing was not an option; I had to be more useful in this situation.

I did not think that telling her that he was now with God and the angels who would look after him would help any. I did not believe that she would take any comfort from that for one moment. I am not even sure that she believes in God, let alone the angels. I did not believe in them either, so how could I hope to convince her that he was now safe?

I crossed to the settee and sat beside her, just out of reach of her flailing arms, which were a clear barrier to any sort of hug. I reached out to touch her hoping that my touch would give some comfort. Instead, she pushed aside my intended comforter with a goodly degree of violence, sending a clear message that she did not want me to come closer. My attempts at lessening her distress seemed to have the opposite effect. If anything, she became more animated, not less.

It was clear that more decisive action was called for. I managed to pass one arm behind her neck and then slip it down to her shoulders. She did her damnedest to extricate herself from the grip I had been able to achieve. Was I succeeding in calming her? Was she finally beginning to trust my embrace? A fist in the face, which took me completely by surprise, told me that I was not. I tightened the handhold which I had achieved and received three or four blows to the side of my head and chest for my troubles.

I knew, or at least I hoped that I knew, that the blows intended no malice but physically, they hurt, and I knew that they hurt and that bruises would follow as sure as night followed day.

I just had to strengthen the foothold, or perhaps more accurately the handhold, which I had achieved, but another well-aimed blow landed on my upper chest and got in the way. Her anger knew no bounds, and her blows had made it obvious. It was clear that the second or two that it took for her to recover before aiming another blow was the only chance I would get. I threw my other arm around her upper body and pulled her into a tighter embrace. I am not sure that it helped her distress, but at least now, her arms could not continue flailing, and her hands were not able to land punches. With her arms locked in my warm embrace, we sat in silence as her emotions began to well up.

Without her arms to emphasise her feelings of grief, her sobs became that much louder. She wept on my chest as I rubbed a comforting hand up and down her back without losing my grip on her arms. This seemed, eventually and gradually, very gradually, to help her sobs to subside.

Suddenly my best friend relaxed into my arms. I thought, at first, that perhaps it was a ruse to get her arms free again. But I maintained my hold on her body, and then it was as if I could feel the tension and at least some of the distress drain from her. The wracking sobs gave way to tears eventually, and this became her sole expression of grief.

Although the tears continued for what seemed like hours, they were surely not longer than half of one of them, and then, eventually, the tears ceased, and the sobs disappeared completely.

My best friend was calmer now. She shifted her position on the settee but was now happy to remain in my arms. She looked deeply into my eyes and whispered, 'Why?'

This indeed was one unfathomable question.

'Why?'

Chapter Two

I remained with my friend for the rest of the night. We talked of this and that, with each of us trying to avoid the one subject that was foremost in our minds – *what happened to her husband?* It seemed as though we had drunk our way through gallons of hot sweet tea, although, in reality, it was considerably less than one gallon. Someone had once told me that hot sweet tea was good for shock, and in truth, it did help but only somewhat.

After a breakfast of scrambled eggs on toast, prepared by yours truly, I told Lyn that I would have to go. After all, it was a weekday, and I did have a living to earn. She protested and begged me to stay a little longer.

'Surely you could take a day off to comfort your best friend. I would if the positions were reversed.'

My best friend found solace in my company, even if we sat for hours without uttering a word. I couldn't bear leaving her alone like this. The pleading expression on her face made my heart melt, and my resolve swiftly followed. Lynda, who preferred to be called Lyn, smiled a little wanly, but it was a smile. She thanked me in a voice just above a whisper.

I washed up the breakfast things, made a fresh pot of coffee, and re-joined Lyn in the lounge. A smile crossed Lyn's face again, which I returned as warmly as I could muster.

Lyn watched me through the steam rising from her mug of black coffee.

'Mal,' she said, 'will you find out why?'

'Why what?' I asked.

'Why David had to die.'

'How the hell can I do that? The police didn't give you any clues, did they?' I asked.

'Well, you investigate things, don't you? Can't you do this much for me?' Lyn asked.

'Well…' I began.

'Well, what? You found out about that break-in, didn't you?' Lyn said.

'What break in?' I asked.

'Surely you remember! The one where the jeweller was stealing his own stock,' she replied.

'Oh, that! That was pure chance.'

'Maybe, but you solved it, didn't you?'

'Well, yes, I suppose so, but that is largely my job, isn't it? Look, Lyn, I am a self-employed insurance adjuster, not a bloody detective,' I said with my voice raised slightly for emphasis.

'I realise that, Mal, but would you? For me?'

I thought long and hard and decided that this vulnerable friend now needed me more than anything else, and I agreed.

'Thank you, Mal. Thank you.'

Where the hell do I start? I had absolutely no idea. I'm not trained for this type of stuff. The police had given neither Lyn nor me any details. Was it a vehicle collision or perhaps manslaughter or even murder; it could, of course, simply have been an accident? Somehow this latter cause did not seem very likely. Surely had it been purely accidental, the police who had called last night would have told Lyn that this was the case. There would not be any reason not to if the death had been an accident. No, it had to be something more serious than that. We can't just call it an accident and wrap the case up. How do I find out what that something was? Clearly, I would have to speak to someone at the police station. There has to be someone in that force who is willing to share more details…

I asked Lyn if either of the officers had left a calling card or a contact number. One of them had, and Lyn handed the card to me and asked if I would make contact on her behalf. I was not particularly eager to point out that she had already asked me to find out what had happened.

She assured me that she would be quite alright to stay on her own. It was something she would have to get used to, I thought.

We hugged lengthily, and I left her to her own thoughts and feelings.

Chapter Three

In the small bedroom, which I used as an office, I started a log of the case I had taken on *pro bono*. I had to do this for my best friend.

After ten minutes or so, I was satisfied with the notes I had made and reached for my office telephone.

A welcoming voice answered my call to the number on the police calling card.

'City police, can I help you?'

'Yes, I am calling on behalf of Lyn Kendall. She has…' I began.

'Ah yes. Just a moment, please,' the voice said.

After a delay of a couple of minutes, a male voice came on the line.

'Mrs Kendall, how can I help?' the voice enquired.

'No. I am not Lyn Kendall; I am her friend Mal Jones.'

'Is that Miss or Mrs Jones?'

It seemed a strange opening question to me. Why did it matter? I decided to return the compliment.

'Who am I speaking to then?' I asked with a grin on my face.

'I am Detective Chief Inspector Carterford. How can I help you, Mrs Jones?'

'It is Miss Jones, not Mrs. The reason I am calling is to attempt to make an appointment to see whoever is dealing with the death of David Kendall.'

'And what is that to do with you, Miss Jones?' Chief Inspector Carterford wanted to know.

'Your colleagues asked me to sit with Lyn Kendall after she was given the news of her husband's death, and she has asked me to look into the death on her behalf. As her closest friend, I will be working on this case. Your colleagues would not tell her anything last night, and that has become a cause of concern for us.'

'Not would not tell her, could not tell her,' he retorted. 'They were from another constabulary and were merely asked to inform Mrs Kendall of her husband's death. They were helping out, so to speak. We were extremely busy last night. She lives very close to the next-door force's border, and they crossed the border and passed on the message on our behalf.'

'What can you tell me about David's death, Mr Carterford?' I ventured.

'Nothing,' he replied emphatically.

'What do you mean nothing?' I countered.

'Exactly that. You are not a relative; therefore, you have no entitlement to know. We're sorry, Mrs Jones, but we can't help you,' he pointed out.

'It's Miss Jones,' I corrected him.

Clearly, this was going to be hard work.

'Look, Mr Carterford, may I come and see you. You know, speak face to face as it were?'

'If you think it would help you understand, Miss Jones, then, by all means, we can meet. Can you make it two o'clock this afternoon? I have about half an hour to spare then.'

'Yes. Is that at the Central Police Station?' I wanted to know.

'Yes, it is. I'll tell the front desk to expect you then.' He terminated the call without further comment.

I stared at the handset for a few moments before replacing it.

Well, I suppose he is very busy, I thought, but even so, that was a little abrupt. Something about this whole case doesn't settle in.

I mentally shrugged and replaced the handset.

I checked my watch; twelve-thirty—just time for a sandwich before leaving for my meeting with Chief Inspector Carterford.

Suitably refreshed, I set off for the Central Police Station.

'I'm here to see Chief Inspector Carterford,' I announced to the officer behind the enquiry desk.

'Yes, of course. He is expecting you. I'll let him know that you are here.'

'Thank you.' I replied.

A few minutes later, a door opened, and an early middle-aged man in a grey but well-worn suit appeared.

'Miss Jones?' he asked.

'Yes,' I replied, taking the extended hand and giving and receiving a welcoming handshake.

Carterford indicated a door off the reception area, which I pushed open and went into what was some sort of interview room. The walls were a pale grey with bright, highly polished red floor tiles. If there were any blemishes to the wall-décor, then the posters portraying missing persons, straying dogs, and foot and mouth disease advice would cover them.

The Chief Inspector indicated a chair on one side of the table and seated himself on the other.

'Right Miss Jones. You tell me what you would like to know, and I'll do my best to answer your questions. You must remember, though, that there will be things I cannot tell you, do you understand? I have to follow the rules.'

'Of course. Well, as you probably know, I was asked by your colleagues to sit with Lyn Kendall after she was informed of her husband's death. I guess it came as a massive shock to her. She has no idea what the cause or what it could have been. She is now almost desperate to find out why he had to die. I am a self-employed insurance adjuster, and she has asked me to find the answers to her questions. My name is Mal Jones,' I told him.

'Mal? Short for…?' he left the question hanging.

I was not in the mood for small talk, but if it helped me get any information out of Chief Inspector Carterford, then I was happy to impart it. After all, it was no secret, just something I didn't normally tell.

'Mallowan, actually,' I enlightened him.

'Hm. That is an unusual name. Where did that originate?'

'Well, my mother was an immense Agatha Christie fan. She chose Agatha's married name for her second-born child without knowing whether I would be a boy or a girl. To her, it sounded neutral and, as you say, unusual.'

'I'll bet you suffered at school with a name like that. Is that why you shortened it to Mal?'

'Yes and no. In primary school, I was always known as Mallowan, and no one noticed me. Then when I went to secondary school, and the teachers called me Mallowan, I had the mickey taken out of me unmercifully. You know how teenagers are. Anyway, by the time we moved into the second year, our class went through a phase where we all took on nicknames. You know, the sort which school kids think describe you. Well, we were studying Richard Brinsley Sheridan's *The Rivals* at the time, and I became known as Malaprop after Mrs Malaprop. I got into the role and often used malapropisms when we were chatting between ourselves. It just seemed appropriate back then to adopt the diminutive version of my given name, so Mal I became.'

I remember the naming game very well. The boys chose biblical names, and we chose The Rivals' names. I remember one boy in my class named after an Old Testament High Priest, Eli. In the way of children, the nicknames gradually fell into disuse. Poor Eli and I were the only ones who, as far as I remember, were known by their nicknames until they left school. Even some of the teachers called him Eli. Strangely when his brother followed him to the school, he was initially called Eli too. That was confusing for everyone, so he became known as Ellie. That nickname stuck with Eli's brother even after he left school! As lame as it may sound now, it was the most fun I've ever had in school.

'Very interesting!' He sounded as if he really did find it so. 'Now, how can I help you?' he asked. It must have been boringly unnecessary for him to know this about me, but he did seem to have the knack of appearing to be genuinely interested. If this was a skill he had developed to gain people's confidence and put them at ease, then he was very good at it.

'I'd just like to know what happened. With your involvement, I take that it isn't a straightforward accident, suicide, or vehicle collision. It doesn't make sense how it all happened,' I ventured.

'Very astute, Miss Jones. No, you are quite right. It is not straightforward.'

He paused, apparently considering just how much to reveal.

'Miss Jones…' he began.

'Mal, please. I know that you would perhaps prefer formality, but I would not,' I told him.

'Okay, then, Mal it is. Mal, how much do you know about Mrs Kendall's husband?'

'Very little, really. Lyn is my best friend and has been since secondary school but David, well I don't know much about him at all. We've dined as a group many times, of course, but that is about all really. As far as I am aware, he had something to do with banking.'

'Banking? Yes, I suppose that you could call it that,' the Chief Inspector said mysteriously.

Clearly, he was very reluctant to elaborate. Confidentiality, the Official Secrets Act or some such obstacle was standing in his way. He hesitated, and I rather gained the impression that he was weighing up the pros and cons of telling me more. For the moment, the cons were winning.

'What do you mean by 'you could call it that,' Mr Carterford?' I asked.

Hesitation again. His face told me David had more to do than he let on…

'Look, please don't start something, and then not carry on with what you were saying. Surely Lyn Kendall is entitled to know what her husband has been up to if indeed he has been up to anything!' I grew frustrated with him sharing information in fragments.

'Let me just say this, Mal, that what Mrs Kendall doesn't know most certainly cannot hurt her.'

'That's even worse, telling me that. Now I know that there is something suspicious about David Kendall's death. What had he been doing Mr Carterford, fiddling the books?' I suggested.

'In a manner of speaking.' Mysterious again.

'Look, Mr Carterford, as I told you, I am an insurance adjuster. I am good at what I do, very good indeed. If it is financial, David's problems that is, then I will find out and get to the bottom of it. I promised my friend that I would find the answer to her question, and I intend to do just that. Do you understand?' I said this as forcefully as I could.

Carterford eased himself back into his chair. He had a small smile on his face, which seemed to be a permanent fixture. The smile widened.

'My, my Miss Jones. We are being the terrier, aren't we?' he said, somewhat mockingly, I thought.

I saw red at this remark.

'How dare you patronise me Mr Carterford. I am not doing any canine impressions. I am merely trying to fulfil a promise I made to a friend. Now, will you help me or not? Because I have other ways to find out.' I retorted.

'I apologise, Mal. I had no intention of patronising you or, indeed, insulting you. I needed to know how sincere you are in your quest for answers. Now I do know. The next thing I must reassure myself about is trust. Can I trust you? How far can I trust you?'

'Apology accepted. While I understand that you cannot take my word for it, you can trust me. I know all about confidentiality and am sincere in what I want to know. Lyn Kendall needs to discover how David died and, much more importantly, why. She deserves closure. Now, if there is no mystery about why he died, why can't you tell me?'

'Therein lies the rub.' Carterford said.

'If you are going to quote Shakespeare at me, Mr Carterford, at least get it right. The phrase is *there's the rub,* and it is from Hamlet.'

'My apologies to Shakespeare too, then,' the chief Inspector said with a grin.

I considered the reply that the detective had given to my question that if there was no mystery about why he died. If indeed there was no mystery, why couldn't he tell me? His Shakespearian misquote gave me the answer. There must have been something mysterious either in the way in which he had died or indeed why he had died. Was he trying to tell me something by telling me nothing? Did that question even make sense? Well, it did to me. And now I have to find out.

'There was something mysterious or perhaps suspicious about David's death, wasn't there? So let me see. It involved his work as a banker somehow or on some level, am I right?'

There was an almost imperceptible nod from a silent Detective Chief Inspector but no verbal response.

'How he died certainly wasn't straightforward otherwise, the Criminal Investigation Department would not be involved.'

Another imperceptible nod.

'What his wife doesn't know can't hurt her, you said, so it must involve fraud in some way.'

No nod this time but a slight widening of the ever-present smile.

'You must know that I cannot tell you which direction our investigation is taking, Mal. Bearing in mind that I have not yet told you anything, what do you intend to do next?' The Chief Inspector wanted to know.

'You must know that I cannot tell you which direction my investigation is taking, Chief Inspector.' I said with what I hoped was an enigmatic smile.

'Indeed, I know you will not. I wish you luck in your enquiries whichever direction they take, and please feel free to consult me further should you feel the need.'

Chief Inspector Carterford stood and crossed the room, holding the door open, allowing me egress before him.

I wished him a good afternoon and proceeded to walk out of the room.

'By the way, my name is Philip,' he said, smiling widely now.

Chapter Four

I returned home.

I made a pot of coffee and took it to my office. I updated my log, which was stored on the computer, and then added a list of some things I felt I should be doing.

The list wasn't very long, in truth, but such as it would serve as an *aide-memoire* very well. Satisfied with what I had added to my enquiry log, I topped up my coffee mug and leant back in my chair to consider my next move.

Just supposing that David was involved in some criminal activity at work, how could he keep it from Lyn? They lived under the same roof! Easily enough, I suppose, especially if they were not in the habit of telling each other how their respective days had gone over the evening meal. I realised that I knew absolutely nothing about Lyn's finances. It had always struck me that the two of them lived comfortably in a very nice house, which must have attracted a fair-sized mortgage, but as this was not really any of my business, I had not thought too deeply about it. I knew that I would have to ask Lyn some questions I had no right to ask and did not relish asking.

Just supposing that David was involved in criminality, then to what extent was he involved? Did Lyn even have a clue about it? How much money was involved? That was indeed a very important question. If it was a few hundred, a few grand even, would that warrant killing him or having him killed? Was he killed to keep him quiet about the crimes, if indeed there were any? Was Lyn in any danger because of it? I felt as if I had started to descend into the rabbit hole. All Lyn wanted to know was why? My list of unanswered questions was growing by the minute, and I had to find answers to them all before I could even begin to guess the why, the one thing which Lyn wanted to know.

There was only one way that I could make a start, and that was to see David's financial records, such as bank accounts and so on. This was a very delicate situation and one in which I hesitated to get involved in but involved I would need to be. After all, if Lyn wanted answers to her questions, then she would have to help me with mine.

I rang Lyn and asked if I could call to see her the following morning. She was clearly crying.

'What's up? I asked.

'Sorry Mal, it's David.'

'Alright, Lyn. I'll come straight round.'

I rang Lyn's doorbell fifteen minutes later, and Lyn invited me into the lounge, where a pot of coffee and two mugs stood on a silver tray. They were surrounded by a cream jug and a bowl of brown sugar cubes. Fairtrade, too, I thought.

Lyn poured coffee, and we sat back into the armchairs.

After a few moments, I asked, 'How did you mean it is David?'

I was genuinely puzzled as to how David, if he indeed was dead, could now be upsetting her to this extent. It seemed to me to be something other than grief.

'What has happened?'

'They won't let me bury him.' She began sobbing again.

'Oh, is that all!' I said, perhaps a little too dismissively.

'What do you mean, is that all,' Lyn expostulated.

'I could have chosen my words more carefully. What I mean is that it is understandable, Lyn, if you think about it. HM Coroner has still to hold an inquest, and there is a shed a load of other formalities to be gone through, let alone any police investigation,' I pointed out.

'What police investigation? It was a car accident, wasn't it?' Lyn suddenly looked up with a look on her face that I could not immediately fathom. It was shock, surprise, and something else too. But what?

'I saw the officer dealing with David's death this afternoon. It was a CID officer, and CID doesn't deal with traffic deaths. He would not tell me anything about what was happening. I am not a relative, Lyn, so that isn't surprising, really.'

Lyn looked me straight in the eyes and said, 'But you said you would find out what happened.'

It may have been purely my imagination but was there a hint of a threat or menace in her face? Surely not. After all, she was my best and oldest friend, and I was only doing my best to help.

'I can only do my best, Lyn, and that I will most certainly do,' I replied.

Her face immediately softened, and whatever that hint on her face was, it had completely disappeared. I was relieved because, for a moment, even I was beginning to feel uncomfortable.

'I know, Mal, and I'm sorry. I must seem very ungrateful, but I need to know what is happening.'

'That's okay. I understand,' I said without understanding at all.

'Look, Lyn. If CID is investigating, there must be some criminality involved somewhere along the line, or there could have been something suspicious about how David died. I don't know which if indeed either of those things is suspected. All I do know is that the police are not prepared to co-operate with me. Lyn, I will ask you a few things now, and I do not want you to get upset. They may be painful to answer, but I do need to know. Are you going to be alright with that?'

'Yes. Anything to help.'

'The first thing I need to know is, were you and David happy in your marriage?'

'How dare you, Mal!'

So much for the anything to help. Some things were going to be harder than others to ask and answer.

'Of course, we were. What are you suggesting that David was having an affair?'

'No, of course, I am not suggesting that. I am asking if, to your knowledge, David was having one.'

'I still do not know how you can ask that, Mal. You know David as well as I do. It wasn't you, was it?' she asked with incredulity written all over her face.

'No, of course, I have not been having an affair with David,' I hesitated and then added as an afterthought, 'or with anyone else for that matter.'

'I'm sorry again, Mal. I really am, but my mind is jumping all over the place, so I am not even making sense to me, let alone anyone else. Please forgive me. David's sudden death has left me confused, alone, and heartbroken.'

'Nothing to forgive, I completely understand,' I assured her.

In truth, I am not altogether sure that I did understand. Was this perfect marriage as perfect a picture as Lyn was painting? Was there something behind her question? Did she suspect David of infidelity? After all, the public face of any relationship could be completely different from the private face, the reality.

I did not really think that there was anything untoward between Lyn and David. Neither had given even the slightest hint. That did not alter the fact that the seed had been sown. Whether it would germinate or not was another matter.

I decided to change tack.

'What about money worries? Did you have any? Did David have any, as far as you are aware?' I asked.

'No. At least David never mentioned any worries about money. I had my own current account, which I used for household expenses and my own needs. David paid a generous amount into that account each month. He never queried anything.' Lyn said.

'I know I have no right to ask, but do you have a few bank statements for that account?' I asked Lyn.

'That's alright.'

She crossed the room to a rather nice reproduction kneehole desk and pulled open a drawer. She removed a sheaf of papers and returned to her chair. She handed the papers to me.

I examined the top sheet, which was the latest statement for the account. At the end of the previous month, Lyn had an eye-watering balance that exceeded fifteen thousand pounds and was fast approaching sixteen thousand. I blinked a couple of times. For someone who did not work, and I feel sure would have described herself *as just a housewife,* this was a small fortune. Certainly, it was to me. I rarely had anything like four thousand in my own bank account, and if I did, that was the exception, I mused. I looked for deposits in the account and found a regular four-thousand-pound deposit on the first of the month. Generous amount indeed. Who could it be from, I wondered.

'Who paid the mortgage and the utility bills? 'I asked.

'Oh, David took care of that side of things. I was responsible for food shopping and other similar household items. You know, the smaller expenses.'

What planet was my friend on if she considered that four thousand pounds were necessary each month for food and so on? Even allowing for the buying of the very nice clothes which Lyn always wore, this still seemed far too much to me. Another thought occurred to me. If David was paying four thousand a month into his wife's account and paying mortgage and utilities, he had to be earning a considerable salary. Unless he was very well placed on the management ladder, something wasn't right.

'What about David's account?' I ventured.

'Oh, I don't have anything to do with that.' Lyn said as though I should know better than to ask.

But surely, I mused, if the couple were so close and happy in their marriage, was there any reason why Lyn should not know about David's income and so on.

'So, you have absolutely no idea what David's bank balance was?' I asked.

'No! None at all.' Then a short pause, presumably for consideration of what I had said, 'Look, Mal, what has David's bank balance got to do with his death?' she asked.

'I do not know that it has anything to do with it. It is just that you asked me to find out why and money is often at the bottom of these things.'

'Oh, I see. Well, I think I do,' Lyn said, 'but surely David would not have been killed deliberately, would he?'

Another hesitation.

'You do think that he was killed deliberately, don't you?' she added.

'Look, Lyn. You only asked me to find out why he died yesterday. I haven't had time to form an opinion yet. The one thing I do know is that a senior CID detective does not deal with a straightforward sudden death, now does he?'

'No, I suppose not.' Lyn said.

'There is no suppose about it, Lyn. In my experience, the everyday uniform branch deals with straightforward sudden deaths. If it is a sudden death involving a vehicle collision, it is usually specialist traffic officers who do the background enquiries. If it is a suicide, then a detective might well be called upon as an advisor, but if there are suspicious circumstances, then it is usually an enquiry for the Criminal Investigation Department. So, my gut feeling is that the death was suspicious.'

Lyn immediately began sobbing and muttering 'no, no, no' between deep sobs. It was as if she did not believe that there could be anything suspicious about David's death and that anyone would want to even hurt her darling husband.

I waited until Lyn's sobs had subsided and then struck again.

'Lyn, can you see if David's bank statements are anywhere to hand? We have to dig deeper.'

'I have no idea where they might be,' Lyn responded.

'Be that as it may be, darling, can you look for me, please?' I almost insisted.

'Alright, if you think it would help, I still do not see how,' Lyn said.

'Thank you,' I said in acknowledgement of this thawing on her part.

Lyn went off in search of the bank statements. If they were going to be anywhere, they would surely be in a drawer of his desk in the bedroom, which served as David's Office. She spent ten minutes or so going through every single drawer in the desk. Nothing. That was strange, she thought to herself. Then Lyn began systematically searching every place she thought it might be a hiding place for his bank statements. Again, nothing. He was pretty good at cleaning up his tracks.

'Mal,' she called. 'Can you come here a moment, please?'

I joined her in what I presumed was David's office.

'What is it, Lyn?' I enquired.

'I have checked everywhere, and I cannot find any bank statements at all. Any ideas?'

I cast my eyes around the room and suggested several hiding places. A hollowed-out book in the bookcase perhaps, I suggested.

'Don't be ridiculous, Mal. Who on earth would go to the trouble of cutting out hundreds of pages just to have somewhere to store something? After all, if it was that important or valuable, David would have put it in the safe.' Lyn reasoned.

'David wouldn't necessarily have gone through all that trouble himself. I remember being on holiday in Lyme Regis in Dorset one year. Anyway, there was an antiques centre on the esplanade. At one end of this emporium, they had stands for craft, hand-made greetings cards, jewellery, little boxes, and the like. I remember being fascinated by a row of books on a bookshelf. They seemed out of place at this end of the shop because virtually every title was a classic. I took one down from the shelf and immediately realised that the book was considerably lighter than a normal hardback book. When I opened it up, I realised that every page had been glued to the next, and there was a space cut in the centre to form a very good sort of safe. Weird yet fascinating,' I told Lyn.

'Even so,' Lyn said, 'I can't see David doing that. It would be too much trouble.'

When dealing with an insurance claim on some valuable books, I asked the detective in charge exactly where an owner would hide valuable books.

The detective said, 'Mal, where do you think the place would be to hide a stolen elephant?'

'That's absurd,' I replied, 'who would want to steal an elephant?'

'Humour me for a moment,' the detective asked of me.

'Alright then. What is the best place to hide a stolen elephant?'

'In a herd of elephants, of course! How would you be able to tell the difference?'

'So, following that analogy, where would be the best place to hide a book?' I asked Lyn.

'Okay. Point taken,' Lyn said and began taking the books out one at a time.

'Come on, Mal, help me, and we'll check, but there are a lot of books, aren't there?' she commented almost to herself.

That was an understatement if ever I had heard one.

'Well, I suppose the longer we delay, the longer it will take us' I assured her that it was worth the trouble.

There was a large bookcase with five shelves laden with what appeared to be quite valuable hardbacks.

'Did David collect books?' I enquired of Lyn.

'Well, not collect perhaps. He did enjoy books, though. To him, these old hardbacks were an investment, nothing else. I don't suppose they have been looked at since he bought them.'

I could believe that. There was a thin layer of dust on the top of the books that I looked at, although the shelf in front of them had clearly been dusted and reasonably recently too.

I worked my way along the top row and found nothing untoward. I checked each book, and virtually each was the first edition, but many were no older than the twentieth century; the author even signed a few.

Meanwhile, Lyn had started on the bottom shelf using the same method I had employed. We reached the end of our respective shelves more or less the same time, and both remarked on how dusty they had become.

'That's because David would never let me take the books out to dust them. He was happy for me to dust the shelves, but he insisted that I not remove the books themselves.' Lyn told me. 'I thought this a bit odd, but I presumed he was just concerned for the books and their value.' That should've been her first clue that he's hiding something.

I suggested to Lyn that we do another shelf each before having a coffee break. Lyn, however, had other ideas.

'No. Let's have a coffee break now, and then I will dust the books and the shelves we have done. Otherwise, it will only mean I have to do it all again.'

'Didn't you find that somewhat strange?' I asked.

'No, not really. Come on, coffee.'

I eagerly agreed to Lyn's suggestion, and we retired to the kitchen, where Lyn switched on the coffee percolator and laid out two mugs, cream and sugar. A plate with a small selection of biscuits on it was also placed before me. I felt a little peckish and reached towards the plate. Then good manners took over, and I withdrew my hand to await an invitation from Lyn.

When the percolator had done its job, Lyn carried the pot to the table and proceeded to pour the hot, fresh coffee into the mugs.

'Help yourself to cream and sugar, Mal. Biscuit?' Lyn invited.

I did exactly as she had invited, and we sat together at the kitchen table, sipping our coffee and munching on our biscuits. We did all of this in companionable silence. It was a nice little break from looking for clues David may have left behind. We may not have been talking, but that did not stop our minds from working. Mine just could not understand why David had collected all these books. Collecting books itself was not unusual, I knew. Many people collected all the published works of Miss Read, Agatha Christie, Dick Francis, and the like. After all, I had collected all of Miss Read's books myself. The difference between David and me was that I had read my collection many times. It did not seem to matter that I knew all the characters and storylines; I could still lose myself in the stories and the times in which they were set. Yet, David's collection seemed untouched. I would bet my life savings that David could not have told me more than one or two of the author's names, and I would equally bet that same amount that he would not know one of the story's subjects, let alone the plotlines.

It was in the centre of the bottom shelf that we hit pay-dirt, as it were. Six extra thick books stood well proud of the others on the shelf. With an intake of breath, I reached for the first of these books, which appeared to be an ancient tome and should have been quite heavy. I gently eased the book and was rewarded with its lighter feel.

I removed it from the shelf and sat back on my knees to open the front cover.

'What is it, Mal?' Lyn asked.

'Don't know. This book certainly isn't what it appears,' I told Lyn.

I looked at the spine and could make the title *Polynesian Researches.* The author was William Ellis. This was not a name that I knew or had even heard of, for that matter.

I took my iPhone from my handbag and activated Google. The search told me that the book had been written during a residence of almost six years in the South Sea Islands. It covered history, mythology, traditions, government, and art and was published in 1829. A bit odd for someone like David to have this book.

One dealer had the book on sale at five hundred pounds. I felt that even David would not have defaced such a valuable book to this extent, but clearly, someone had.

Lyn shuffled alongside me. We looked at each other, and I raised a questioning eyebrow in her direction. Lyn nodded in response, and I carefully opened the front cover. There appeared to be nothing untoward at first glance.

It was only when I turned over the tenth page that the treasure, well, not treasure perhaps, but booty certainly became apparent. For there, carefully folded was a sheaf of bank statements. *Bingo!*

Lyn reached out to take them, but I stopped her.

'Be careful,' I said, 'there may be fingerprints or DNA on the sheets of paper. Have you got any plastic gloves?'

'I've got the thin gloves I use when cleaning the bathroom furniture,' Lyn said.

'Bring two pairs, lovey, would you?'

Lyn returned within a few moments and handed me a pair of gloves. I carefully took one sheet out, holding it by one corner, and equally carefully handed it to Lyn. She opened it out fully and laid it flat on the floor.

There was a very sharp intake of breath from my friend. She nervously flipped the pages.

'Mal,' she whispered, 'look at this.'

I looked more closely at the sheet of bank statement. On this page, the opening balance was £950,000, and the closing balance on the same page was just short of two million pounds. If I had thought Lyn's bank balance had been eye-watering, these were eye-deluging amounts of money.

'Where the hell did David get sort of money?' I whispered to Lyn, although I knew it was none of my business.

'How the fuck should I know,' Lyn retorted with her voice raised more than a little.

It was more than apparent that Lyn was as gobsmacked as I was. We couldn't believe what we had stumbled upon.

Neither of us envisaged any career in banking that brought this sort of reward. Those at the very top maybe, although even that was doubtful. David may have been in banking, but at no time had there been anything to suggest that he held any real high-up position.

Lyn took out the next sheet of the statement, and the two-million-pound mark was soon passed, and by the last entry, the balance had exceeded three million pounds. This pattern continued through the ten sheets ending at just short of forty million pounds as the final balance.

Words failed us both. Lyn just stared at the statement sheets looking from one to the other. We were both dumbfounded. Neither of us could've imagined David would be handling this much money.

'What the f...' escaped her mouth, but she cut the expletive short.

'How the hell...?' was the next of Lyn's utterings.

I just could not take in what I was seeing. To use more modern parlance, I would say that I just could not get my head around it.

I picked up the first sheet again and tried to ignore the balances. I concentrated instead on the dates. All the dates shown were at least five years previous. The most recent sheet had dates that were two years old. Next, I turned my attention to the heading on the first sheet.

It was a Swiss Bank. One of the infamous numbered Swiss bank's accounts, no doubt. NUMAC seemed innocuous enough. The international dialling code was evidence that the bank had little to do with the engineering company of the same name. The only details shown on the header were the main title of NUMAC with the telephone number, including the international dialling code and the account number. There was nothing to show whose account it was, just the account number.

Alarm bells began ringing in my head, and they were deafening. This was high stakes for both of us and something I did not wish to get involved in.

'We've got to hand these to the police,' I said to Lyn.

'Why? If this was David's money, surely, it comes to me now?' Lyn exclaimed.

'Lyn, get a grip. You know as well as I do that this money is almost certainly dirty in one way or another. There is no way that David earned this sort of money, and he certainly would not have come by it by buying and selling antique books.'

'Well, until I know differently, the money is mine!' Lyn said.

'Lyn!' I shouted. 'Get real. Of course, it is not yours. Apart from any other consideration, how the hell are you going to get your hands on it. It's in a numbered Swiss bank account, and it is certain that there won't be a record of the passwords needed to access the account. How do you plan on getting it without alerting whoever is involved in this?'

'Mal, don't you shout at me. For Christ's sake, I have just lost my husband. Am I not upset enough without you adding to my misery?' Lyn said with a raised voice, though not shouting as I had. 'I don't care what you say. I am his wife, and I am entitled,' Lyn said.

'Look, Lyn. I'm sorry to say this, but technically, you are now David's widow, and his executors will have to determine ownership of his property. While you may have a claim on David's money, you cannot touch it for the moment because this account is a numbered one and not in David's name, certainly not in joint names.

The exchange between us seemed to take ages to sink into Lyn's grieving brain. When it finally sank in, Lyn began crying again, and the tears flowed freely down her cheeks.

'I do realise that, Mal,' Lyn said, 'but I am still going to ring that bank in Switzerland, whatever you say. Surely, they will need to know that David is dead, won't they?'

'That is as may be, Lyn, but let us just stop and think about this for a minute. Firstly, where the heck did all the money come from? It sure as hell did not come from a banker's salary, nor did it come from buying and selling rare books, so where?' I pointed out. 'I'm afraid there might be dangerous people involved. Please think about it with a clear head, Lyn,' I begged.

Lyn stood up and moved towards the table where the telephone was located. I held out a restraining hand, but Lyn continued towards the telephone table.

'Lyn, don't!' I said loudly. 'Look, lovey, I know that you are all over the place at the moment but think about this account as clearly as you can. If the money did not come from salary or book dealings, there are a couple of other possibilities.'

'Rubbish! What other possibilities could there possibly be?' she said shortly.

'Think, woman, think!' I implored her.

'I am thinking, but I cannot think of anywhere else the money could have come from.'

God help me, I silently intoned. I know she is grieving, but surely, despite that, she must see the possibilities.

'Lyn. You are my best friend, and I love you very much, but you must see that this money's most likely source is money laundering or some other crime. It must be one or the other, can't you see that?'

Lyn turned away from the telephone and offered to get us coffee. While she was out of the room, I looked again at the bank statements one by one, hoping to find extra information we may have missed. There were what I would think of as massive amounts of money going into the account and slightly less huge amounts going out. The difference would presumably be David's commission. I did not like what I saw one little bit.

Lyn returned with a tray on which sat two cups and saucers, a coffee pot, a jug of cream, and a little bowl with fancy lumps of brown sugar. She placed the tray on the low coffee table and crossed to a sideboard. She returned with a bottle of white wine and two tall glasses.

'Just in case we need it,' Lyn said, sitting beside me on the settee.

'We might need it soon enough,' I whispered.

We both went through the bundle of statements again, but nothing jumped out to explain the high balances.

I looked away from the balance sheets in front of me. I had been studying the bank statements so closely for so long that the numbers were beginning to merge. I obviously needed to rest my eyes. I leant back onto the back of the settee and closed them. Lyn thought that I was feeling sleepy and said nothing. My eyes might have closed, but my brain most certainly was not. I tried to sort the facts I knew with certainty into some order.

Suddenly my eyes flew open.

'Lyn!' I exclaimed.

'What?' she replied.

'The other books. We haven't checked the other books. We need to finish the job.'

We both went back into David's office and crossed to the bookshelf, and I noticed Lyn held back. She let me get on with the job at hand.

The next book was exactly what it purported to be. None of the pages appeared to have been cut out. The third book yielded the same result. The fourth, however, was also hollowed out. I knew this before I even opened the cover. In the hollowed-out inner were several soft leather bags. It did not take a genius to find what I was going to find. I asked Lyn to get several sheets of paper and to lay them flat on the floor.

I opened the first bag and emptied the contents onto one of the sheets of paper. About forty or fifty dirty little pebbles fell out. They were each, I estimated, about six or seven millimetres across.

'Why would David keep stones like this?' Lyn asked.

'I don't know much about these things, but I guess these are not just any old stones; these are uncut diamonds!'

'How many are there?' Lyn wanted to know, suddenly interested.

I counted them. Forty-four.

'What are they worth?' Lyn wanted to know.

'Well, I have no idea, but I know someone who will know,' I told Lyn.

I reached for my mobile and found the number of Klass Van Janssen. Klass was a diamond dealer I had dealings with in the past when I looked into a case involving diamonds.

'Klass can help us get some clarity over this diamond situation,' I assured Lyn.

I pressed his contact on my mobile, and the number went directly to the answerphone.

I disconnected.

I checked the time on my mobile. Nine o'clock! Stone me, no wonder I was feeling hungry. I had not eaten since… I realised that I could not remember when I had last eaten a meal.

'Lyn. Look, I must go. I suggest you replace everything we have discovered in the same places we found. We can have another go at it tomorrow,' I suggested.

Lyn agreed and suddenly sat back on the settee and, leaning her head back, closed her eyes.

'I think you ought to get yourself to bed, lovey. You need sleep,' I advised.

'I think you are right. Can you find your way out? I am going straight to bed; I feel exhausted.'

I assured her that I could and watched as she mounted the stairs. I left.

Chapter Five

I was woken a few minutes after seven by my mobile's loud ringtone. It rang for the third time before I finally picked it up.

I didn't even look at the caller's details but instead held the phone to my ear without even opening my eyes.

'Yes?' I said, fully expecting Lyn's voice.

Instead, an accented male voice asked, 'Mallowan? Is that you?'

I was suddenly wide awake, Klass Van Janssen!

'Klass! Lovely to hear from you again.'

'I am sorry I missed your call last night, but I was in bed and fast asleep at the time your call came in.'

'Yes, I am very sorry, Klass, but I didn't think about the time difference. I thought that when we went into Europe, we would all come under the same time zone.'

Klass laughed. He had heard that one before, I thought.

'How can I help Mallowan?'

Klass Van Janssen was one of the few people who knew my proper name and used it.

'Klass, I wonder if you could do me a no questions asked favour?'

'For you, Mallowan, I will make an exception. What would you like to know?'

'I have been helping a friend who has just lost her husband, and she has in her possession a leather bag containing what I think are rough diamonds. I need an estimation of their worth.'

'I can do that; however, it is difficult, Mallowan, without seeing the actual stones. Is it possible to photograph them and send me the picture? That will give me an idea.' Klass wanted to know.

'I am sure that I can. I will go to her house after I have eaten, so you should get the photographs by about eleven o'clock my time. Will you be able to do that?'

'That's fine; send them over whenever you can,' Klass said.

'Okay, Klass, thank you for your help.'

We ended the call. The one thing you could say about Klass is that he did not indulge in small talk; instead, he would get straight to the point. No beating around the bush.

I dragged myself out of bed and padded along to the bathroom. After completing my morning ablutions, I descended to the kitchen, made a pot of tea, and put two eggs on to boil. I felt it was a morning for fortification of the inner person, so I put three slices of toast into the toaster. I relished my toasted soldiers, my eggs, some toast, and thick-cut marmalade.

While I waited for the eggs and toast, I rang Lyn. No reply. Initially, I found it worrisome. But she had been emotionally exhausted last evening, so a lie-in was the probable answer. I tried to put Lyn to the back of my mind and concentrated on a leisurely breakfast.

Just after ten o'clock, I rang Lyn again. This time a very sleepy-sounding voice said, 'Hello.'

'Lyn? It is Mal. Can I come around to see you? It's about the diamonds.'

'Yes, of course. Come as soon as you like.'

Lyn opened the door to my first ring of her doorbell and invited me in. She certainly seemed much brighter and much like her old self. I presumed that it was the good, long sleep that had been responsible. For the first time since her husband's passing, Lyn looked well-rested and more like herself.

'Lyn, those stones we found, do you mind if I take some pictures of them? I have a contact in The Netherlands who is a diamond dealer, and he will give me a rough value, but he needs to see the stones.'

'Of course.' Lyn assented.

She opened the hollowed-out book and extracted the soft leather bag. She poured the stones onto a sheet of paper and spread them out. I then checked my purse and found a couple of five pence pieces and a couple of twenty pence pieces. I placed these coins strategically around the page and took five pictures from above. It then occurred to me that Klass may not be familiar with the size of British coinage, so I asked if Lyn had a small ruler. With this placed alongside five different stones, I took five more photographs. The ruler gave us a clearer idea about their size.

Satisfied that they all seemed clear enough, I sent them to Klass for closer examination.

Lyn and I sat chatting about this and that. It gave us something to concentrate on besides David, his money, and the diamonds. I don't know about Lyn, but these things were to the fore of my mind, although I did not give voice to my thoughts. I still could not get my head around the biggest question of all; how had David accumulated his not inconsiderable bank balance and the equally not inconsiderable sum required to buy precious stones. What was he up to, and how did Lyn stay completely unaware of his activities all this time?

Around half an hour later, my mobile activated again, and Klass' voice came on the line.

'Just a moment,' I told him and went to the kitchen. I do not know why but I did not want Lyn to overhear my conversation with Klass.

'Mallowan. I have reached an estimate for those stones, but you must understand that this is just that, an estimate.'

'That is understood, Klass. Do I need to sit down?' I chuckled as I asked the question.

'That depends on what idea you already have of the value, but yes, I would advise it. It's probably more than anything you imagined.'

'As far as I can tell, the value of those rough diamonds would be about forty thousand pounds. Of course, that could be more depending on the quality of the stones, but it is not likely to be less.'

'How much?' I screeched. My jaw dropped open, and Klass probably felt it through the phone.

'Forty thousand pounds at least. Are you sure you are sitting down?' Klass chuckled down the phone.

'I am now,' I told him.

'Why would someone who apparently has no connection with precious stones have so many diamonds in his possession?' I asked.

'Well, Mallowan, the only reason I could think of is that these are being kept as an investment.'

'Yes, that makes sense, but what would someone have to pay for that number of uncut diamonds? Could he be keeping them for someone else? Because where did he get the money for these?' I asked Klass.

'That is where I got the approximate worth from. If I were buying that number of stones, I would expect to pay at least forty thousand pounds,' he explained.

'Bloody hell!' I exclaimed. 'Look, Klass, there are four more of these bags, but we haven't opened them yet. Can I perhaps send you some more pictures of whatever we find in the bags?'

'You can, of course, but it may make more sense to bring them to me in Amsterdam. Perhaps I can then give you a more accurate estimate of their value.'

'I need to find out whether these stones are legitimate, Klass. I cannot, no, will not explain all over the telephone. If I come over, I can explain much more to you. You're right. Let me make the arrangements, and I will come to see you.'

'That is good, Mallowan, and will be much appreciated.'

I rang the KLM offices and was able to book a flight for the following day. It would leave London Heathrow at ten-thirty, which should get me to Amsterdam Schiphol before noon. I made the booking, rang Klass, and confirmed when I was travelling. He offered to send a car for me, an offer I gladly accepted. My next problem was getting Lyn to agree to my taking the bags of stones to Amsterdam. Of course, it would be a concern for her. I also remembered that we had not checked all the bags and still had some books to check.

I returned to the lounge where Lyn was waiting patiently.

'Well?' She wanted to know what Klass had to say about the diamonds.

I told her what Klass had told me, and she just stared open-mouthed at me. Her reaction was no different than mine.

'You have got to be kidding me, Mal. You have got to be!' Lyn exclaimed.

'Not unless my Dutch contact is kidding me. I'm not,' I told her.

'But that was just one bag! We still have more!'

'Yes, I know.'

'We, or rather you, have to get the rest valued too, and if they are in your possession legally, then you will need a true value for probate,' I pointed out.

I could see disbelief written all over her face.

'What do you mean, Mal? What exactly do you mean by 'if they are in my possession legally?' Of course, they are legal.' Lyn was getting herself worked up again, and tears were beginning to form in her eyes once more.

I waited for the exchange to sink in. She glanced at me every so often as though she were trying to come to terms with what I had told her.

I broke the extended period of silence between us.

'Look, Lyn, do you think that I could take the bags of stones to Amsterdam to be properly valued?'

Again, Lyn's mouth dropped open. As expected, she didn't seem thrilled about the idea.

'Take my diamonds to Amsterdam? Take them? What do you take me for, Mal? Look, I am not an idiot. What is to stop you from taking my diamonds and selling them without me knowing,' she said with a raised voice. I realised that she was hurting and not thinking straight, but nonetheless, her apparent mistrust of me, her best friend, hurt me deeply.

A period of complete silence then began between us. I glanced out of the corner of my eye and could see Lyn's lips moving as if chatting to herself. No sound emanated from her, however. I was disappointed with her reaction, maybe overreaction, but we had to dig deeper. I pushed Lyn again to discuss them.

'Lyn, we have to talk some more about these stones,' I said softly.

'No, no more! No more! No, no, no, no,' she said, although not with a raised voice which was something I supposed.

'Lyn. Listen to me.' I began.

'No, you are not my friend if you are scheming to steal my diamonds,' she said levelly.

'But Lyn, darling. I am not scheming to steal anything. You asked me to find out about David and what happened, and this is what I am trying to do,' I countered. 'You're my best friend, and I'm only trying to help you find clarity in an otherwise messy situation.'

'I think we ought to leave it all to the police. I no longer want you to investigate anything.'

'If that is what you really want, what you really, really want, then I will, of course, do as you ask. Let me ask you something, though, Lyn. Other than telling you that David had died, how many times have they been to see you?'

'Don't quote Spice Girls' song's lyrics at me!' Lyn said indignantly.

'Okay, but how many times have the police been to see you?' I persisted.

I knew the answer before I asked the question. A long-serving detective had given me that advice once. Only ask questions of a suspect or would-be suspect if you know the answer beforehand.

Was Lyn a suspect? I asked myself silently.

Yes, she was, I decided until I knew differently. I hated having these thoughts about a friend of so many years. If Lyn had been open with me, I might have had a different viewpoint. She was starting to seem more and more like a suspect at this point.

Lyn had obviously been turning over my question in her mind, and it was ten minutes or so before she spoke again.

'Mal?' Lyn said very softly, barely above a whisper.

'Yes, lovey,' I replied in a low voice.

'What have I done to our friendship?' She wanted to know.

'Nothing,' I replied, 'well, at least nothing that cannot be mended.'

'But how could you let me blame you like that without defending yourself?'

'It is the grief talking and not my friend,' I assured her.

'I know that I said some hurtful things. Can they ever be put right?' Lyn's voice was almost normal again.

'Lyn. Until you can accept the fact that David's wealth may not have been accumulated lawfully, then whatever I suggest is going to seem like I am against you. I am not against you; I want to try to protect you from harm, but I can only do that if you are completely honest with me and trust me,' I told her. 'I would never do anything to hurt you.'

'I think that deep down, I know that everything is not as it should be. I also know that you are on my side. So, what exactly is it that you want?' she asked.

'Firstly, we need to check the remainder of the books in the bookcase. When we know what we are dealing with, we can decide what to do next.' I pointed out.

'Okay, let's get on with it.' Lyn was fully recovered now and crossed the lounge to the bookcase. The remainder of the books were still in place, and only the one with bank statements and the one with stones lay open. The other four were still in place on the shelf. Two of these were whole books. Nothing cut out. The next book had been cut into and contained four soft leather bags, similar to the ones which contained the diamonds.

These bags contained well over a hundred stones and meant absolutely nothing to the amateur eye. We were in complete disbelief at what we were witnessing.

The last book was the same as the second containing four soft leather bags containing stones of some sort.

My mind was running riot. If one bag of stones was valued at forty thousand pounds and the remainder were somewhere near the same value, then, in front of us, we were looking at the biggest part of half a million pounds worth of precious stones. Of course, my calculations could very easily be way out, as that is as far as my mind could go, but that had to be our starting value.

We kept the contents of each bag separate, and having counted the stones in each bag, we made a note of the numbers and placed them back in their bags again.

'Mal? What do you think we should do next?' Lyn enquired.

'We must know exactly what we are dealing with. I have a friend in Amsterdam who is a diamond dealer, but he handles other precious stones too. That is what I wanted to take that bag of stones to Amsterdam for. He believes he can give us a better estimate by looking at the stones in person. What do you think?'

'I'm still doubtful, but, I agree, we do need to be certain. Let's go to Amsterdam!'

I had no wish to curb Lyn's newfound enthusiasm and did not point out that I had already booked a seat on a KLM flight for myself. Now, I had to book one for her as well.

'Okay, I'll book us a couple of seats.' I assured her.

Thankfully, Lyn busied herself in the kitchen making some sandwiches, and I took the opportunity to ring KLM. They were pleased to confirm that I could book an extra passenger to travel with me and that we could have adjoining seats. I confirmed the booking quickly and got us seats by the window.

Lyn came back into the lounge, and I told her that we would be taking the ten-thirty flight to Amsterdam and that we would be arriving about noon. Lyn was enthusiastic about our little trip to northwestern Europe.

'I had better let Klass know that we are both going and approximately how many bags of stones we are taking with us,' I told Lyn.

Klass was happy with the arrangements and even offered to book a hotel for us. I did trust Klass implicitly, but I stopped short of giving the go-ahead for the hotel booking. I would feel happier if we did this ourselves. One could never be too careful.

Chapter Six

We sat side by side on board the KLM Embraer 175 aircraft. We had taken economy class seats for the short flight. I had to admit to myself that I had never heard of the Embraer 175, but the KLM website told me that they were used for European flights. Smaller planes are usually preferred on this route due to the shorter duration of the flight. It seated eighty-eight passengers, and I estimated that the aircraft was a smidge over half-full. Fortunately, it didn't seem too crowded.

The flight was smooth as ever, and we landed at Schiphol Airport at noon without incident. We were met in the arrivals lounge by no less a person than Klass himself.

Klass Van Janssen was in his early sixties and looked every year of his age. I thought that he may well have added a few more years to his age. His dress style was certainly not that of a wealthy diamond dealer but more of an ordinary working Dutchman. His clothes were tidy with well-pressed trousers, but one could never attribute the adjective smart to his appearance.

We greeted each other like long-lost friends, and I introduced Lyn to him. Lyn's eyebrows briefly moved skywards as she shook Klass's hand and glanced at me as if she was trying to understand how we became friends in the first place. I returned her glance with the briefest of smiles in acknowledgement of her unspoken comment. Klass was obviously an admirer of young women in the purest possible sense. He was almost fawning over us but managed to stay just on the correct side of propriety. He led us to the car which was waiting on the airport apron. Beside the large black car and holding door open was a uniformed chauffeur. He made sure that Lyn and I were settled before closing the front passenger door on Klass and returning to the driver's door. As he began to lower himself into the seat, I caught the briefest glimpse of the butt of a handgun under one arm. I made no comment to either Klass or Lyn, but it started a tiny warning bell in my head. Carrying bags of possibly illegal diamonds all the way to another country was no easy task, nor was it safe. There was next to no volume to the warning bell, but I could hear it quite clearly. I felt it best not to enlighten him as to how the bags of stones had come into her possession. I had warned Lyn on the flight over not to reveal too much to Klass. I could not explain my unease. After all, my dealings with Klass had been several years before, and there was nothing but that to associate us. It was just that something was ringing a tiny warning bell somewhere in my brain. I may well be wrong, but I decided that we ought to be playing it safe, so to speak.

On the journey from Schiphol into the city centre the only conversation was of a desultory nature. It was by design on our part, but how Klass viewed it was impossible to read.

Once ensconced in his smart but sparsely furnished office, we were offered coffee and stroopwafel, the rightly famous Dutch pastry. The stroopwafel is now almost iconic within The Netherlands, and its popularity is now spreading to the United States of America. While the United States of America may seem a strange choice of country to come under the influence of a Dutch food, it must be remembered that Dutch settlers were early occupiers of what is now New York; having been named New Amsterdam by the settlers, presumably in memory of their homeland. Traditionally the stroopwafel is circular and consists of two thin wafer-type cookies with molasses between the layers. The name stroopwafel literally means *waffle in syrup.* Fitting if you think about it. Food names shouldn't be that complicated.

A paper napkin was thoughtfully provided just in case any of the delicious syrup leaked from between the layers. This was my first experience of the stroopwafel, and I vowed that it would not be my last. So far, Amsterdam has been quite welcoming, I admitted to myself.

Niceties over, Klass carefully wiped his mouth with his napkin, smiled, and turned towards me.

'Mallowan. Have you brought the stones?' He wanted to know.

I looked over at Lyn, who, in return, held my eyes with hers for a few seconds. I nodded to her, and she nodded once to acknowledge my permission to show Klass. I proceeded to fish the bags out of my purse and brought them to Klass.

'This is the bag of stones which I sent you the pictures of,' I told Klass.

I again looked at Lyn. She was carefully watching what Klass was doing with what she saw as her stones. Keeping an eagle eye on him to ensure his intentions weren't malicious.

Klass picked up the stones one by one. He looked at each one carefully and examined them with a magnifying eyeglass. Apart from an occasional 'hm' and 'oh', he said little, so engrossed in his work was he.

After half an hour or so, he removed the eyeglass and placed it carefully on the desk. He studied the stones again without touching them this time.

He looked up, first at me and then at Lyn.

'Where did these stones come from?' he asked.

Lyn opened her mouth to reply but caught the very slight shake of my head. I had already warned her not to let on too much. She picked up on my signal and stopped before sharing more than what was necessary.

'I can't tell you, Mr Van Janssen. Not yet anyway.'

'Mal?' He turned his head towards me.

'I'm sorry, Klass, but as Lyn said, we can't tell you now. All I can say is that they came into Lyn's possession after her husband died,' I told him.

Klass again muttered a 'hm'.

'When? Can you tell me that?'

'Yes. Last week.'

'I see,' Klass said.

Klass pursed his lips and asked, 'You said that you had more bags, Mal. Is that correct?'

I nodded across to Lyn again, and she took the remaining seven bags from her bag.

She handed them, one at a time to Klass, who emptied each in turn onto the large sheet of paper in front of him. Klass was clearly anticipating a repeat of the first bag, and even I had mentally calculated that if the value was anywhere near the value of that first bag, then we were looking at around four million pounds worth.

An hour passed. Lyn and I sat in silence, and Klass busied himself with the stones, carefully setting aside those which he had examined. I began to shift uneasily in my chair. I almost feared what Klass would tell us about the value of the stones.

I felt moved to break the silence as Lyn stared at me with nervous anticipation.

'Well?' I asked.

''Well, Mallowan. You have appeared to have hit the jackpot. If I was offering to buy this little lot, I would be offering you three and a half million pounds. I must add, though, that I am not making an offer. I could never afford that.'

'Why not Klass?' I could not stop myself from asking.

'I don't know their provenance, Mal. It is as simple as that.'

'Are they all diamonds then?'

'Yes, every one of them!' Klass exclaimed with enthusiasm.

I let this sink in for a few moments while my mind turned somersaults. What the bloody hell had David been doing to possess these stones? Perhaps I should leave insurance adjusting and become a book dealer! Common sense told me that this would be sheer folly. I thought of David and his two-million-dollar bank balance and then his diamonds worth four million or so. Six million! No man following a legitimate career would have this sort of wealth unless they were the owner of a large business conglomerate. In David's case, rather secretly. Six million, I thought, what would I do if I had that kind of money? Something was wrong, very wrong indeed. The dilemma I now faced was whether Klass was on the side of the angels or not.

Everything I knew about him pointed to the fact that he was one of the good guys. Having said that, though, I didn't really know that much about Klass. How the hell did I go about investigating Klass without him knowing? I had no idea off the top of my head.

'Would you like me to keep these diamonds safe for you, Mal?' Klass asked.

'We cannot agree to that, I am afraid. They are all part of Lyn's husband's estate, so they are all subject to probate. Sorry, and thanks for your help,' I replied.

'I understand,' Klass said, but I am not at all sure that he did or that he wanted to hand the stones back.

He carefully replaced all the stones in their appropriate bags and reluctantly, or so I thought, passed them across his desk to Lyn. Lyn, in turn, put them into her bag, around which she clutched both arms. Carefully tugging it so no one dares take it away from her.

I thanked Klass profusely, and he offered to use his car to return us to Schiphol Airport.

This offer presented me with a dichotomy. Is Klass straight? Is Klass bent? If he was the former, it would be alright to accept the offer. If he was not, well…

It was Lyn who saved me from having to make that decision. She presented him with an excuse and paved our exit from his office.

'We are going to spend some time in Amsterdam, thank you, Mr Van Janssen.' Lyn said.

'Zeer goed,' Klass said. 'Shopping or taking in the sights?'

'A little of both,' Lyn explained.

'Where are you staying?' Klass asked.

Now I thought that was an odd question. Why on earth would a diamond dealer want to know where we were staying? What possible interest could it be to him? My doubts about his character started to grow stronger, and I again turned to Lyn for a signal.

'We haven't found anywhere yet, but we will when we have had the opportunity to talk more about it,' Lyn told Klass.

The tiny alarm bell I had heard previously began clanging just a little louder. It was apparent that Lyn had picked up a warning bell, too, if her somewhat evasive answers to Klass' questions were anything to go by.

We made our farewells to Klass, offering to keep in touch, especially if or when Lyn decided to sell 'her' stones and left.

We did not want to carry the stones with their high value around with us. Neither Lyn nor I felt that hotel safes would be secure enough either. I suggested that we find a branch of

Lyn's bank and ask to leave the stones in their vault, so we went off searching for one.

I began to sense a sort of itching at the nape of my neck. I looked around several times but could not ascertain whether we were being followed. I knew the feeling I was experiencing and had felt it before when dealing with insurance claims where something was wrong. The itching increased in intensity, and I stopped, signalling to Lyn by touching her arm to do the same.

'Don't do anything other than appear to be having a touristy chat,' I warned Lyn.

'Why? What's wrong?' She understandably wanted to know.

'I really don't know, Lyn, but I have this itching that is telling me something is not as it should be.' I nervously told Lyn as I tried to maintain composure and not appear suspicious.

Lyn had known me long enough to be able to trust my instincts without my having to explain them.

Instinctively she began looking around her.

'Don't do that, Lyn,' I cautioned her. 'We are just two tourists having a chat, remember? Just smile and act like a regular tourist.'

Lyn immediately stopped her somewhat furtive looking. However, I could tell from her body language that she was uncomfortable.

From the corner of my eye, I caught a glimpse of the same man who had acted as Klass's chauffeur. He was on the opposite side of the road but was watching us. I did not want to think ill of Klass, and the charitable side of me wanted to think that perhaps he had arranged for his chauffeur to watch out for our welfare; the logical side of me said otherwise. His hesitance to let go of the stones did seem strange, and so did his curiosity to find out where we were staying.

'We have a watchdog, and we need to try and lose him if we can, Lyn,' I said.

'I agree,' she said but added, 'as long as we don't have to split up. I don't know Amsterdam at all.'

'Well, I've only been here once, and that was some years ago, so I don't know it very well.'

'Let's take a taxi and try to find a hotel.'

I waved at the next taxi which passed by, but it did not stop, and neither did the next nor the next. I was on the verge of developing a complex about taxis and Dutch hospitality when one that Lyn hailed pulled up beside us.

Most Dutch people are taught English as a second language, at least that is what I had been told by a particularly pleasant Dutch couple I had met on my last visit. The husband was fluent in Dutch, English, and German and could speak passable French too. His wife could speak Dutch, English, German, French, and Spanish fluently and worked as an occasional interpreter for the International Court of Justice, which is part of the United Nations Organisation.

Our taxi driver was not up to those standards but could understand us, and we could understand him.

'Where to?' He asked the same question asked by cabbies the world over, it seemed.

'Amsterdam main railway station, please,' I told him.

There was no polite conversation, but although I watched his rear-view mirror, he appeared only to be using it as any driver would. I turned and watched the man in black suit following us. He had clearly given up the chase but was talking animatedly into what appeared to be a mobile phone. Co-incidence? On balance, I thought not.

Once we were well out of sight of black suit, I asked the taxi driver to pull in and told him that we had changed our minds. We paid him his minimum charge with a hefty tip, which appeared to placate him. He seemed rather displeased as he drove off quickly. We hailed another taxi and made our way into the centre of Amsterdam. We decided against asking the taxi driver for hotel recommendations and walked instead to the Stationsplein overlooking the Westertoegeng. Near one end of the Westelijke Toegangsbrug, we located the Ibis Hotel and went inside. As far as I could tell, we were not followed, and I went to reception and was able to book a twin-bedded room.

We were shown to our room, and to be fair to the staff we encountered, no one raised even an eyebrow at the absence of any luggage or why we looked pale with fear. We closed the hotel room door and ensured that it was locked. It was time for a secret conference.

We each sat on a bed and faced each other. For no reason at all, we simultaneously burst out laughing. Afterwards, neither of us knew why exactly and put it down to relief at being in a reasonably safe place.

'What was all that about, do you suppose,' asked Lyn.

'Your guess is as good as mine, lovely, but if I were to guess, then I would say that it had something to do with the stones which you are carrying in your bag.' This was the only explanation I could immediately come up with.

'But why did we get a taxi and travel a little way before alighting and catching another? What the hell was that all about, Mal?'

'Did you not spot black suit on the opposite side of the road before we got into the first cab? He was on the phone and seemed to be following us,' I told Lyn.

'No. I took your word for it that we had someone following us, but I didn't bother to look. Look, Mal. I am getting seriously concerned about all this. What the bloody hell was David involved in? More to the point now is what do they, whoever they may be, want from us? We need to get home as soon as possible.' Fear was showing clearly on Lyn's face. The reality was beginning to kick in, and the initial euphoria at inheriting the very healthy Swiss bank account and the valuable stones was beginning to be pushed to the rear of her mind. With me, it was the opposite. The itching at the nape of my neck had not let me down, I felt sure. Something was very, very wrong.

'It seems to me that the first thing we must do is stash these stones away somewhere safe. Any ideas?'

Lyn thought and then said, 'Well, we were on our way to try to find a local branch of my own bank when this cat and mouse stuff started. Why not there, at least for the time being?'

'Right. But how? Do you have idea where the nearest large branch of your bank might be?' I asked.

'Hang on,' Lyn said and reached for the telephone on the small table between the beds.

'No!' I exclaimed, raising my voice sufficiently to stop Lyn in mid-reach.

'What? What?' Lyn asked.

'Look, Lyn, I am not becoming paranoid, honestly, but it would be better if we didn't make any calls via the hotel switchboard, at least until we know what is what. This call could trace back to us and get us in deep trouble,' I advised Lyn.

'And you reckon you are not becoming paranoid?' she retorted.

I grinned, 'Well, perhaps a little.'

Lyn opened her bag and extracted her mobile phone before dialling her own bank back in the UK.

She introduced herself and asked to be put through to the manager or at least one of his assistants.

'Good afternoon, Mr Stokes. This is Lyn Belmont,' Lyn said into her phone.

She caught my raised eyebrow and smiled.

She mouthed the word 'later' towards me, and I nodded.

'Mr Stokes, do you have a branch in Amsterdam?'

'Not to my knowledge, Ms Belmont. What is your problem?'

Lyn explained that she had something which is considered valuable, and she wanted somewhere safe to deposit the item temporarily.

'I would suggest the Delta Lloyd bank in Amsterdam. I have a very good contact there, and I will gladly ring him and ask if it is possible to fulfil your request. Would that suit?'

'Excellent. Thank you, Mr Stokes. May I call and see you on my return to the UK probably in a few days?' Lyn enquired.

'Most certainly, Ms Belmont. I will ring you back as soon as I have spoken to my contact. Is there anything else I can assist you with?'

'Thank you, Mr Stokes. Not at the moment. Goodbye for now.'

Lyn ended the call and looked across at me, 'Did you get all that, Mal?'

'Yes, I did, but what is all this Belmont business?' Who the hell is Lyn Belmont?'

'It's me, of course. Lyn, or to be more precise, Linda Belmont, was my maternal grandmother's maiden name. Long before I met David, I wanted a bank account into which I could pay money as and when I could afford it. It was a sort of secret savings account, if you like. I had no idea what I was saving for, and in fact, I still haven't. The bank, though, is useful, as you have seen.' Lyn told me.

I was learning more and more about my friend. I thought that I knew her so well too, but clearly, I did not know her at all. Lyn was smarter than I had imagined. And having a secret bank account for savings was certainly proving to be useful.

'If you don't mind me asking, how much have you got in your secret account?' I asked.

'No, I don't mind at all. There are about one hundred and twenty thousand pounds in it at the moment!'

My mouth dropped open and stayed open, almost as if it was weighted down. David and Lyn were certainly good at keeping their money a secret.

'A hundred and twent…' I began.

I have wealthy relatives, you see, and each time they left me a few thousand in their will, I paid it into my secret account. Simple really!' Lyn said.

'Oh, very simple!' I replied somewhat sarcastically but with a smile on my face. 'The only thing I have ever been left was a small coffee table belonging to an elderly aunt. I had always liked it and had said so on several of my visits. When it was delivered to me after my aunt's death, I found that it was a reproduction table and almost worthless. I had, of course, kept it for sentimental reasons. Anyway, its value or otherwise had not been why I admired it. I simply kept it as a reminder of how much I loved my aunt.'

Lyn's mobile beeped out its ringtone before we could say more.

'Lyn Belmont,' she announced.

She listened and made a note which turned out to be an address for the Delta Bank in Amsterdam. She thanked Mr Stokes profusely and promised to keep in touch. The call was terminated.

'Right,' Lyn announced. 'First things first. I am hungry. What about you.?'

'Hungry I am; let's find a café somewhere.'

We left the hotel with Lyn clutching the bag with the bags of stones therein, and we found a small coffee shop just a few hundred yards from the hotel. I had carefully, and I hoped surreptitiously, been keeping an eye open for unwanted followers. There were none that I could see, and neither were there any slow-moving vehicles that could have been tracking us. I slowly relaxed and reminded myself that it was just paranoia. We weren't being followed. Who else knew we were carrying these stones with us, anyway? Who else but Klass…

With the inner-man or rather inner-woman replenished, we set off to find the bank and did so without too much trouble.

Lyn went to what appeared to be an enquiry counter and asked to speak to Mr Bakker, the contact of Lyn's bank manager.

We were immediately taken into a quiet office away from the normal foot traffic of the bank and asked to be seated.

'Mr Stokes has been in contact and said that you want help. I will gladly provide that help if I can', Mr Bakker assured Lyn.

'Mr Bakker, I have something in my bag that I now know is worth a considerable amount of money. I do not know the history of these items other than that they belonged in some way to my husband. He died recently, and I discovered them with my friend Mal here, who is helping me find out how and why my husband died. We came here this morning to get an estimate of their actual worth. What I would like is to place them on deposit here until further notice. This will both keep them safe and allow us the time to find out exactly what is going on. Is that possible, please?'

Mr Bakker pursed his lips and appeared to be considering Lyn's request.

'Miss Belmont. That is a lot of information to take in. You must understand that I need to know at least the value of the item or items, if nothing else. I also have never met you, and so from that point of view, I cannot vouchsafe for your identity. May I ring Mr Stokes in England while I have you here?'

'Of course, anything.' Lyn replied.

Mr Bakker dialled a sequence of numbers, and within seconds the call was obviously answered. Mr Bakker then put his handset into a machine, and the voice at the other end could be clearly heard by all of us.

'Hello Luuk. How are you?'

Mr Bakker, or Luuk as we now knew him, told Mr Stokes that he was in his office with Ms Belmont and her friend.

'Hello, again, Ms Belmont. I do not know your friend, though. I do not think,' Mr Stokes said.

'Hello, Mr Stokes, I am Lyn's friend Mallowan Jones, and I am helping her with her problems.'

'Good afternoon Ms Jones. My apologies for my bluntness; we have to ensure the person we're speaking to is legitimate. Now Luuk, what can I do for you?' Mr Stokes enquired.

'Can you please describe Ms Belmont to me?' Luuk asked.

'Certainly, she is about five feet nine inches tall, approximately 1.75 metres, with dark brown hair which hangs to her shoulders, green eyes, and a tiny mole just behind her left ear.'

At this, Lyn stood, held back her hair, and showed the mole to Luuk.

'Yes, that appears to be in order. Do you have a security-type question I can ask?'

'Ask Ms Belmont the name of the aunt who left her a half share in a cake shop.'

'Lettuce,' Lyn replied immediately.

Luuk smiled at the name, as did I, and appeared satisfied with what he had been told. After the usual niceties, the call was terminated, and the handset was replaced to its correct place.

'Very well, Ms Belmont. I am happy to provide safety deposit facilities to you in the short, medium, or long term. There is a set fee which I am happy to charge to your account with Mr Stokes' bank in England. Does that suit you?' Luuk asked.

Lyn looked over at me for my approval, although, of course, she did not need it.

I smiled and nodded to Lyn, signalling to go ahead, and she opened her bag. She took out the soft leather bags and placed them on Luuk Bakker's desk. She opened one and shook the stones onto his blotter.

There was an audible gasp as Luuk Bakker took in what he was seeing. A normal reaction for anyone who saw them for the first time.

'And do the other seven contain similar numbers of stones?'

'Yes.' Lyn confirmed.

Luuk cleared his throat before he continued. 'Have you had them valued by a reputable diamond dealer?' Luuk wanted to know.

'Yes,' I said, 'the stones are worth approximately four million pounds sterling which is about four and a half million Euros.'

'Are they legitimate, though,' Luuk Bakker asked.

A reasonable question, I suppose, from a reputable bank representative.

'As far as we are aware. They legitimately came into Lyn's possession after the demise of her husband recently. How they came into his possession is not certain at the moment. This is subject to enquiries. We brought the stones to Amsterdam for a fair valuation from a diamond dealer I have dealt with before during my work as an insurance adjuster. They are still a subject to probate, though.'

'I see. May I ask who the dealer was?' Luuk wanted to know.

'You may ask, but I will not tell you his name for now. We do not want to be transporting this value package about Amsterdam and indeed on an aircraft. You ought to know that I suspect that someone is watching us; we do not know whom.'

'I see,' Luuk Bakker said and paused.

'We will put them into a safety deposit together, and please leave them with us for as long as you wish. We will keep them safe for as long as you find stability in your situation.'

'Dank je wel, Mr Bakker,' Lyn said and stood.

'I followed suit, and Lyn collected up the soft leather bags which had not been opened, returned the other stones to their bag, and we both followed Luuk Bakker to the safety deposit area of the bank.

With the bags of stones safely locked away, we left the bank and returned to our hotel. There was no sign of black suit on the short journey back, and we felt safer now that we weren't carrying the stones around with us. We entered the hotel foyer, and Lyn went to reception to collect our room key. I noticed a man wearing a sports jacket and pale grey trousers. He was clearly watching us but was trying to disguise the fact. I took Lyn's arm, and we walked, arm in arm, towards the lifts.

As the lift door opened, I saw the sports jacket man take out a mobile phone and begin to speak. I told Lyn that I wanted to get something from reception and if she would wait at the lifts for me. As soon as the sports-jacketed man saw me turn, he hastily, or I thought hastily, replaced the mobile in his pocket. I went to the reception desk and picked out a few touristy leaflets before returning to the lifts and

Lyn. I watched sports jacket man out of the corner of my eye and saw that he still had his mobile phone in his hand. I pretended to read some of the leaflets while standing at reception. He was watching Lyn more than me, but there was absolutely no doubt that he had us under observation. The question was, who the bloody hell was he? Was he with Klass or somehow related to David and the diamonds? More to the point, perhaps why was he watching us so closely.

I crossed the foyer and joined Lyn back at the lifts. We entered the lift and were the sole occupants. As the doors softly closed, I caught a very brief glimpse of sports jacket man talking into his mobile phone once more.

We got out at our floor and saw no one in the corridors. Our room was only a few yards from the lifts, and as I inserted the key card into the lock, I realised that the door was not fully closed. Now, I was certain that the door had been properly closed when we had left that morning. Something was very definitely not right. Someone had been here while we were away, or perhaps, waiting for us to return. I laid a warning hand on Lyn's arm and put a finger to my lips in a silent shush.

I very, very slowly pushed the door open, but when I ventured to put my head around the door jamb, the room was empty. That, however, is where the relief ended. Every item of our possessions had been emptied out of our bags, drawers, and wardrobes. It was an absolute bloody mess. All our things were all over the place.

I crossed to the telephone on the bedside table and dialled reception. I asked the receptionist if there was a man in a sports jacket and pale grey trousers in the foyer appearing to be waiting for someone. The receptionist came back on the line within seconds and told me the man had left, closely followed by another man.

'Were they together when they left?' I asked the receptionist.

'I think that they probably were, although they seemed to be doing their best to give the appearance that they were not together.'

'Can you call the police for me, please?' I asked. I am certain that someone had broken into our room.'

'Yes, madam. At once.'

It was barely ten minutes later that there was a tap at the door, and it swung open. A tall blond-haired man in plain clothes came into the room and held out an ID card.

'I am Hoofdinspecteur Van Hoorn of Centrum Amstel Police. Are you both English?' he asked with barely a trace of an accent.

'Yes, we are,' Lyn answered.

'What has happened here?' Van Hoorn asked.

'We went out into Amsterdam on business, and on our return, this is what we found. Our door was unlocked, and our bags had been emptied out.'

'And you saw no one?'

'Not here,' I told him.

'What exactly do you mean, not here?'

'Well, when we entered the hotel foyer, there was a man who appeared to be watching us. When he saw us going towards the lifts, he started speaking on his mobile phone. When he realised I had seen him, he stopped what he was doing and put his phone back in his pocket. After we saw what happened in our room, we called the reception to look for him, but he had already left.'

'Are you certain that he was watching you?'

'Obviously, I cannot be absolutely certain, but the probability is that he was.'

I knew in my mind that he had been watching us, but I would never be able to convince the Hoofdinspecteur or anyone else for that matter.

The questioning continued for about fifteen minutes before Van Hoorn sent for his forensic experts to come to check for fingerprints and the like. I doubted they would find much, but I wasn't going to disabuse him.

'Now Ms Jones, Mrs Kendall, what exactly is all this about? You have not told me the truth, have you? If you're hiding something, please tell us now.'

'Hoofdinspecteur Van Hoorn, you are clearly a very shrewd man,' I began.

Van Hoorn inclined his head to acknowledge the compliment and was clearly waiting for me to enlighten him.

'Can we go somewhere a little more private, do you think?' I suggested.

'Certainly. Would you be so kind as to come with me to Centrum Amstel Police Station?' Van Hoorn asked, indicating that we should precede him from the room.

Chapter Seven

Once ensconced in an interview room at Centrum Amstel, Van Hoorn seated himself on the opposite side of the table to Lyn and me. I had no way of knowing whether this was by design or coincidence, but it suited us both. We waited for him to begin the interview.

'Well, Ms Jones?'

'It is a somewhat complicated story, but I feel that we should be telling someone the truth. One week ago yesterday, I received a telephone call from an English policeman asking me if I could go to Lyn's home to be with her because she had just been given some distressing news. On my arrival, I was told by the police officers there that Lyn's husband had died. They would not or could not tell Lyn or me any more than that. It transpired that they could not because they were from a different constabulary and were just helping by delivering the message on behalf of Lyn's force. I found it odd, and indeed I still do, that the officer investigating Lyn's husband's death has not interviewed her or, in fact, been anywhere near her since then. I, therefore, took it upon myself to go to speak to him. To say that he was evasive was an understatement. He clearly knew, or at least suspected, a lot more than he was telling but refused to share any more than he had already.'

I explained to Van Hoorn the gist of my conversation with Detective Chief Inspector Carterford. While I didn't deliberately leave anything out, I only told him what I considered pertinent.

'And you said that your English policeman has not been to see you, Mrs Kendall,' Van Hoorn said.

'No, he has not been near me. I have to say that I find that odd.' Lyn told Van Hoorn.

'How do you mean odd?' Van Hoorn wanted to know.

'Well, when Mal, err Ms Jones went to see the police to try and find out what happened, she was referred to a Detective Chief Inspector. Now I do not know what things are like in Holland, but I am certain you would not allocate a senior officer to investigate a straightforward death, natural causes, I mean. This tells me there's more to David's death than what they're letting on.'

'First of all, Mrs Kendall, it is the Netherlands, not Holland. Many still refer to the Netherlands as Holland, but it was in medieval times that the Netherlands was also known as Holland. For the sake of accuracy, there are now two provinces that bear the name Holland. Those are Noord-Holland and Zuid-Holland. So, unless one is referring to either of these provinces, it would be more accurate to describe our country as the Netherlands.' Van Hoorn told us.

'Oh, I'm sorry for my ignorance. I'll try to do better next time,' Lyn said with a grin.

Hoofdinspecteur Van Hoorn also smiled widely and dipped his head to acknowledge Lyn's apology.

'Anyway, Mister Van Hoorn, would a senior detective be given a natural causes death to investigate?'

'Please call me Jens. Hoofdinspecteur Van Hoorn is a bit of a mouthful after all!'

'Yes, that's true,' Lyn said somewhat shyly. It was indeed a mouthful for non-native speakers.

'Well, to answer your question truthfully, no, we would not allocate a senior policeman or police officer, if you like, to investigate such a death. Things do not work that way in the Netherlands. Having said that, I cannot anticipate what another police service will do. I do find it very strange, though, that after having gone through the trouble of allocating a senior officer, that officer has not been to see you yet. Do you have any idea why that might be?'

I decided that I ought to answer that question.

I piped in, 'Look, Jens, there is something that you should know. We are here in Amsterdam for a very explicit reason. We came, or rather, Lyn came, into possession of a large quantity of precious stones. I am an insurance adjuster; I investigate insurance claims, in other words. I had some dealings with a diamond dealer called Klass Van Janssen several years ago and felt he was a man I could trust. For that reason, we contacted Mr Van Janssen and sent him a photograph of one of the bags of stones. The stones were contained in several soft leather bags. The estimate he gave Lyn would have valued the stones at about three and a half million pounds sterling if he had to buy them on the open market.' I paused, and Jens Van Hoorn pursed his lips in surprise.

'That is an awful lot of money to be hidden in your home. I take it they were hidden,' he enquired.

'Yes, they were,' Lyn told him, 'And that is not all. I also found several Swiss bank account statements hidden in a similar fashion. If you thought that three and a half million pounds worth of diamonds was eye-watering, the final balance on the bank statements would have provided an absolute waterfall from the eyes. They showed my husband as having about forty million pounds in his bank account.'

'Forty million pounds! Are you sure?' Jens asked in disbelief. His jaw dropped upon hearing Lyn's confession.

'Yes, forty million,' Lyn confirmed.

There was a short period of silence. Lyn turned to look at me with a puzzled expression, anticipating Hoofdinspecteur Van Hoorn's response.

'What does, sorry did, your husband do to earn a living?'

'He was in banking. Do not misunderstand me, though. He was not in a position that paid millions in bonuses. He was just someone who was employed by a bank. I know that he bought and sold old books, but I cannot think this would be responsible for the sort of money he had in his account; well, his Swiss bank account anyway.'

'Have you looked at his everyday bank account? I take it he did have an everyday bank account.' Jens wanted to know.

Lyn admitted that she had not found his current account statement. So taken had she been by the discovery of the stones and the Swiss Bank account statements.

Why the hell not? I thought to myself. *Why the hell had neither of us thought about his day-to-day banking? Surely that should have been our first thought.*

'Where are the stones now?' Jens enquired.

'They are in a bank safety deposit box here in Amsterdam,' I told him.

'Which bank?' Jens asked.

'That isn't important. What is important, though, is that while we were out this morning, someone entered our hotel room and turned the place upside down. I believe that they, whoever they may be, were after the stones. We're unsure if they were Klass' men or had unfinished business with David. Either way, it is suspicious.'

'That is when you called the police?'

'Yes, Jens,' I assured him. 'We feared we were in danger.'

'Well, Lyn, Mal, what do you want me to do exactly?' Jens asked us.

'At this moment, investigate the break-in to our room. No more. We intend to return to England this evening, and we will be making enquiries at our bank tomorrow; I can assure you.'

'And you'll let me know?' Jens asked.

'Of course,' Lyn said. Do you have a number I can guarantee to get you on?'

Jens handed us both a card with contact details on it. On the rear of each card, he added another number.

'Cell phone,' he said by way of explanation. 'You can call me on this number any time. I keep myself available on it.' He continued, 'Oh, by the way, are you going to see the English detective too?' Jens wanted to know.

'Yes, we will, although not straight away. Of course, we don't know whether he will want to speak to me,' Lyn told him.

'No, of course. If I get any information, I will contact you if you can give me your cell phone numbers. I am not sure that we will get very far with our examination of the crime scene, but you never know. We might find something useful to help your case.'

He rose to his feet, thus signifying that the interview was at an end. We shook hands and left.

Once outside the Centrum Amstel Police Station, we hailed a taxi and took a circuitous route to our hotel. We checked with reception and were told that the police were still in our room. It seemed a good idea to try booking a flight back to the UK via reception. There was a flight leaving Schiphol Airport at ten-fifteen, and we booked seats on that. We dined in the hotel dining room, a reasonably good meal and not too expensive.

By the time we had finished our meal, we saw the police leaving the hotel.

We went to our room, packed our clothes and toilet things, and went to reception to settle our account. No one appeared to be watching us, but obviously, we could not be certain. I felt a constant tingle at the back of my neck, fearing the men who broke into our room were still around.

Well, if anyone was watching, they did not show themselves, and we made it to Schiphol without incident.

Chapter Eight

The next morning, I sat at my desk and wrote my notes. I usually like to do this daily, but with the activity of the past few days, I had not had the opportunity to do so. With all the happenings, it took me the best part of the forenoon. I did, however, have a lot to write about the recent events. I glanced at the clock on the wall above my desk and noted that it was just fifteen minutes before noon. So engrossed in my writing I had been that I had not stopped for refreshment since half-past eight. I got up and walked to the kitchen to prepare myself a meal.

I made coffee and made myself a cheese sandwich and was munching my way through the second of these when the telephone on my desk shrilled out its tone.

'Mal Jones,' I announced.

'Mal! Mal! It's my dad!' sobbed my friend Lyn.

Oh God, I thought to myself. *What now?*

Out loud, I said, 'Lyn, calm yourself, calm yourself!'

The sobbing continued for several minutes, and eventually, I could tell Lyn had calmed down. I tried again.

'Lyn, what on earth has happened?' I asked.

'It's dad. It's dad,' Lyn shouted hysterically.

'What is?' I asked her.

'They've got him.'

'Who has got him?' I asked. I was at a loss as to what bearing Lyn's father would have upon the matter in hand.

'I had a call from my mother just after seven. She said that dad was not in the house. Nowhere! And he doesn't have a mobile phone either.'

'Perhaps he had just gone out for a newspaper or some other trivial reason. Why all the histrionics?' I was trying to pour oil upon what Lyn obviously saw as troubled waters.

'Dad doesn't just go out for newspapers. He just doesn't. He seems to rely on my mother more and more these days. He's much more likely to ask her if it is alright for him to go to the shop. I'm worried, Mal. I think I'm going to be sick.'

'Alright. Sit tight. I'll come over. Are you at home or with your mother?' I wanted to know.

'At Mum's. Do you know where she lives?' Lyn asked.

'No. Give me the address.'

I noted the address and immediately left to be with Lyn.

I rang the doorbell of Lyn's mother's address, and Lyn herself opened the door.

'Thank God you've come.'

Lyn stood to one side, holding the door open to allow me access. I stepped inside, took my coat off, and handed it over to Lyn, who hung it behind the door.

'Mum is in the lounge,' she said, indicating an open door next to the hall.

'Mum, this is my friend Mal. I have asked her to see if she can help,' Lyn told her mother.

'I do not see how you can help. Can you find my husband?'

'What shall I call you. I can't keep calling you Lyn's mum, can I?'

A smile played around her mouth, and she replied, 'No, I suppose not. Please call me Susan, not Sue, but Susan,'

'What do you think has happened to your husband, Susan?' I asked.

'I just don't know. I woke up and found him gone. It's so unlike him. I have absolutely no idea what has happened. I just hope he's okay.'

'Have you called the police yet?' I asked.

'No, why should I?' Susan wondered.

If this was how it was going to be, it was going to be bloody hard work.

'Susan, please,' I pleaded, 'try and think logically. This could well be a missing person case. How old is your husband?'

'He's over sixty.'

'Does he still drive? Does he enjoy good health?'

'Yes, he still drives, and for his age, he is in pretty good health.'

'Is his car gone?'

All I got from mother and daughter were blank looks.

'Well, has it?' I insisted.

'Go on, tell me. You haven't checked, have you.' I expressed my surprise and tried to keep the disbelief out of my voice.

'No, I'm afraid that we haven't.'

God help us! I thought to myself.

'Where is the car garaged?' I enquired. 'It should have been the first place you checked.'

'About four or five houses down is a narrow lane. You can't miss it; it has grass growing along the centre. If you turn left at the end of that lane, there are six garages, and my husband garages our car in number five.'

There was no movement by either mother or daughter to go to check for the car, so I held out my hand for the garage and ignition keys.

'What?' asked Lyn.

'The keys, please!'

'They are on a hook in the kitchen at the side of the draining board. They are on an owl keyring,' Susan told me.

It came as very little surprise to me that the keys were not where Susan had said that they should be. *Does this woman know nothing about her husband?*

I returned to the lounge and sat down again.

'No keys!' I stated.

'But they must be there!' Susan said.

'Well, I can assure you that they are not,' I reiterated.

'In that case, I have no idea.' Susan said, and Lyn merely shrugged her shoulders.

' How could you not? I'll go out and check the garage in case the keys had been left in the ignition.'

I went outside and located the narrow lane. At the end, I turned to the left and quickly found one marked number five. The lock was still attached to the hasp but was open. I slowly opened the garage door, and the garage was empty. What was going on?

'Look,' I said, 'the keys are gone, and the garage is empty. The door wasn't even locked.'

'Well, that I do not understand,' Susan said, 'my husband is meticulous about locking the garage door.'

'I think that we ought to call the police. This is concerning,' I opined.

'No, no police,' Lyn said.

'Lyn. This is your father we are talking about. He could be in danger! Do you not remember telling me that they…'

Before I could complete my sentence, Lyn interrupted.

'I've changed my mind,' she told me.

'Changed your mind about what?' Lyn's mother asked.

'Doesn't matter, Mum.'

'Well, clearly, there is more to this than what first meets the eye. So come on, Lynda, tell me.'

Silence.

'Lynda?' Susan persisted.

'Yes, Lynda, tell us,' I supported Susan.

Silence again. I noticed Lyn shot daggers at me from across the room.

'Is this connected with what we found at your house, Lyn?' I pushed her.

'What did you find, Lynda?' Susan prompted her daughter.

Silence again. Lyn struggled to come up with a viable explanation for her hesitance.

'Lyn. If you are not prepared to answer your mother, then I shall feel I cannot continue to help you.'

Of course, I didn't mean it, but I thought it would be helpful for us all to know exactly what was what.

'Lyn?' her mother spoke softly. 'Tell me.'

There was a prolonged pause, certainly too long to be called a pregnant pause.

Lyn gave a very heavy sigh and then took a deep breath.

'Okay. I'll explain.'

'Mal, firstly, I'm sorry, but I did not tell you all that I suspected, not knew, mind you, just suspected.'

'Lyn,' I interrupted, 'We can deal with all that side of things later. For now, your father has to be our priority. We must tell the police that he is missing. Just tell them that for now, don't elaborate. If we report him missing from home, then they can at least put his vehicle registration on the Police National Computer. That way, if there are any checks made by the police anywhere in the country, the police we report him missing to will get to know. That must be the least we have to do.'

It was an ultimatum of sorts, I knew, but if it took that to get any action out of either of them, then it would be worth it. Lyn and her mother's reaction to her father's disappearance was shocking, but I wasn't giving up.

Lyn crossed the lounge to the telephone and dialled the local police station. I heard her giving details of her father and his car. The officer she spoke to promised to get things moving and promised that someone would be around later in the day to complete the missing person report.

Lyn carefully replaced the handset and returned to sit on the sofa beside her mother. She made to put her arm around her mother's shoulders but found her attempts at comfort rejected. Lyn was shocked by her mother's rejection but nonetheless accepted it.

'Mum?' Lyn whispered but would not look at her mother.

'Lyn. You have not been honest with me, have you?' Susan asked Lyn.

Another pause. This time a much shorter one.

'No,' Lyn whispered her reply, clearly ashamed of her actions.

'Tell me, Lynda, tell me.' So, her mother was still a bit mad at her. And rightly so, in my opinion.

Lynda was obviously considering most carefully what she should tell her mother. I wondered, too, whether she would let anything slip that I was unaware of.

'Mum, it's David.'

'David. What about David? How does he come into things?' Susan asked with clear astonishment.

I, too, could not believe what I was hearing. She had not even told her mother that David was dead! Why on earth not? What's going on with you, Lyn?

'Well,' Lyn continued slowly, 'three days ago, the police called at my house to tell me that David was dead. They were not able to tell me what had happened, though. So that is all I know for now.'

I realised that Susan was watching her daughter, and I could clearly read the disbelief in her eyes. Susan sat there, shell-shocked at the revelation. There, Susan and I were in total agreement. I didn't believe Lyn either. Well, I believed that the police had told her that David was dead, but I definitely did not believe my best friend when she told her mother that that was all she knew. Clearly, there was more. The diamonds, or whatever the stones were, the bank statements, and the fact that both were hidden. For some reason, Lyn had decided not to tell her mother about these. I did not want to ponder over why she didn't tell her, but I suppose, thinking as charitably as I could, Lyn may have been trying to shield her mother from concern about what David had been up to because up to something, David had most definitely been.

'I am still waiting to be interviewed by the police,' Lyn told her mother.

This was true, I knew, but the possible if not probable reason behind that fact was conveniently withheld. That was perhaps unkind of me. After all, there was no real evidence to suggest that Lyn knew more than she was telling her mother or me. That said, there was something niggling in the back of my mind. Had Lyn said something which would point to the fact that she had almost let something slip? I went back over our conversations since I was first summonsed to support her in her loss and the time she lashed out at me for trying to evaluate the diamonds' worth. The main point that was niggling me was that she never thought to question the fact that David was in a financial position to allocate four thousand pounds a month for food and clothing. I felt sure that if it were my husband giving me that sort of money, then I would certainly be questioning it, to myself if no one else. How could Lyn let it slip? Surely she isn't that naïve. Lyn was nobody's fool, and yet apparently, she had accepted the income to her personal bank account as not in the least bit suspicious. I remembered that we had not found David's account in this country, always supposing that he had one, of course. I would ask Lyn about that as soon as we had left her mother or if an opportunity arose before that.

My musings were interrupted by the jangling of Susan's telephone.

'Could you answer that please, Lyn?' Susan asked.

Lyn did as she was asked.

Lifting the receiver, she announced herself, 'This is Lyn Kendall.'

We learned later that the caller was an officer from the local police division station calling in regards to her father's disappearance, and the conversation had gone something like this, 'Mrs Kendall. Was it you who reported your father missing?'

'Yes, that's right. Why do you ask?'

'Well,' the officer had said, 'we have found his car.'

'You have! Where?' Lyn's voice had gone up in volume somewhat.

'Looe, in Cornwall.'

'Where?' Lyn was almost shouting by this time.

'Near The Sardine Factory Restaurant, Quay Road at West Looe.'

'What about my father? Where is he? Is he okay?'

'I am afraid I can't answer that. Devon and Cornwall Police rang us after carrying out a Police National Computer check on the car.'

'Well, someone must be able to tell me!' Lyn exclaimed.

'Of course, they can. If you ring the Plymouth police station, they will get the officer to contact you directly. The incident number is 2022 of today's date,' the officer said and helpfully furnished the contact number.

'Thank you,' Lyn said and terminated the call.

She turned and saw Susan looking enquiringly at her.

'Well?' Susan urged her to share the information.

'The police in Cornwall have found Dad's car in West Looe,' Lyn told us.

'And…?' Susan asked again.

'And that's all that police officer knew. He took a call from Devon & Cornwall Police to say that the car had been found near a restaurant in West Looe. He didn't say anything about Dad because he didn't know. He has suggested that we ring the Plymouth Police and ask the officer finding the car to ring us direct. Do you want me to make the call, Mum?' Lyn asked.

'Yes. You do it. Get as much information as you can.'

Lyn dialled the number for Plymouth police station and within minutes had given the incident number and was speaking to someone in their communications department.

'Is there any news of my father?'

The operator could not help as she did not have that information.

'Is it possible to speak directly to the officer who found the car?' Lyn asked.

'Yes, you can,' the operator assured her. She has left her mobile number on the incident log for you to do just that. You can call her now. She's available.'

'Thank you very much.' Lyn said and terminated the call.

She replaced the handset, immediately picked it up again and began dialling. The officer's mobile number, I presumed.

She stopped dialling before she had completed the number.

'I think I will use my mobile. That way, I can put it on speaker, and we can all hear the conversation.'

'Sounds fair,' I responded in acknowledgement.

The ring tone stopped, and a female voice answered the call announcing that she was Police Constable Wyatt.

'Hello,' Lyn said. 'Are you the officer who found my father's car?' she asked.

'Who is this?' Constable Wyatt again.

'Sorry, yes, this is Lyn Kendall. I have been asked to ring you about my father's car. I believe that you have found it.'

'Yes, that is correct. I located it on The Quay at West Looe, near the Sardine Factory Restaurant.'

'What about my father? Is he alright?' Lyn asked.

'Well, I'm afraid we cannot answer that at the moment. We haven't actually located him yet. We are out making door-to-door enquiries as we speak. We're trying our best to locate him as soon as we can.'

I indicated to Lyn that I would like to ask a question, and she nodded her assent.

'Hello, Constable. My name is Mal Jones. I am an insurance adjuster, and I am helping my friend Lyn Kendall with enquiries about her husband's death, and we feel that this incident could be connected.'

'Please call me Amelia, and can I call you Mal?' the officer wanted to know.

'That's fine; Mal is alright. Was there anything to suggest anything untoward as regards the vehicle?'

'Such as?'

'Signs of a struggle, for instance.'

'No, nothing like that. Nothing indicates that the driver left against his will. The keys were still in the ignition. If I didn't know that the owner had been reported missing, then I would have gone with my first instinct, and that was that the driver had either been drunk and abandoned the vehicle or that it had been left there and the driver had merely forgotten to take his keys.'

'Lyn, here again, Amelia. Is the car still there?'

'No, we had to recover it to a local garage. The road is very narrow along here, and it was causing an obstruction. That was, in fact, the reason that I was sent here, because of the obstruction.'

'Thank you. Could you let me know when we can collect the car on this number? I'll be waiting for your call.'

'Yes, we will. We would like to hang on to it for the time being until we know what has happened to your father.'

Susan gave a sharp intake of breath and said, 'Is that a suggestion that something untoward has happened then?'

'No, absolutely nothing. We just don't know anything at this time. Is there any particular reason for your concern for his welfare?'

Lyn interjected, 'No, nothing at all. It is just that this is not like him at all. He never leaves the house without telling Mum, that is why we panicked.'

'We will be in touch, Mrs Kendall, goodbye for now.' The officer terminated the call.

I looked at Lyn and raised a questioning eyebrow.

Nothing from Lyn. She stood there staring at the wall blankly.

I suggested by a movement of my head that I wanted to speak to Lynaway from her mother. She was quick enough on the uptake and said she had to get some air in the garden. I offered to accompany her, and Susan said that she would make us some tea.

Once safely outside and away from Susan, I asked Lyn why she had not told the police the whole truth.

'But I did,' she protested.

'You told me this morning when you rang me that 'they've got him.' If you truly believe that, then surely you should have told the police.'

'Look, Mal, I don't know what has happened to my father, so I wasn't lying to the police,' Lyn maintained.

'Lyn, you must be in your own little world,' I said with exasperation. 'Stop hiding things from everyone. What's going on?'

'What the hell do you mean by that? Don't you believe me?' Her question sounded genuine.

'Look, Lyn, let me just point out a few facts to you:

1.   You haven't heard from the police about your husband's death. You do not seem surprised or concerned about that. If that were me, I would be chomping at the bit to get some answers from the police, but you don't seem that concerned. At all.

2.   You did not seem too surprised when we found all those diamonds hidden in the books in David's study.

3.   You certainly were not overly shocked at David's bank balance and the fact that it was a Swiss bank account.

4.   You must have just thought that David was involved in something illegal, yet you do not seem surprised.

5.   Your monthly allowance for food and clothes is considerably more than I earn from my job, yet you accept this as normal. Did it ever occur to you to question David where he was getting his money from?

6.   You didn't seem surprised when Klass put his value on the diamonds.

7. Anyone else would have been almost frantic at finding that their hotel room had been ransacked. You did not seem that concerned.

'Lyn, you have to tell me what is going on. If you don't, then I am not that sure that I can carry on helping you. So come on, Lyn, give me the truth! What are you hiding from me, from us?'

Chapter Nine

I could see that Lyn was visibly shaken by my outburst, and I understood why. I rarely castigated her. She just stood there looking at me, I thought in disbelief. I saw her eyes turn to the kitchen where her mother stood busying herself with cups and saucers and a teapot and kettle. She must surely have heard my raised voice even if she could not clearly hear what I had been saying.

'Come on, Lyn. This is your last chance with me. I mean it. It is the last thing I wish to do, but I truly mean that if you cannot be honest with me, then we are over. I've been trying to help you find closure, but I cannot continue unless you tell me the whole truth.' I told her with as much emphasis as I could.

'You wouldn't, would you?' Lyn asked, still not convinced that I really did mean what I said.

'Yes, I would. Don't push me to do this.' I said with what I hoped sounded sincerity in my voice. 'I don't want to terminate our friendship, but I will if you cannot be completely honest with me. We have always told each other everything, all our innermost secrets, and thoughts. We have shared information about each other which a man and wife probably wouldn't even share, and yet you're hesitant to share this, whatever this is.'

I paused to let what I had said sink in. Clearly, it was penetrating her brain and processing what I had said.

'Alright, you win. I will tell you as much as I know, but I do not want Mum to hear everything about her son-in-law, at least not yet. Let's go for a drive and find somewhere quiet, and I promise I'll tell you.'

I told Lyn that I accepted this for now and was about to turn to re-enter the house when Lyn's mobile rang. It was the police officer we had spoken to earlier, Amelia Wyatt.

'Lyn, it's Amelia Wyatt. I believe that we have located your father. Can you describe him?'

I saw Lyn's eyes widen with hope. 'Well, I don't know what he was wearing, but he is aged sixty-four, about six feet tall, slim build, greying dark brown hair cut short. He wears pale brown tortoiseshell glasses that have bi-focal lenses. Oh, and he has a scar on his left forearm, about three inches long,' Lyn told the officer.

'In that case, Lyn, we have definitely found your father.' Amelia Wyatt said reassuringly. 'We'll tell you when to come down and take him home.'

'Is he alright?' Lyn's mother asked.

'Yes, physically, he is absolutely fine. However, we are a little concerned about his mental health. He doesn't seem to know who he is, where he is, or how he even got here. We are therefore taking him into Plymouth Crown Hill Police

Station so that we can get a doctor to have a look at him and assess his mental health state.'

'But my husband is not mad!' shouted Susan.

'No one is suggesting that he is. What we are duty-bound to do is to satisfy ourselves that he is not a danger to himself or indeed to others. It is not an infrequent action, I assure you.'

'Can we see him if we come down right now?' Susan asked.

'Certainly, you will be able to see him. How long before you get to Plymouth?'

Lyn looked quizzically at me, hoping I'll drive them both to Plymouth.

'About four to four and a half hours, I should think,' I told Lyn.

Lyn passed this on to Amelia Wyatt, and she seemed happy with this.

The call having been terminated, Susan said, 'At least he is safe.' She said this with relief in her voice.

'Yes,' I said, 'at least there is that. I do wonder how he got to Plymouth, though,' I whispered under my breath.

I considered my earlier conversation with Lyn in the garden again. I stood by what I had said but decided that the news of Lyn's father's safety took precedence.

'Shall we take my car?' I offered.

'Yes, please,' Lyn spoke on behalf of herself and her mother.

'I'll just pop down to the petrol station and top up with fuel,' I told them. 'Do you want me to bring back some snacks for the road?'

'I don't think that would be necessary. Before we leave, perhaps we ought to have this pot of tea, and I'll cut some fruit cake. That ought to keep us going.' This was from Susan, who immediately made her way to the kitchen to collect the food and drink.

'I suppose I can fill up when we leave. Is there a petrol station between here and the motorway?'

Both Susan and Lyn nodded yes.

We had our fill of fruit cake and tea, made sure that we were comfortable for the journey, and were on our way.

I glanced at the dashboard clock of my car as we drew away from the kerb outside Susan's house. It was just four fifteen. 'Sit back and relax, you two. It's going to be a while,' I announced as we finally hit the road.

The first part of the journey would not be as fast as the latter part of it would be. There was the rush hour traffic to contend with and any roadworks we might encounter. There would inevitably be torpedoes; as it were, there always are.

I told my two passengers that it would be very unlikely that we would be at Plymouth before eight-thirty, maybe later. I also opined that trying to find a hotel near the police station in Plymouth might be good as well. Both agreed that it was a good idea and began the task of finding one via Google.

She chose the Travelodge Plymouth Roborough, which was only about ten minutes from Crownhill Police station. We booked two rooms, one double for Susan and one twin for Lyn and me. Lyn booked the double just in case her father was able to join us.

We made good time until we hit the M5 motorway. Leaving the M4 and joining the M5 was an absolute nightmare. There were major roadworks between the turn off for Cribbs Causeway Shopping Mall and Gordano Service Area. The speed we were able to make made a snail seem speedy. My guesstimate of four to four and half hours seemed like a dream now. I reckoned it would take much longer. The one consolation was that at least we were moving, just.

I took this opportunity to remind Lyn of her promise to tell me all that she knew. This seemed a good way to pass the time, some of it at least. I glanced in my rear-view mirror and saw that Susan was asleep in the rear passenger seat. I pushed Lyn to use this opportunity and start talking.

'But Mum!' Lyn said, jerking her head towards the rear seat.

'She is asleep,' I told her. 'Come on, give!'

'What if she wakes up?'

'Then I'll keep my eyes on her from here and indicate to you,' I told her.

'Right. It started…' she began.

'What started?' I interrupted.

'If you wait, I'll tell you. Just don't interrupt me.'

'Sorry,' I said to Lyn, indicating that she should continue.

'As I was about to say, it all began before we were even married. I met David at a party to celebrate a mutual friend's marriage. To say it was love at first sight would be overstating things. Perhaps a better description would be lust at first sight. We were both instantly attracted to each other's energy. We danced for several hours and partook of the free bar liberally. We decided to get some air. Oh, it must have been at about eleven-thirty. Well, once outside in the garden, he put his arm around my waist and pulled me closer to him. I didn't have a boyfriend at the time, and when he turned me into his arms and kissed me, I did not resist his advances. If anything, I wanted it more than David, and when he placed his hand over my breast, I not only did not object but also actively encouraged it. We managed to make our way around a hedge where there was an arbour seat. We were out of sight of the wedding party, and it was then a race between us as to who got their clothes off first. I think I beat David by a few seconds.' Lyn chuckled as she recalled their first encounter. I noticed her lips break into a shy smile before she continued. 'I felt for him and found that he was hard, as hard as steel it seemed to me. My touch was enough to light the blue touch paper as it were, and before I could think about whether what I was doing was the right thing, he entered me. It was the most marvellous feeling that I had ever experienced. David said that he felt the same way. We did it once more before we decided that we ought to get back to the party. We dressed, which took longer than it should have because we just could not keep our hands off each other. We made our way back to the party, and it seemed that no one had missed us. The following day, which was Sunday, we met up again. We spent the whole day and evening in bed, making love at regular intervals. It was as if we could not get enough of each other, and from my point of view, that was true. I wanted to be around him all the time. It was the following Saturday before we were able to get together again. David did not seem as keen on our lovemaking as he had been the previous weekend. In fact, it was all I could do to get him upstairs! After we had made love, David lay on his back, staring at the ceiling. He said nothing. I thought at first that he had not gotten the same satisfaction from our lovemaking as he had before. Clearly, he had something on his mind. I asked him what the problem was, and he just looked over at me but said nothing.'

Lyn paused at this point in her narrative as if she was considering what to say next.

'Go on, Lyn. Susan is still asleep.'

Lyn glanced back at her mother to ensure her mother wasn't listening.

'Well. I climbed out of bed and went to make coffee. When I re-entered the bedroom, David was buttoning up his shirt. I asked him what was wrong, and he refused to reply to me. I asked him again, and he froze. His hands were quite still on his shirt buttons, and he was looking at me most intently. I could see the worry in his eyes. I got the impression that he was trying to make his mind up about something. It wasn't exactly frightening, the look on his face that is, but it was certainly unnerving. I asked him again what the matter was. He hesitated again for what seemed an age, then ignored looking me in the eye and answering my question. Then he leaned over and picked up his trousers from the chair at the side of the bed. He then put his hand into the inside of the waistband. When he extracted his hand again, I could see that he was holding a small bag with a pull-string closing. David pulled the top of the bag open and poured the contents into his hand. There was a small pile of what appeared to be small stones. They were quite dirty and held no particular attraction that I could see. I looked up into David's eyes, and they had literally lit up. It must have been the stones; there was nothing else. I didn't react at all, and David obviously was surprised a bit, I think. I asked him what they were, and he just smiled back at me. I asked him again, and he whispered the word diamonds. I was unable to hold back a gasp of disbelief. He said that the diamonds in his hand were worth tens of thousands of pounds. I wondered why he was showing them to me, considering we barely knew each other. In the end, I asked him just that. He said that he needed someone to keep them safe and would I be willing to keep them for him. I was taken aback, but I agreed, without knowing anything about the diamonds or why he wanted someone to keep them. I know now that I should have asked, and had I not been satisfied with the answer, I should have refused to take them. I should have done that, but I didn't. Well, one thing led to another, and a few days later, he brought two more bags of stones for me to keep for him. I asked him what he wanted me to do with them, and he said he would think about it and let me know. This went on until I had six bags of the things. Yes, all six bags. I knew about them.'

I looked at Lyn in disbelief. How could she keep this from me? I thought to myself.

She continued narrating her story. 'One night after David had been round and we had made love, he told me that he had found a method of hiding them. That was the cut-out books. We were engaged to be married within a few weeks and had set a date to be married six months later. On the evening before our wedding, David handed me a cheque for four thousand pounds. He told me that as soon as possible after our marriage, he would transfer in the same amount as the cheque each month, and he did. After the honeymoon, we settled down as a married couple, and everything was going swimmingly. We were happy, and things continued as normal.

Then one day, I happened to catch sight of a strange-looking bank statement sheet on the floor of David's study. I wasn't prying; I had gone in there to vacuum through. I looked at the balance. Well, I couldn't help myself, really. The figure made me gasp out loud again. It was well up into six figures. I pondered what else he was hiding from me. I asked David about it when he came home, and at first, he accused me of prying in his study. I assured him that I had not been prying, just vacuuming his study like I usually did.

Then I turned the onus on him and demanded that he tell me what was happening. I knew that he had diamonds hidden inside the cut-out books worth millions. So, what with that and the bank balance, something was going on, I knew. I asked him outright, and to my surprise, I might even say shock, he told me. The money was the result of illegal trading, he said. He couldn't do much with the money at present because if the bank ever discovered what he was doing, he would end up in prison. What was worse, he said, was that I would be sent to prison too for aiding and abetting him by hiding the diamonds. After he told me, I got stressed about getting in trouble. The diamonds had been bought so that he could convert some of the cash. He told me that he wasn't alone, that there were five of them involved in the trading and that he was the designated banker for the group. This explained the huge bank balance and the fact that he had possession of so many diamonds. He was asked to hand over four-fifths of all the money he was holding to the other group members, and to begin with, he told them that it wasn't possible. He told me that he had always intended to withdraw the monies owed to the others but couldn't do so for the time being. I have no idea why he could not or would not repay the money; he never told me. All I do know is that he told me, a few days before his death, that he had been threatened. He didn't say by whom, but I assumed it was one or more of these people. So, there's your whole truth.'

Lyn paused again and looked around to see her mother's mouth wide open in astonishment. We were not aware that she had already woken up from her slumber. She had not heard everything Lyn had told me, but she clearly had heard enough.

'Lyn, how could you!' her mother shouted. 'If you want to put yourself in danger, then I cannot stop you. It's your life; you can do what you think is best, but if you have endangered your father in any way, then I will never, ever forgive you, and I will go to the police myself. Do you hear me?'

'Yes, Mum. I hear you,' Lyn whispered, clearly ashamed of what she had done to protect David.

'Hang on a moment, Susan. At this time, we do not know exactly what has happened to your husband. There may be a perfectly logical explanation.' I tried to sound reassuring.

'What possible logical explanation can there be? I heard Lyn when she rang you asking for help. She said, 'they've got him.' What else is that supposed to mean?'

'Yes, that is true, she did. But still, we shouldn't jump to conclusions. I know of an oldish chap who went out one morning to get petrol and a newspaper from his local garage and was missing for two days. He turned up eventually at a seaside town where he had spent holidays as a child. He had no idea why he went there and had no recollection of going there. It turned out to be a very mild form of dementia, nothing more sinister than that. So, let's just wait and see, shall we? The important thing right now is that he is safe, and we have to bring him home.'

I am not sure that Susan was convinced by my assurance, well, assurance of a sort. I was watching Lyn out of the corner of my eye, and I was not absolutely certain that she had told us the story in its entirety. I was convinced that there was more and wanted to dig further. I may well have been wrong, of course.

The journey to Plymouth seemed almost never-ending, but we eventually arrived just after nine-thirty. I felt it was too late for us to see Susan's husband, but she was adamant that she wanted to see him.

We went to Crownhill Police Station and asked to speak to Constable Amelia Wyatt. The enquiry desk clerk told us she had gone off duty at nine o'clock.

'Are you Mal Jones?' she wanted to know.

I confirmed that I was she, and the clerk handed me a note.

'Please ring this number. Amelia Wyatt', the note read.

'She left her number in case you arrive late and need to speak to her,' the clerk said by way of explanation.

I rang the number on the note and was immediately rewarded with a reply.

'Amelia, hello. This is Mal Jones,' I announced.

'Hello, Mal. Are you within earshot of Lyn and her mother?'

'Yes, I am.'

'Could you go outside, do you think?' she asked. I stroked my furrowed brow, wondering why she would ask me to step away from them. Regardless, I agreed to her request.

'Of course, hang on.'

'Lyn, I need to take this call, but it isn't a very good signal. I'm just going outside.'

'Okay, Mal. We'll wait here,' Lyn said.

I left the building and went a few yards along the street.

'Right Amelia. I am outside, and the others are still in the foyer. You can talk to me now.'

'Mal. We called a doctor in to examine Mr. Wright. He seems to be in very good health, both physically and mentally. There were no signs of dementia and, initially, nothing to explain why he should take it upon himself to drive to Looe. The doctor who carried out Mr Wright's assessment was a mental health specialist, so we called a police surgeon in to examine him. The police surgeon said that she could find nothing untoward either. However, as she said, Mr Wright is very alert and in good health. To be on the safe side, blood samples were taken. They will, of course, be subjected to various tests, alcohol, drugs, and so on. If these were to be used in criminal proceedings, the tests would be carried out at the Forensic Science Laboratory, but the police surgeon has a good relationship with the pathology department at Plymouth Hospital. We are not going to use these in criminal proceedings, so she asked her contact to do a rush job, as it were. The upshot of this is that the blood samples were clear of alcohol. The worrying thing is that the blood sample did show traces of Rohypnol. He may have been drugged.'

'Date rape drugs, you mean?' I said with puzzlement and disbelief all rolled into one sound in my voice.

'Yes,' Amelia confirmed.

'It doesn't make sense. Not to me anyway. Who would drug him, and why?'

'Nor me. So, I consulted the police surgeon again. She said that if this had been administered in sufficient quantity, then Mr Wright could easily have been abducted, the drug, in liquid form, could be given to him, and when he wakes up, he is miles and miles away in Looe. It is also known that Rohypnol can cause forgetfulness. So, Mr Wright should regain all his memory, but no one seems to know how soon it will be. We have taken the precaution of admitting him to the hospital overnight, just for observation at this stage. May I suggest you leave it until tomorrow morning to visit him? We have to ensure he is out of danger before his family meets him. I am back on duty at eight o'clock in the morning, so I could meet you outside the hospital main entrance at about nine if that suits.'

'Yes, thanks, Amelia. I think that would be best. I'll tell Lyn and her mum some of what you've told me but leaving out the Rohypnol bit, I think.'

'Good idea, Mal. I will see you in the morning then. Bye.'

The call was terminated, and I returned to the police station foyer.

'Everything okay, Mal?' Lyn wanted to know.

'Yes. That was Amelia. She says that your father has been admitted to the hospital overnight. Just for observation, that's all. He has been seen by a mental health doctor and a police surgeon, and he seems in tip-top condition, physically and mentally. There's nothing to worry about at the moment.'

'If that's the case, then why is he in the hospital?' Susan wanted to know.

'Just for observation, I told you,' I assured her. 'The police needs to be sure nothing untoward happened to him.'

'Yes, but if he is okay mentally and physically…' she left the question hanging in the air.

'The thing is, Susan, no one has been able to explain your husband's odd behaviour satisfactorily.'

'Odd? What do you mean, odd?' Susan asked.

'Well, going missing from home and then turning up miles and miles away with no recollection of how he got there could be thought to be at least a little odd, don't you think?' I pointed out.

'Yes, I suppose so. When you put it like that.'

'Amelia Wyatt says that your husband has already been admitted and that he ought not to be disturbed tonight. She will meet us at the main hospital entrance at nine in the morning. Until then, we can only wait and hope nothing untoward happened to him.'

Neither Sue nor Lyn made any further comment, and we made our way to our hotel in absolute silence.

As we approached the hotel, Lyn suddenly pointed out that we hadn't eaten since the hasty snack lunch much earlier in the day.

Doctor Google gave us directions to a Chinese restaurant; fortunately for us, they were still serving meals late at night.

After a delicious meal, we again made our way to the hotel. A good night's sleep was what we all needed after a long day.

Chapter Ten

Refreshed from our slumbers, we met up in the dining room shortly after eight o'clock. The breakfast was well-cooked and tasty and set us all up for the day.

By nine o'clock, the three of us were waiting outside the hospital's main entrance. We didn't say much. There didn't seem to be much we could say, but everyone appeared to be holding back their thoughts. Once Susan and Lyn had the chance to speak to Mr Wright, they would almost certainly be far more talkative.

True to her word Amelia Wyatt arrived, and all four of us went into the hospital. She led us to the ward where Mr Wright was waiting for us. He stood up as we approached his bed and threw his arms around his wife and daughter. Amelia stood back and watched the reunion. All of the emotions displayed appeared genuine enough to me, although I was nowhere near an expert in these things.

As we watched, there was a soft tap on the door, and a staff nurse poked her head around it as it opened.

'Constable Wyatt?' she asked. Well, it was a part question and part statement. As Amelia was the only one of us in a uniform, it must have been fairly obvious.

'Yes,' Amelia said.

'Could you come with me, please? The doctor would like to speak to you before Mr Wright is discharged,' the nurse said.

'Oh, alright,' she said to the nurse and then turned to me, 'you had better come as well, Mal.' Lyn and Susan looked at me intently, wondering why the constable would ask me to join them, but Mr Wright soon turned their attention away.

We followed the nurse a short way along the corridor to another door on which the nurse perfunctorily knocked before opening the door and going inside.

'Ah, Constable Wyatt, I presume. I am Doctor Francis, Paul Francis,' the doctor said, extending his hand to be shaken.

'Yes, doctor, and this is Miss Mal Jones, a family friend of the Wrights who is looking into his disappearance.' The doctor shook my hand too. 'Nice to meet you, Miss Mal.'

'I thought that you ought to see this, Miss Wyatt.' He extracted a sheet of paper from a file.

'Injection?' exclaimed Amelia.

'Yes, we found this injection site during a routine examination of Mr Wright prior to his admission,' the doctor informed us. 'So that explains how Mr Wright was persuaded to go to Looe. He didn't know anything about it. He was brought here unconscious and drugged.'

'The question which remains unanswered though is, who persuaded, if that's the correct word, Mr Wright to go to Looe and perhaps more importantly, why?' Amelia Wyatt was clearly pondering everything.

She looked at me, 'Mal?'

'Amelia?' I replied.

'Don't mess me around, Mal. You know more about this than you are saying, don't you?'

'Yes and no.' I pondered what I could say to assist Amelia.

'Come on, Mal, don't prevaricate. You do, don't you?'

Amelia Wyatt was clearly not prepared to let the whole thing pass. She suspected that things were not straightforward, at least not as straightforward as they seemed.

'Doctor, is there an office I can use to interview Miss Jones, please. Somewhere where we won't be disturbed.'

'Yes, of course. Use the one next door. There is an engaged sign, and no one will come in unexpectedly. Suit you?'

'Thanks, doctor. That will be fine. Mal, can you let the Wrights know what is going on?'

I went back to the ward, and although the hugging was over, they were still very close. I told them that Amelia wanted to interview me without elaborating. They seemed happy enough, so I left them to it.

Once ensconced in the office with the 'engaged' sign illuminated, we sat on opposite sides of the table.

'Now, Mal. Come on. Out with it. What is going on? I know you're keeping something from me,' Amelia asked.

'How much do you know?' I wondered.

'All I know is what we have found down here. I am still trying to find out exactly why Mr Wright ended up down here. You heard what the doctor said about finding an injection site?' she asked.

'Yes, I did hear,' I told her.

'Well?' Amelia wasn't going to accept any old story, but I didn't know all the answers. The only information I had was a mixture of what I had been told by Lyn, which I don't know is the entire story, and what I had seen in David's study.

'Look, Mal. If Mr Wright had been injected with Rohypnol, it could only have been for one reason, and that is kidnap. If that was the case, as it appears to be, there must have been a reason for the kidnap. Do you not agree?'

'Yes. I do. If you listen to what I have to tell you without interruption, then I will tell you everything that I know or suspect.'

'Go ahead, but is it going to take long?' She wanted to know.

'A while!' I told her.

'I think we had better tell Lyn and her mum that they can go back to the hotel and that I will bring you back later when I have finished with you.'

Amelia Wyatt returned to Mr Wright's ward and spoke to the two ladies.

'Lyn, Susan, I want to interview Mal about this incident, which may take a little while. You go back to the hotel, and we will join you in about an hour. Is that alright?'

Neither made any objection, but I learned later that Lyn's face had a strange look when she knew the police were speaking to me without her presence. Perhaps she was wondering how much I would tell Amelia and how much I would hold back. In truth, that was exactly what I was thinking too! I had no idea what to do with all the information she had just shared with me.

Amelia came back into the office and closed the door behind her.

'Do you mind if I record our conversation? Only it will save me having to write it out as we go along. I don't want writer's cramp halfway through now, do I?'

'No, I suppose not. Yes, you have my consent. You can record it, and I will do the same if I may. That way, I shan't have to try to remember what was said. Lyn and Susan will almost certainly want to know.'

'Fine by me.'

Both Amelia and I took our mobiles out and placed them on the table between us, and simultaneously we switched on the record buttons.

'Right, Mal. Now give! Tell me everything you know.'

I decided that honesty would be the best policy, and that seemed to include only those facts which I knew for certain. I did not want to get caught out in a lie later. So, with all that in mind, I began the story as I knew it.

'Well, Amelia. As far as I am aware and concerned, it all started a week ago. I received a call from a police officer who, or so it transpired, was at Lyn's house. He asked if I could come over to be with Lyn as he and his colleague had just told Lyn of her husband's death. Lyn and I have been friends since school, and I did not hesitate to be with her. She's my best friend, and I felt it was important to be there for her for support at a time like this.'

I continued with my narrative and told her about finding the bags of stones and the bank statements. This may have been disloyal to Lyn, but I was more interested in covering my own backside. The only thing I left out was the name of the bank in Amsterdam where the stones were safely under lock and key. I am not sure what made me hold back, but I did.

When I had finished my narrative, Amelia just sat and stared at me. It was clear that she had some difficulty processing what she had heard.

It was a full five minutes before Amelia asked, 'Have you spoken to Detective Chief Inspector Carterford again?'

'No, I have not. I am finding it difficult to know exactly who is investigating what. At the moment, we had West Sussex Police delivering a death message, Thames Valley Police investigating the death of David Kendall, the Dutch Police are investigating the break-in to our hotel room, and you are investigating the finding of a missing person. You can appreciate my dilemma, I feel sure. We're a bit all over the place at the moment.'

'Yes, I realise that it must be difficult for you. If it helps, at the moment, we cannot be certain that any crime has been committed at Looe, so you can perhaps discount us at this stage. As soon as the situation has been resolved to our satisfaction, I am perfectly happy to liaise with Chief Inspector Carterford. Does that suit you?'

'That really will be up to Lyn, but as far as I am concerned, yes, that will be fine. Thanks, constable.'

We both switched off the recorders on our mobile telephones and leaned back in our chairs.

'Mal?' said Amelia. 'May I ask you a question?'

'You can ask, of course, you can. Answering will remain my prerogative.'

'That goes without saying.'

'Go on then, ask away.'

'Do you trust Lyn? One hundred percent trust her, I mean?' Amelia wanted to know. I mulled over her question before I could speak up.

'Would I trust her with my life? Yes wholeheartedly. Do I trust what she has told me about David's affairs? Probably not. It may be that she thinks that she is being wholly honest with us, you, and me. If she is being honest, then the truth will almost certainly be out. If, however, she is not, then who can say what the truth is?'

'I have much the same thoughts, to be frank with you. I think that when we have resolved the incident over Mr Wright, then after I have updated Susan, Lyn, and yourself, I will liaise with Chief Inspector Carterford. From what you have said, and he has not said, I suspect that he and his colleagues are looking at a pretty serious incident and or offence.'

'You may be right, Amelia. I just worry how much Lyn could be involved in this whole affair. Her source of income will be stopped now, but she does seem to have legitimately squirrelled away a fair sum of her own money. This means she should be alright financially for a while.'

'Well, that's one thing, I suppose. Anyway, I will be in touch, Mal. Thank you for your time.'

Amelia shook hands, we exchanged calling cards, and I left.

I didn't raise the subject of her coming to the hotel with me to meet up with Lyn and Susan. Either it had slipped her mind, or she had decided against it at this time.

The hotel was a short taxi ride from the police station, but it was nearly two hours before the three of us were together again.

Lyn was the first to spot me entering the hotel and waved at me as I entered the foyer.

I joined them at their table before deciding to find a pub, and we made our way to the nearest one. We soon found one, and over drinks all round, Lyn asked me how the interview had gone. Her question felt like an attempt to discover if I had told Amelia anything that would shed a bad light on Lyn.

'Before I say anything about that, where is your father, Lyn?'

'The doctor decided they wanted to keep him for another twenty-four hours, so we have decided to stay at the hotel for another night. Now, what happened?'

'Nothing happened, Lyn. It was just an interview,' I told her.

'If it were just an interview, why wouldn't she let me sit in?'

'Well, that is what it was. An interview, no more, no less,' I told her. 'Maybe she wants to interview each of us individually.'

'What did you tell her, Mal?' Lyn wanted to know, and I had the feeling that there was the slightest something in her voice. I detected fear and perhaps menace.

'Only what I know and no more. I was not going to tell any lies to the police. I don't want any of it coming up to bite me on the bum later. I didn't tell her anything that could get us in trouble, Lyn.'

'What did you tell her about David?'

'As little as possible. I don't know much about him, anyway, do I?'

'No. I suppose not.'

I thought Lyn had exhausted her questions for the time being, but I was wrong.

'What did you tell her about the diamonds?' she asked.

'Only that we found them hidden and that they are now safe. All fact and all true.'

'What about the value of them?' Lyn asked.

'What about the value?' I retorted.

'Did you tell her the value of the stones?'

'No, I didn't. After all, we have, sorry, you have only been given an estimate of their value, not an official valuation,' I pointed out.

'That should be alright then.'

Lyn seemed satisfied with my answers but appeared to be at the end of her questions, and we began chatting about normal things.

After about twenty minutes of inane conversation, Lyn suddenly switched back to our previous conversation and asked if Amelia was still coming to see herself and Susan. I truthfully said that Amelia had not mentioned coming to the hotel but that she had said that she would be in touch at a later date.

'What of your dad?' I asked Lyn.

'Doctor Francis said that he wanted to keep him there for another twenty-four hours as he was still not happy with the blood test results. So, we'll collect him when they say it is okay.'

'That makes sense.'

Chapter Eleven

We arrived back at Susan's house. I pulled into the driveway and was surprised and more than a little afraid to see that the front door was not completely closed.

'I'll get the kettle on,' Susan said.

'No!' I said in a raised voice but without shouting.

I did not know whether whoever had entered the house was still inside. I alerted Lyn and her mum that someone had broken in.

'The front door!' I said with as much urgency in my voice as I could muster.

'What the…' Susan's sentence was left hanging in the air.

I noted that Lyn said nothing. I could not detect any emotion which reached her face. She just looked at me. Like me, she had probably guessed.

'Stay here, both of you, and call the police,' I instructed them.

I hurried over to the wall of the house and began making my way carefully and slowly towards the window. I chanced a very swift glance into the room, the lounge. There was no one there, but every drawer had been opened, and the contents of each just scattered on the floor. It was a hell of a mess. Whoever broke into the house clearly knew what they wanted. I continued my way as silently as possible towards the front door. And then stood upright to one side of it. I looked back at the car to make sure that Lyn and Susan were still sitting tight. I was relieved to see them remaining there still. Fear showed clearly on Susan's face, but Lyn's face still showed no emotion at all. She did, however, hold up one hand with a thumb pointing upwards. I took this to mean that she had called the police.

Should I go in on my own, or was this foolhardy in the extreme? I decided it probably was, so I crossed the door as quickly as possible and continued my slow and stealthy way along the wall to the next window, the dining room.

I quickly looked into the room but again could see no one. The culprits, whoever they might be or might have been, had also repeated their search of every drawer in this room. The mess was just as upsetting in this room. At least it would be to Susan when she saw it. Again, there was no sign of anybody in that room.

As far as I could remember, there was only one other room with a ground-floor window, and that was the kitchen. This window was around a corner of the house. I looked in through this window and could not believe my eyes. I should think that every speck of flour, sugar, cereal, biscuits, dried fruit, and the myriad of items one would find in a well-stocked kitchen had been strewn across the floor. There was barely an inch of the black and white floor tiles, which could be clearly seen. The whole scene was a disaster.

Even with all the crime scenes I had visited as an insurance adjuster, I was not prepared for this. I suspected that if I had been willing to enter the premises, I would have found exactly the same mess in every room upstairs and any other room which I could not see from outside. Susan was certainly in for a massive shock when she eventually went in. I only hope she doesn't faint when she does.

I heard a vehicle approaching and glanced at the road. There were two cars, the first of which was a marked police car. The second car followed the first and two plainclothes officers stepped out.

Clearly, they had not seen me because they went straight over to my car and started talking to Lyn and Susan. Lyn was pointing towards the house, and it was then that the officers noticed me. One of the officers held up his hand at me as if they wanted me to stay where I was. I was only too happy to oblige.

When the plainclothes officers had crossed to where I was, one of them placed a restraining hand on my arm. I have to admit that I didn't need any encouragement to follow their instructions. I do not frighten easily, but even so, I could see no reason to put myself in danger unnecessarily. I remained silent and followed their orders.

The first plainclothes man crept in through the front door, keeping low as he did so. Ten minutes or so passed when the only activity had been when the second plainclothes man had followed his colleague into the house. He had again indicated that I should stay put, but nothing had been heard since. Lyn, Susan, and I stood in the driveway waiting for the officers to step out with some information.

I was getting concerned for the officers' safety. It seemed a long time for two people to check a house for intruders, so I straightened myself up and was about to move towards the front door when one of the officers poked his head out of the door. He told me there was definitely no one in the house and beckoned to Lyn and Susan. They joined us outside the front door.

'Well, Mrs Kendall, Mrs Wright, Miss Jones, we have checked the inside of the house, and there is no one inside, so it is safe to go in, although I would prefer it if you didn't. We need to get the crime scene investigators down here to go right through the house.

'What, for a simple break-in?' Lyn asked.

'Nothing very simple about this break-in, Mrs Kendall. Every single drawer, cupboard, and bookcase has been turned out, and all the tins and packets in the kitchen have been emptied over the floor. There is very little damage, and once the mess has been cleared up, it will be almost back to normal.'

'Look, Mrs Kendall, I have been a detective for nearly fifteen years, and I have been to hundreds of burglaries, and I can tell you that this is anything but a simple break-in. Now can you shed any light on it?' the other officer interrogated.

'No, I'm sorry. I can't,' Lyn told the detective but cast me a warning glance which I interpreted as being a request, an instruction even, to say nothing.

'Mrs Wright, this is your house. Can you think of any reason for this?'

'No, none.' The expression on her face suggested that she was being perfectly honest.

I suggested I go to a takeaway coffee establishment and buy coffee for us all. We couldn't go into the house yet, and we couldn't just stand about. It was a very mild day, so I suggested Lyn and Susan sit out on the patio while I got the coffee. I asked the detectives too, and they eagerly affirmed that coffee would be very welcome.

I drove to the out-of-town shopping centre and quickly found the Costa Coffee drive-thru. In a matter of minutes, the coffees were passed through the serving hatch, and I was on my way.

On the spur of the moment, I decided to return to Susan's house via Lyn's home. It was not that far out of the way after all. I wanted to ensure it wasn't broken into as well. As I pulled into the driveway, it was no surprise to find the front door open. A silly thought went through my mind about waiting for buses, and two came along at once. They had to be connected, without a doubt. What should I do? The sensible answer is 'nothing'. But I wasn't feeling very sensible, so I closed the car door as quietly as possible and crept over to the front door. As I peeped around the door jamb, a large, gloved fist caught me full force in the face. I fell backwards, and the last thing I remember is banging my head on the gravel of the driveway. I blacked out.

I next became aware of my surroundings when I felt moisture on my face. I blinked my eyes open and immediately became aware of a violent headache. I reckoned it was due to the fall earlier. It was raining too, hence the moisture on my face.

I had no idea how long I had been lying there, but my clothes were soaking wet. I looked at my wristwatch. It was only fifteen minutes since I had alighted from my car. I found my mobile telephone on the drive. It was very wet, but thankfully when I switched it on, it worked. I rang Lyn's mobile, and she answered almost immediately.

'Mal, where's that coffee, for God's sake?' was her opening remark.

'Bugger the coffee, Lyn, can you get the police to come around to your house. It has been broken into, and I am certain that I disturbed them. I got a bashing in the face for my troubles.'

'You what! Oh, Mal, what are you doing? Are you alright?'

'Yes, yes. Just get the police around here. I'll see you shortly.'

Within ten minutes, the same two plainclothes officers got out of their car on the drive. By this time, I was sitting up, still a little dazed, and leant back against the house wall.

One detective looked at my face and immediately summoned medical help.

'You've got a nasty cut just above your eye and another on your upper lip as well blood coming from your nose. I don't think it is too serious, but no point in taking chances, is there? You just sit there. We'll get you some help.'

'Thanks. It's not too bad.'

'Why the hell didn't you just ring the police instead of going in.'

I remember my mother was a big fan of Ken Dodd as a singer. She didn't rate him highly as a comedian but admired his singing voice. His first album, 'Presenting Ken Dodd', was her favourite album, and the track *Fools Rush In* was her favourite track. As I sat there, it went through my mind, and I thought how bloody appropriate the song was. Why didn't I take Ken Dodd's advice? Why?

An ambulance arrived some ten minutes later, and a paramedic examined me. After much prodding and poking and a few hmms, she declared that there was nothing very seriously wrong with me. She followed the concussion protocol, and everything seemed as it should.

'I wouldn't look in the mirror for a few days if I were you. I put butterfly stitches on the cuts. The cuts are more superficial than anything; they'll just be unsightly for a while. Your nose isn't broken, but I am certain that you will have two lovely black eyes by tomorrow.' The paramedic tried to make her report as light as possible; after all, in the greater scheme of things, my injuries were minor indeed. I took it lightly, and we both had a laugh.

The first detective came outside again and asked if I was feeling better. I assured him that I was feeling fine, well, reasonably so anyway.

'Have Lyn and her mother come too?' I enquired.

'Lyn, sorry, Mrs Kendall has, but Mrs Wright has stayed at home waiting for the crime scene investigators to finish their work. Someone had to stay back and keep an eye anyway. I think that she wants to start clearing up as soon as possible.'

'What have they done to this house?' I wanted to know.

'The same as Mrs Wright's, basically. Look, Ms Jones, I have got the feeling that there is far more to this than meets the eye. I do not believe in coincidences, do you?'

'No. I do not,' I replied.

'Well?'

'Well, what?'

'Is there more to this than meets the eye?'

The detective clearly was not going to just accept my silence. He believed I was keeping something from them, and maybe he was correct... I guess.

'Look, Ms Jones, there have been two break-ins to two houses, both belonging to members of the same family. The mess in each house was almost identical. That ain't coincidence now, is it?'

'No, I see what you mean,' I said as noncommittally as I could.

'I see what you mean!' said the detective very sarcastically. 'You see, what I mean doesn't actually mean anything, does it? You know much more than you tell me, don't you?'

I decided that silence would be my best friend at the moment, so I said absolutely nothing to the detective.

'Where is Lyn now?' I enquired.

'At the rear of the house on the patio.'

'Is it alright if I go and see her?'

'Of course,' the detective replied. I gained the impression that he was a bit miffed by my silence.

Lyn was sitting at the patio table and had a glass of something in her hand.

'You want one, Mal?' she asked.

'Not for me, thanks. I'll have a cup of tea when we can get into your kitchen.'

I pulled another chair over to the table and sat as close as possible to Lyn.

'Lyn,' I said, 'I think that we, and I do mean we, ought to be straight with the police. We can't go on like this. Someone is going to get hurt if we don't do something. Enough keeping secrets. The sooner the truth is out, the sooner we'll be free from this mess.'

'Straight about what?' Lyn asked.

'Everything. You still haven't been completely honest with me, have you?'

'Yes, I have!' Lyn smiled, but the smile remained on her mouth and most certainly did not reach her eyes.

'Lyn! Come on, this is me you're talking to. We have been friends since school, and I can read you like a book. You are not telling me everything. Oh, I don't doubt that what you told me is true, but you have not told me everything. Now come on, please, my love, please tell me everything. You remember what I said some time ago. You know that I would do no further investigations for you unless you were honest with me. Well, I meant it then, and I'll say it again, and I can assure you that I really do mean it this time. Lyn, unless you are completely honest and tell me everything, then you can kiss our years of friendship goodbye. Do I make myself clear?'

There was nothing from Lyn, not even a flicker of anything on her face. She just sat there and stared at me poker-faced.

'Lyn?'

Still nothing. 'Lyn!' I raised my voice in an attempt to get through to her.

Still nothing. Not even a whisper.

I stood up as if to go.

'Lyn! This is your last chance. If I leave now, our friendship is over, I'm telling you.'

Still nothing.

I turned to leave.

'Mal, don't go,' Lyn said in barely more than a whisper.

Well?' I said as placatingly as I could.

'Not here,' Lyn said.

'Where then?' I wanted to know.

'Let me clear it with the police, and then we'll go to the downs car park.'

Lyn went off to locate one of the detectives and returned to the patio a short while later.

'Well?' I asked.

'Come on. Let's go on to the downs. They will be at least an hour, maybe two. It's time I come clean about some things.'

Chapter Twelve

We got into my car, and twenty minutes later, I pulled into The Downs Car Park. Mine was the only vehicle there, oddly enough.

After a few minutes of me taking in the view and Lyn just staring straight ahead, I began to think Lyn had brought us here on a fool's errand. Then… she suddenly spoke.

'You know all about the diamonds, don't you?' Lyn asked.

'Of course, I bloody well do, as you very well know. And believe me, Lyn, I could not be more shocked.'

'Yes, of course.'

'Come on, Lyn, don't prevaricate with me.'

'Alright, Mal. The whole truth as I know it. No holds barred; I promise you.' Lyn took a deep breath and let it out slowly.

'Okay, Lyn. Let's have it.' I did my best to encourage her, although, in truth, my heart was not in it.

'Well, I first met David at a friend's wedding. He was with another guest. I think that he was there as a plus one. I don't know how well he knew the bloke as they didn't seem to spend too much time chatting to each other. I was there as a friend of the bride and didn't have a plus one. It was as if we were two people in the same boat as it were. It seemed completely natural that we would drift towards each other, and that is exactly what happened. We got on well from the very first time we spoke. He was an absolute gentleman. After the wedding feast, we spent the rest of the afternoon and evening together, drinking and dancing. He could certainly dance well. I had the most amazing time that night. We both danced as if we had no worry in the world.

Well, I fully expected him to want to spend the night with me. If he had made any approaches in that direction, I would have jumped at the chance. I fancied the absolute pants off him. He called a taxi to take me home and offered to accompany me. I agreed and began to feel quite excited at the thought of a night of lovemaking. I couldn't wait to kiss him and run to the bedroom. When the cab pulled up outside my house, David turned into me and kissed me deeply. Ah! I thought, the first move. Just as I imagined it. He kissed me, then drew apart and said he would call me the following day, which he duly did. We spent the whole of that glorious Sunday together and ended up in bed this time. He was a caring and thoughtful lover, and I was more than satisfied, if you know what I mean!

Well, within two months, we agreed that we were deeply in love and that we should marry. I had no hesitation in accepting his proposal. He was everything I wanted in a husband. The date was set, and exactly one year later, we were married. It was a low-key affair at the local registry office with just my mother and father and his mother as the only guests. I admit to being a little surprised at his choice of venue and the whole affair. It wasn't exactly my taste, but I didn't think too much of it. Be that as it may, I was so loved up that I was happy to agree to any suggestion he made. We honeymooned in the Maldives, and it was an absolutely blissful three weeks. I did think that three weeks was a little extravagant for a honeymoon, but David assured me that money was not a problem. I could hardly believe my ears; my choice of a husband had certainly been spot on.

When we got home from our honeymoon, David said he wanted to sell his flat and move in with me. It suited me very well, and I was happy to contribute this much to our relationship. It didn't make a difference to me if we stayed at my place or his. David moved in and seemed to have very few belongings. For a few minutes, I thought that a little odd, but David explained that all his furniture and knick-knacks had been sold with the house; it went for a little extra because of all the furniture. All he brought with him was his clothes and personal papers. I know that one of the people mentioned in the lyrics of Ralph McTell's *Streets of London* was an old lady carrying her whole world in two carrier bags. But this was real life, not a song verse. Three suitcases did not seem much by way of possessions for his life so far.

Be that as it may, I fully accepted what David said, and that was that. I was somewhat surprised when David suggested I give up work to keep the house full-time. This, again, I thought rather strange. At no time had we spoken of starting a family; indeed, some comments David had made in our everyday conversations led me to believe that he didn't really like children very much. I presumed that he wanted children, which was why he didn't want me to work. I handed in my notice at the office and worked the month out. I was quite sad to leave because I enjoyed my job and relished the friendship and companionship of my colleagues.

Obviously, I did not need to raise the subject of money with David. After all, he paid me £4000 every month and confirmed that this amount would continue to be paid into my account. The amount was rather unusual, but I guess my love for him had put a blindfold over me. He had given me a cheque for that amount and asked if it would be alright if he paid housekeeping into the account directly each month. It seemed the most convenient way of doing things, and I readily agreed. I did think that four thousand pounds every month were an exceedingly generous amount but thought that David must be able to afford it; otherwise, he would never have suggested it

When we had been married for about two months, David asked if he could convert one of the bedrooms in the house into an office. Well, there are four bedrooms, as you know, so I said that he was welcome to. We only used one room, and the rest were usually empty. Once the conversion was done, David spent more and more time in his new office. He had a separate telephone line installed, and I have to say I was a little jealous of his office, daft as that may seem. How the hell can you be jealous of a room?

Then, one day, David was in his office as usual and had been there since returning home several hours earlier. I thought he must be hungry, so I made him a plate of sandwiches. I entered the office without knocking. Well, why would I knock in my own house? I saw that David was leaning over what appeared to be a sheet of paper. I could not see what, if anything, was on it, but he certainly tried to cover up whatever it was. I presumed that it was some sort of gift that he didn't want me to see. Maybe he was planning to surprise me later. I thought about asking him but decided against it. After all, if it was a surprise gift for me, then the surprise would be spoilt.

Time passed, and it must have been, oh, a couple of months later again, that, when I was doing a complete clean-through of the house, I went into David's office. I am sorry to admit that curiosity got the better of me, and I began checking the drawers of David's desk. I don't know what I was hoping to find, but I checked all of them. All seven were locked. Odd, I thought. What on earth had David to hide from me. I just could not make any sense of this. I began to hear warning bells ringing in my head, although at this stage, I could not see any reason for them. Other than the locked drawers, I had no real reason to have doubts about David. I believed, truly believed, at that time, that the drawers of the desk were locked to keep secure some confidential papers to do with his work.

I silently debated whether or not to ask David about the locked drawers but decided that, on balance, it was really none of my business. He would probably think that I had been snooping. Of course, I had to a certain extent, but it was a spur-of-the-moment thing. I had not deliberately gone into David's study to search it, had I?'

I nodded, not wanting to interrupt Lyn's story. It seemed honest, so I let her carry on.

'Then the bottom of my world fell out when the police called on that fateful night to tell me that David was dead. That, Mal, is when I suggested that the police ring you and the rest you know.'

'That is everything, yes?' I enquired.

'Yes. On my honour, I have told you everything. This is the whole truth, Mal. I'm sorry I lied before.'

'The thing now, Lyn, is where do we go from here?'

'I don't know,' Lyn replied almost in a whisper. It was as if telling me everything had completely drained her. I could understand that. Lyn had suffered the break-in to our hotel room in Amsterdam, the break-in at her mother's home, and then the discovery of the break-in at her own home. All this trauma was certain to take a toll on her emotionally, if not physically and mentally.

I decided not to press her further, allowing her to breathe a bit and take a break from all the stress of the last few days.

'Well, lovey, I think our first job will be registering David's death. Do you have a death certificate yet?' I enquired.

'No. I do not. I don't know how to get one.'

'Right,' I said as masterfully as I could, 'we'll start with that. I will make an appointment for us to see Detective Chief Inspector Carterford in the morning, then we will see where we should go or what we should do next, yes?'

Lyn agreed, and I was about to start my car when she opened her door and got out. She walked a few yards away, facing out across the beautiful vista of the downs. I made to follow but then thought better of it. I watched Lyn, and after a few minutes, I could see her shoulders going rhythmically up and down. She was clearly crying, and I felt my presence at her side would not be welcomed or necessary. I allowed her to take this time and let it out on her own.

After almost a quarter of an hour, I noticed that her shoulders had stilled, and clearly, she was coming to terms with everything. Perhaps it was the relief of sharing her fears with someone. I don't know which it was, but she turned and walked back towards the car. She opened the door and climbed in. She fitted her seat belt without a word or even a glance in my direction. I started the car, and we returned to Lyn's house.

Drawn up on the drive was a rather expensive-looking Rover saloon.

Lyn and I looked at each, and as one, we shrugged. Neither of us recognised the vehicle. Our hearts began to beat faster as we wondered if we had some uninvited guests.

As we stopped, a tall man exited the front door. I may not have recognised the vehicle, but I certainly recognised this man, Detective Chief Inspector Philip Carterford.

'Well,' I said to Lyn, 'that'll save us seeing him tomorrow, won't it?'

'How do you mean?' Lyn wanted to know.

'Because, my dear friend, that is Chief Inspector Carterford!'

Lyn and I alighted from my car, and Philip Carterford immediately ceased his conversation with the uniformed officer guarding the door.

'Mrs Kendall?' the Chief asked.

'Yes, I'm Lyn Kendall.'

'Firstly, I must apologise for not being in contact with you before now. We have had certain enquiries to make into your husband's death. Is there somewhere we can talk?'

'The inside is a mess, but if your men have finished in any of the rooms, then we can go to one of those and talk. I'll make you some snacks.'

'The kitchen is certainly the messiest, but the dining room is not too bad. I think the crime scene investigators have finished in there. Come along.'

All three of us set off towards the front door, and the chief inspector spoke quietly to the officer on guard, and we entered the dining room. Lyn picked up three chairs and swished them off with her hand before indicating to the chief inspector and me to sit down.

Once we were settled, Chief Inspector Carterford took a portable voice recorder from his pocket.

'I would like to record our conversation if you don't mind. And I would prefer that we were alone.'

'You can record it by all means, but Mal stays. She knows everything that I know, and I want her here. She can be my, what do you call it, my responsible adult?'

'Responsible adults are usually only present where juveniles or mentally ill people are concerned, but if you want Ms Jones here, then I can see no objection. Shall we begin then?'

'Before we start, Chief Inspector, what about David's death certificate? We can't register his death without one,' I enquired.

'All in good time, Mal.'

The chief inspector's use of my diminutive first name caused Lyn's eyebrows to raise. I did not comment.

'Mr Carterford, am I under arrest or suspicion?' Lyn wanted to know.

'No, you are not Mrs Kendall. The recording is just to aid me in recalling our conversation later. It helps us take notes on things of interest.'

'I see. Very well, what would you like to know? By the way, you may as well call me Lyn, seeing as how we are all on such chummy terms,' Lyn said somewhat sarcastically and looked at me.

'Very then, Lyn. Do you know how your husband died?'

This was not the first question either Lyn or I had expected.

'No. No one has told me anything, well, only that he was dead.'

'Very well, Lyn. Well, first of all, I am very sorry for your loss, and I am even sorrier to have to tell you that he was killed unlawfully. He was a young man, and I'm sure it must've been hard on you.' The chief inspector paused either for effect or, as I preferred to think, to let Lyn take this information in.

'You mean he was murdered?' Lyn's mouth was hanging open in utter astonishment.

'We haven't established the offence at this time, but he was certainly unlawfully killed.'

'How? Where?' Lyn asked.

'As to the first part, I am afraid I cannot confirm that until all of our enquiries have been completed. As to the where, well, that is a little easier to answer. Tell me, has David ever been to Somerset? Did he have any business there?'

'I have absolutely no idea. We certainly haven't been there as a couple. Why?'

'Because, Lyn, David was found at the foot of Ebor Gorge near Wells, in Somerset. It appears that he fell from top to bottom and then rolled some distance before a tree arrested his descent. He was reported there by a man walking his dog early one morning. When the police arrived about an hour after his body was found, he was already dead. He was fairly battered about, as you can probably guess. It took us a while for us to identify him.'

'Is that why you haven't spoken to me yet?' Lyn wanted to know. 'Why didn't anyone tell me about this before?' Lyn questioned the inspector with a crack in her voice.

'Not exactly, but I will come to that in due course. Anyway, as I said, your husband was found by an early morning dog-walker. That was on the day that you were informed of his death.'

'How did you identify him if he was battered?' I interrupted.

'Fingerprints, Ms Jones.'

'How come you've got David's fingerprints on your files?' Lyn asked, clearly surprised by this revelation.

'I would rather not go into that for the moment, but the police have their ways. Suffice it to say that is how we identified David.'

I looked over at Lyn, and tears were in her eyes, but she was showing quite a good degree of control, and they were not yet flowing.

'Do you know what happened to David?' Lyn asked.

'Before we speak about that, I want to ask you when you last saw your husband. Was anyone else with him at the time or on the trip to Somerset?'

'Three days before your people came to say that David was dead, why?' Lyn asked.

I thought that I could see where this line of questioning was going. Was the chief inspector going to try to hang the death on Lyn? Surely not. Since the police had come to tell Lyn of David's death, there were quite a few things that I doubted about them. Both of them. But killing? No, absolutely not. For a start, I don't think that Lyn would be capable of any such thing, and from Lyn's point of view, I am certain that she saw her marriage as a very happy one and had every faith in David. She seemed to have no reason to murder him.

'Well,' the chief inspector continued, 'I can tell you with absolute certainty that it was not an accidental death,' the chief inspector said.

'How do you know that?' Lyn asked.

'The post-mortem revealed that he had been shot, for a start. I am sorry to have to tell you this, but David could not have inflicted the shot on himself; the angles are all wrong. So that rules out suicide. It would have been quite convenient to whoever the killer was to have us believe that it was suicide when you think about it. If it gives you any comfort whatsoever, we are one hundred per cent certain that this is not the case. Then there was the location where he was found. It is an isolated spot to some degree, and had the body not fallen as far as it did, then it may have gone undiscovered for well, who knows how long. Whoever did this had it all planned out. The fact that, as far as you know and as far as we can ascertain, he did not know the Ebor Gorge even existed is in itself suspicious. After all, it has to be a three-hour drive, at least from here, if not more. Why would he make all this effort to kill himself? It is not the sort of place one happens upon to visit; one almost certainly would have to know of its existence. Incidentally, can you tell me where he normally garages his car?'

'Yes, we rent a garage over in the next street,' Lyn told the detective.

'Have you checked it to see if David's car is there?'

''No. I have had no reason to. He left the house at seven-thirty and, as I thought, went off to work as normal. That was the last time I saw him.'

'Do you have any objections to one of my officers checking the garage?' he asked.

'No, none at all,' Lyn said.

'Barry,' he called over his shoulder.

'Sir?' said a plain clothes man I took to be Barry, as he poked his head around the door jamb.

'Barry, this lady will tell you where her husband's garage is. Take the keys and have a look inside. You know the drill. Let me know straight away if the car is or is not there, please.'

'Yes, sir,' Barry said. He listened to Lyn's directions, took the keys, and went off on his errand.

Chief Inspector Carterford continued his questions to Lyn. 'Didn't you think it odd that he didn't come home that night?'

'No, not really. He often worked long hours or was called away on business to other parts of the country and even abroad. I was used to him coming late.'

'I see,' said Chief Inspector Carterford, 'but doesn't he let you know that he is going to be late or even going away? I know that if I had not let my wife know I was working late, there would have been hell to pay.'

I noted the use of the past tense in Carterford's remarks. Was he widowed or divorced, I vaguely wondered? I quickly dragged my mind back to the conversation.

Lyn had obviously not given any thought to the detective's question and had now to come up with a reply which made sense.

'Mrs Kendall?' prompted Mr Carterford.

'Well, it wasn't an infrequent occurrence for him not to come home at night and be away for several nights. So, I didn't really take that much notice. Although we loved each other very much, our marriage was, to a degree, open. By that, I mean that I didn't keep track of David, and he made no attempt to keep track of me as far as I know. We trusted each other.'

Lyn thought that she had answered the question as though it was quite natural not to know where one's husband was, but Mr Carterford was not easily satisfied.

'Come now, Mrs Kendall, I am not convinced that you knew absolutely nothing of your husband's comings and goings. Please do not take me for a fool because that is one moniker that no one can hang on me.'

'I'm sorry, Mr Carterford, but that is God's honest truth. I have no idea whatsoever as to where David was. All I know with certainty is that he left home to go to work at the usual time. My husband was a good man; that's all I know.'

Unlikely as it may have seemed to any, what I might have described as a right-thinking person, I knew that Lyn's marriage was strange, to say the least. I don't mean that either of them had any strange sexual habits or anything untoward like that. Or at least I didn't think so. Whatever their marital situation, I did not have intimate knowledge of their relationship to comment on what may or may not have been.

'Mrs Kendall, please do not take offence, but I do not believe you for one minute!' Carterford said.

'Mr Carterford, if you do not believe me, then that is your prerogative, but it does not change anything or affect anything. What I have told you is the truth as far as I know it. You can choose to believe it, or not. Other than what I have told you, I am as much in the dark as you are.'

The look on the chief inspector's face spoke volumes. It was saying that despite assurances of Lyn as to the veracity of what she had told him, something just was not quite right.

The chief inspector's mobile warbled its ringtone, and he answered it. On the other end, Lyn sat in her seat, maintaining her confident posture.

'Yes, Barry. Right, well, get it on to the PNC as soon as you can.'

There was obviously a question from the other end.

'At this stage, just say that we wish to locate the vehicle in connection with a serious assault and get the operator to put our incident log reference on as well. It is our enquiry now, so we don't want Avon and Somerset muscling in, do we? Make sure to take care of it, so we don't have anyone meddling in our case later.'

He terminated the call and replaced his mobile in his pocket.

'Right, now, Mrs Kendall, where were we?'

'You didn't believe what I was saying,' Lyn said, her voice heavy with sarcasm.

'Oh yes. Look, Lyn, you have to admit that what you have told me seems unlikely in the extreme. Try and see it from my point of view, and you may be able to see what I mean.'

'Oh, I see where you are coming from, and as unlikely as it may seem, what I have told you is the absolute truth as I know it,' Lyn said reassuringly.

'Okay. Now, on a different tack, we would like to access your bank account and that of your husband.'

'Why do you want that?' Lyn asked.

'Well, his bank accounts may show whether or not your husband was suffering any financial problems. You know whether he owed money to anyone, that sort of thing. Anything really which might reveal a motive for killing your husband. A victim's bank history can tell a lot about their case.'

I began to blush. I knew about some of his financials, and I didn't think this would help David's cause. I just hoped that Philip Carterford wasn't watching me. I had averted my eyes from his face, but I just couldn't hide the blush.

Chief Inspector Philip Carterford was an astute detective. Unbeknownst to me, he had been watching me almost as closely as he had been watching Lyn. I don't know whether or not he felt that I knew something which I wasn't telling or whether his interest was more personal. I thought it was probably the former but vaguely hoped it may just be the latter. I shook my head to try to clear my thoughts and hoped that Philip Carterford didn't see and try to impose his own interpretation on it.

Lyn remained silent. The chief inspector was clearly becoming a little impatient with her.

'Look, Mrs Kendall, Lyn. If you know anything, then I think it best that you tell me now. It will help us solve your husband's murder sooner. I do not believe that you are involved in your husband's death, but your reticence is beginning to tell me that you could be.'

Lyn was about to speak when he held up a warning hand.

'Lyn, if you deliberately do not reveal information that may have a bearing on David's death, there may be a criminal offence. I do not wish to even consider prosecuting you for that but believe me; I will not hesitate to do so.'

Lyn looked over at me and raised an enquiring eyebrow. I knew that the detective chief inspector would not miss it; he was far too shrewd for that. I made a decision that may or may not signify the end of our friendship. I considered it necessary to save Lyn from herself as much as anything else.

Lyn gave a barely perceptible nod in my direction.

'Chief Inspector Carterford, I have some information which may help you.'

He turned his attention to me.

'Well?' he asked encouragingly.

I hesitated.

'Mal? Tell me. It's alright.'

I looked over at Lyn again. She was clearly considering something, and then she said, 'Tell him, Mal. What do you know?'

'Yes, tell me, Mal!' Philip Carterford said with a grin on his face.

'Okay. As you may know, I was called by your colleagues to come sit with Lyn when they advised her of David's death. Well, the following day, Lyn rang me and asked me if I could go over. It transpired that she had tried to obtain a death certificate to register his death. No one would give her such a document, and she was very upset at not being able to begin the process of laying David to rest. To try to make some sense of David's death, Lyn began looking around David's study. I think that she thought that perhaps he had taken a mistress and was trying to find some letters and things. Every drawer in the desk was locked, which she found a little odd. I mean, what was he hiding in there?

When I got there, we both checked the study. Then I noticed this very large bookcase which was crammed with books. I suggested we check the books shelf by shelf to see if anything had been hidden inside one or two of them. Well, we checked all the shelves, except for the bottom shelf. This shelf contained larger books than any of the others. That's when we discovered it. The largest of these books, right in the centre of the shelf, had been hollowed out by cutting a sort of picture frame on almost every page. The only exceptions being two or three pages at the front and the same at the rear. Well, folded up in half and neatly was a pile of about ten pages of bank statements. These were for several accounts at a bank in Switzerland. The final balance was just short of forty million pounds.'

'Forty mi…' the chief inspector seemed lost for words.

'Lyn, where on earth did David get that sort of money from?' He wanted to know. 'And how come you never questioned it, Lyn?'

'I have absolutely no idea. Mal will be able to confirm that I was as gobsmacked as you clearly are. To me, forty million pounds, well, it is just numbers, isn't it.'

'That is as maybe, Mrs Kendall, but forty million pounds, that is a massive amount of money in anyone's language. You don't get that sort of money working in a bank, now do you. You're not that naïve.'

I noted the change in Chief Inspector Carterford's approach, from informal to formal.

'Do you still have the statements?' he asked.

'Yes,' Lyn told him. 'They were put back into the book in David's study.'

'Let us hope that this is still the case. If that is what the intruders were looking for, then they have almost certainly gone.'

'That's not all, Philip.' I decided on informality in case it might help in some way.

'What do you mean?'

'We found that some of the smaller books were also hollowed out. Inside we found lots of little soft leather bags. Each of these bags, except one, contained forty dirty little stones. We knew that if David had gone to the trouble of concealing these bags of stones, then they most certainly were anything but worthless. Well, a while ago, I had dealings with a diamond dealer in Amsterdam, and he had shown me uncut diamonds, you know, straight out of the ground. I recognised the stones which we had found. I tried to get an approximate value from the diamond dealer by sending a photograph. He suggested that I go over to Amsterdam with the stones so that he could give me a reasonable estimate of the value of the stones. Lyn and I did just that, and the dealer gave us the approximate value of four million pounds. We were both speechless when he told us the value. He offered to keep the diamonds safely for us, but Lyn turned the offer down. She contacted her own bank, and they gave her the name of a bank they regularly used in Amsterdam. The diamonds are deposited there. We came back as soon as we knew they were safe.'

'I see. What are your intentions now, Lyn?' Carterford wanted to know.

Before Lyn could answer, I continued with my narrative.

'Before Lyn answers your question, Philip, I do have a little more to tell you. Well, it was after we had deposited the diamonds safely that we returned to our hotel room. I noticed a man sitting in the hotel's foyer, and I didn't like his look. As Lyn and I approached the lift, I noticed this man take his mobile from his pocket. Something made my neck itch, so to speak. I made an excuse to Lyn so I could go to reception and surreptitiously watched the man. Whoever he was calling, the call did not last very long. I followed Lyn to the room, and when we arrived at the door, I noticed that it was very slightly ajar. I carefully entered the room, but there was no one else in the room. All the chest drawers had been ransacked, the wardrobe contents were spread on the floor, and every drawer or other orifice where something could have been hidden had been turned out. It was a mess, like someone came looking for something specific. The police were called and arrived quite quickly, really. Once we were given the go-ahead, we packed the clothes and other bits and pieces as quickly as we could and went downstairs to reception. They were able to get us on a flight from Schiphol to London Heathrow later that evening. We found a restaurant and had an early dinner before catching our flight without further incident.'

'Is that all?' Chief Inspector Carterford asked.

I told him there was nothing else until we found the two break-ins at Susan's house and then Lyn's. Clearly, he was aware of these.

'I know this is an obvious thing, but do you think all of these happenings are connected?' the chief inspector asked.

It seemed a ridiculous question, and I presumed it was rhetorical.

'Mal?' Philip prompted.

'I'm sorry, but I thought your question was more of a statement,' I ventured.

'It was to an extent but are you of the opinion that all of this is connected?'

'Yes, of course, they are. Why don't you? Why would anyone break into our hotel room, then both the houses without a purpose?'

'Yes, I am convinced, but I just wanted to know that we are singing from the same hymn sheet. What about you, Lyn. What is your take on this?'

'I agree with everything that Mal has told you. I still do not understand very much of it all; I have to admit,' Lyn replied.

'Hm. There are certain aspects which still puzzle me too,' the chief inspector admitted.

'How much longer before I can go back into my house properly?'

'Later today, but it would be better if you could find accommodation elsewhere just for tonight,' Philip advised.

'I'll ring Mum,' Lyn suggested.

I nodded my agreement, and Chief Inspector Carterford raised no objection.

Chapter Thirteen

We spent the night at Susan's house. To say that we slept there would have been overstating things. I don't think any of us had that much sleep after our conversation with Chief Inspector Carterford. I certainly didn't and spent the night dozing in the armchair. I didn't feel refreshed when dawn eventually lightened the sky, and I treated myself to an early morning cup of tea. I took it outside onto the patio and sat thinking. I just could not get my head around the possibility that David may have been murdered. What the hell had he got himself involved with? What other secrets was he hiding? Whoever was running whatever it was must be pretty powerful and certainly ruthless. Were Susan and Lyn in danger? Or me, for that matter; you know guilt by association. My concern for our safety grew by the hour.

The sun eventually showed its face, and I was startled when I suddenly heard the sound of running water. I was half asleep, I suppose, but I couldn't immediately locate the source in my head. I put my mug on the patio table and stood up. As I turned towards the house, I noticed that a water feature had suddenly sprung to life. It was an attractive two-barrel set-up with a miniature village pump atop the two barrels. The water was pouring out of the spout of the imitation pump, which ran into the upper barrel. This, in turn, overflowed into the lower barrel and was then pumped back up again. It was the flow of water from the spout hitting the surface of the upper barrel which had disturbed my reverie. I smiled to myself. After all, I loved the sound of water, be it the waves of the sea, the trickling of a stream or river, the pitter-patter of rain sprinkling on the roof, or even a garden water feature; I loved it.

The sound of the running water made me feel a little sleepy, and, placing my mug on the patio table, I closed my eyes. Within minutes, my head had flopped down onto my chest, and I was asleep. There were no dreams to disturb my outdoor slumber, and I woke up two hours later feeling refreshed.

I went back into the kitchen to brew more tea and found Susan and Lyn engaged in that task.

'You're about early, Mal,' Susan remarked.

'I didn't sleep too well. I don't think it was the armchair that was comfortable enough. It was more what was going through my mind which kept the sandman away. I made a mug of tea, fell asleep on the patio, and woke up when the water feature burst into life with the sun. I feel fine now.'

'What happens next, do you think?' Lyn asked me.

'Well, lovey, I think the first priority is to get David's funeral organised, don't you think?' I suggested. 'Everything else comes after.'

'But I don't have a death certificate,' Lyn pointed out.

'Well, ring the Coroner's office and see what they say. Even if they can't issue a death certificate yet, they may well be able to authorise David to be buried. I doubt they will give the go-ahead for cremation, though, at least not until the police enquiries are complete. You can only ask.'

Lyn rang the local coroner's office and was told politely that they were very sorry for her loss, but David's death had occurred in another coroner's area, so their office could not give any go-ahead. The staff member Lyn spoke to suggested she ring the coroner's office at Wells, Somerset, to see if they could give the go-ahead for a funeral.

As I had anticipated at this stage, the Somerset coroner's office said the same thing. The police enquiries were still ongoing, and until they were complete, they could not permit the funeral to take place. This was about as I had expected, and the only advice they could give Lyn at this stage was to speak to the police. We were certainly in a pickle, but we had to remain patient and keep trying.

Lyn rang Detective Chief Inspector Carterford, and he gave us much of the same story. He did go on to explain that as this was a murder enquiry, David could not be cremated nor, at this stage anyway, buried until all the enquiries are complete.

'But why not? The post-mortem examination has been done, hasn't it?' Lyn sighed and asked him in frustration.

'Well, yes, it has. This isn't very pleasant for you, I know, but if and when a culprit is apprehended and charged, the defence team will be entitled to have an examination of your husband undertaken by their own pathologist. Therefore, it is extremely unlikely that you will be able to bury David or cremate him. Not until the investigation is over, at least.'

'I see,' Lyn said. I suppose that is all that she could say, really.

'Lyn,' Chief Inspector Carterford asked, 'would you be able to call and see me at 3 o'clock this afternoon?'

'Yes. I do not have any plans. Can I ask why?'

'I would rather explain face to face if you don't mind.'

'See you then,' Lyn said as she terminated the call.

'Well, that is one thing we have to put on the 'To Be Done' pile, I'm afraid,' Lyn told us.

'Why, what did the coroner say?' asked Susan.

'The person I spoke to said they cannot authorise cremation or burial in case the culprits are found and charged, and the defence wants to do their own post-mortem. That means it could be weeks, months even before we can bury David,' said Lyn with a defeated look on her face.

Lyn began to sound quite tearful at this. I have to say that I was surprised how practical she had been this morning, but this had proved one drop too much in the bottle, as it were.

Manfully, or should that be womanfully, she held the tears back and said she felt like going to the bank to report David's death and see exactly where she stood financially.

'It occurs to me, Lyn, did David have life insurance? I know that it is not a good thing to talk about, but you have to think of your immediate future, too, you know.'

'I haven't actually found an insurance certificate. In fact, apart from the bank statements we found hidden inside the books, I haven't seen any of David's personal papers.'

'What about the desk?' I asked, 'I don't think the intruders got a chance to break into that. My arrival must have disturbed them. Maybe we'll find something there.'

'Yes, but I don't have a key,' Lyn pointed out.

'We could always force the locks on the drawers. It might cause some damage, but surely you've got to know what is in there,' I suggested.

'Yes, I suppose so. Come on then, let's go!' she said with a sudden burst of energy.

She said goodbye to her mother, as did I, and we hot-footed it over to Lyn's house. The police had obviously finished their examination of the crime scene and removed the crime scene tape. Her house was safe to step into by the time we got there.

Using her key, Lyn opened the door and then stood aside.

'You go in first, Mal,' she invited.

I entered the house and made my way to David's office. I turned around to tell Lyn that the desk appeared to be intact and found that she hadn't followed me inside.

I returned to the front door and found Lyn standing there, just looking into the house's interior and trembling. It was as if fear had taken over her. With concern, I motioned towards her.

'Lyn?' I asked.

'Is it clear, Mal?'

'Yes,' I assured her, holding out my hand towards her, 'it's all clear.'

Lyn and I went through to David's office, and I showed her the intact desk.

'How are we going to open it?' Lyn asked.

'Hang on a second,' I said, dropping to my hands and knees. I crawled as best I could under the desk. It was a fairly tight fit, and I could not manoeuvre very well in the confined space. I reversed my way out and lay down on my back. Using shoulders and heels, I edged my way back under the desk and stopped as soon as I could see all of the undersides.

My efforts were rewarded. I spotted a tiny brown envelope, no more than three inches long and an inch wide, tucked right up in one corner. No one would have found it unless they had done what I had. I managed to ease one corner away from the underside of the desk, and gradually, the envelope came loose enough to fall into my hand. I felt it. It felt like a key to me! *Bingo!*

Using heels and shoulders, I extricated myself from beneath the desk and gracefully stood upright. Triumphantly, I held up the envelope and pasted the widest grin I could muster onto my mouth. Lyn returned my excitement with a smile.

'Is that the key?' Lyn asked. It felt like a strange question until I realised she didn't know what was in the envelope.

'Seems like it. It is a key, anyway.' I put forward.

I handed the envelope to Lyn. After all, it was hers, and the desk was her property, not mine.

'No, you do it,' she said emphatically.

'But…' I began.

'No, please, Mal, you see if it fits, and if it does, open the drawers. I want you to take a look inside first.'

'If you are absolutely certain.'

'Yes, absolutely.'

I extracted the key with some difficulty from the envelope; it had been stuck to the envelope interior with sticky tape.

I slowly tried the key in the keyhole of the top drawer. It turned with ease, and I pulled the drawer completely out of the desk and handed it to Lyn. She began to riffle through the pile of papers which is what the drawer contained.

'Car registration document, car insurance, car MOT certificate, passport. Hang on; there are two more passports here,' Lyn said with surprise.

'Are they all in David's name?' I enquired.

'No. One is, the other in the name of Robert Dickson and a third in the name of Gillian Dickson. Who are they?' Lyn asked.

I reached out and took the passports from her. The two with the male names contained David's photograph, and the one in the woman's name had Lyn's photograph. I gazed at the documents in my hand, wondering what the hell I was looking at. Why the heck did he want false passports for himself and Lyn? I let this discovery churn around in my mind for a few moments trying to make sense of it. I suppose this was my equivalent of Hercule Poirot employing his little grey cells. The only thing that came to mind was that David and Lyn might have to make a hasty getaway and would need false passports to aid them in this. Nothing else made sense… but why would they need to make a run?

'Did you not look closely at the photographs, Lyn?'

'No, only at the names.'

'Well, look again,' I suggested.

Lyn took the passports back and studied the details again.

'Bloody hell, this is me, and the other two are David! But why would we want…' Lyn suddenly paused in her question. The truth had obviously dawned on her.

'Look, Mal, I knew nothing at all about these; you have to believe me.' Lyn said, almost accusingly.

'I believe you,' I said. 'Let's see what else we can find.'

I extracted the second drawer and emptied the contents onto the desktop. There must have been over two dozen bank statements. They were all from the same bank, and it was not the anonymous Swiss Bank but a high street bank. The branch shown was in the next town from where we both lived. The balance was considerable, although nowhere near as much as the Swiss numbered account. It was certainly well up into six figures. It brought a 'phew!' from Lyn when she read it. We collected the statements together, and Lyn found a large brown envelope to keep them together.

The third drawer was more pertinent to Lyn as it contained a copy of a last will and testament for David Kendall and a life insurance policy, taken out the week before David and Lyn married. It was in the sum of two million pounds, and Lyn was named as the sole beneficiary.

The last drawer we found contained a heavy-duty cash tin. I tried the lid expecting it to be locked, but it opened with ease. Inside was a single envelope containing a hand-written letter addressed to Lyn.

I handed it to her without looking at it, believing she would like to read it on her own. This was too personal to share. She scanned the letter and then read it out loud.

My dearest darling Lyn,

If you have found this letter, then I am dead. I have left a copy of my will and an insurance policy in the next drawer if you have not already found them. It was always my intention to ensure your safety, but I could not guarantee it completely. I earnestly hope that you have not been injured at all and have not been traumatised by anything that may have happened.

When I got myself into this affair, I fully understood the risks I was taking, and I hope you will forgive me.

Hidden in the bottom row of books in the bookcase, you will find some bags of stones. These are diamonds, and they are worth a fortune. Retaining them will put you in the gravest danger, so you must pass them on to ensure your safety. Whatever you do, you must not tell the police of the stones' existence.

I know that you will be grieving now, but you must do this one thing for me and protect yourself. You should go to the address at the end of this letter and take some identification with you. You should ask for Harry Haraldsen. Speak to no one else about the reason for your visit. Harry will advise what to do about the Swiss account and the diamonds. Whatever you do, do not tell the police about that account or the stones.

Please follow these instructions, and you will be safe. The life insurance policy will mean you never suffer financially, and there is no mortgage on the house for you to worry about.

Please always remember that I loved you and did so from the moment I first saw you. I am so sorry that I have mixed you up in this matter, and I can only hope that you will forgive me in time.

I know that you will be desperate to have some sort of explanation for the Swiss bank account, the diamonds, and the money in my personal account. Lyn, my dearest Lyn, please do not seek answers from any source other than Harry Haroldsen; it will not be healthy to ask too many questions.

Stay well, my dearest love, be happy in your life, and I hope you will find someone else with whom you can enjoy the rest of your life.

Forever and always, I will love you.

David.

The letter followed an address in Sussex, presumably Harry Haraldsen's home.

I found it difficult to take in. How could David have done this to my oldest and best friend? He must surely have realised the danger that he was putting Lyn into. Either he had not given Lyn any thought at all, which I could not believe, or he had been totally reckless in his actions. Either way, he had put not only his wife, whom he said he loved so much but his mother-in-law and Lyn's best friend in danger too. I suspected that Lyn would be able to forgive him, but I would find it more difficult to do so.

'Bloody hell, Mal!' Lyn suddenly exclaimed. 'The bloody police already know some of this, don't they? We told them about the diamonds, didn't we? Oh, fucking hell! And the Swiss bank account! What am I going to do now? David said that we must not tell the police, and we bloody well have. Is this going to get us in trouble?'

I knew Lyn must be extremely upset because I rarely heard Lyn swear, and then it was usually bloody or an occasional bugger. Certainly not the F word. She must be really concerned if it had come to this. I suddenly heard in my head William Moore, Ronnie Corbett's on-screen father in Sorry!, shouting 'language Timothy'. A half smile briefly did its best to reach my lips but didn't quite make it. It came across as more of a twitch, really.

'As I see it, Lyn, we only have two options. We either tell Carterford everything or clam up and say nothing more. Considering what we have already told him, I believe we should take option one. The only proviso I would make is that you don't show Carterford the letter from David. I've got an awful foreboding about that, and I don't particularly relish the possible outcome of that course of action.'

'I think that we should do that too, Mal. I admit to being a bit scared of what we have told the police already. I hope we can keep this covered, though.'

Chapter Fourteen

At her request, I went alone to keep Lyn's three o'clock appointment with Chief Inspector Carterford.

Having discussed things with Lyn, we had agreed that more harm than good would come from attempting to retract what we had already told him. I sat in the foyer of the police station where Carterford was based. I anxiously rocked my leg while I waited for him to appear.

A door opened, and Philip Carterford's head appeared around it.

'Come through, Mal,' he said in a very friendly tone.

We were seated in his office when there was a discreet tap on the door, and a female brought in a tray with three cups and saucers and a tea-plate with assorted biscuits on it.

'Help yourself to a cup of tea and some biscuits if you would like them.'

'No biscuits, thanks, but the tea will be welcome.'

'Go on, spoil yourself, have a biscuit! You're my guest.'

'Oh, okay then, thanks. I'll have a bourbon if I may.'

'Of course, just take whatever you would like.'

I took a sip of tea, and as I did so, I glanced at Carterford over the rim of my cup. I blushed slightly when I realised he was doing exactly the same thing!

I quickly looked away and tried to figure out exactly why I had reacted the way I did. I cursed the fact that I could not control the reactions of my body. I did blush quite easily, and it had let me down in the past. The main problem I found was that many men, indeed some women, would misread the sign. On this occasion, I didn't even know why I had blushed, but it may have been that both Philip Carterford and myself were free people and that this had sparked something at some level between us. I looked away nervously, waiting for him to begin speaking.

The chief inspector broke the silence.

'Mal, I am grateful for the opportunity to see you away from Lyn. It is about David's death. I want to share something with you.'

'Oh yes!' I replied as non-committedly as possible.

'Yes. I have been down to Somerset and attended the post-mortem on David Kendall. I was asked to attend because of the connections David had with my force area. The upshot was that the cause of death, as I intimated, was indeed shooting. The murderer used a small calibre handgun, judging by the shell case that was found at the scene. How the shooting was carried out suggests strongly that this was a professional hit and, not to put too fine a point on it, it had all the hallmarks of an execution.' The chief inspector paused perhaps for effect but certainly to let the remarks sink in. I stared at him wide-eyed in disbelief.

'Execution! What the bloody hell was he involved in, Philip?'

'There is certainly an element of money-laundering involved, but what else, we just are not sure. Do you have any ideas? Did you happen to find something else in the house?'

'That is what has been going through my mind, I admit. But I just cannot help thinking that there is more. I am being honest when I say I don't have any real ideas.'

'No more do we! It's amazing, really, with all the intelligence which we have at our disposal, we still cannot keep tabs on the major criminals.'

'Are you saying that David was mixed up in major crime?' I asked, suddenly realising that this was really serious.

'Yes, I believe that he was. Exactly how, we have yet to establish, and that is where you may be able to help.'

'Go on,' I encouraged.

'Do you remember when you first came to see me and told me that David was involved in banking?'

'Yes, I do. You said, 'Banking? Yes, I suppose you could call it that,' if I remember correctly.'

'Spot on. That is exactly what I said, and I suspect you may now have an inkling of what I meant by that remark.' It was a statement rather than a question, but I wanted to reply.

'Yes, I think I do. The problem is that there is no one to ask to check anything, is there?'

'Indeed, there is not.'

'So, what do we do now?' I enquired.

'That is the crux of the matter, to be frank. I do not know. The ball is, in some ways, in your court or Lyn's perhaps more accurately.'

'How do you mean exactly?' I asked.

'Well, I would like access to that Swiss bank account,' Philip said.

'I'm sorry, Philip, but I do not have any access to that myself, nor am I privy to any of the account details. I cannot ask Lyn to help you either. I don't know how to get the details for you.'

'Why ever not?' Philip asked.

'Because,' was my curt reply.

'Is there something you are not telling me, Mal?'

'Yes, there is, but I just cannot say what. I'm very sorry, but I just can't.'

'Look, Mal, all I am interested in is finding David's killer and establishing how he was taken, why he was taken, who pulled the trigger, and why.'

'That is quite a lot, though, isn't it?'

'Yes, I know. The money and the diamonds are someone else's concern, not mine.'

'If that be true, then I would ask why you are interested in David's murder when it didn't even occur in your force area?'

'That is a little easier for me to answer. Avon and Somerset are dealing with the murder, and I am dealing with the apparent kidnap. I have been made lead detective in the two separate enquiries. I'm just trying to do my job.'

'I see,' I said, but in truth, I didn't really see at all. I was wary of Carterford's interest in the case and hesitated before saying anything more.

'Tell me about the diamonds then.'

'Look, Philip, for reasons I cannot reveal, I cannot tell you more than I already have. I'm very sorry, but I just can't.'

'You will have to tell me sooner or later, Mal,' he said.

'That may well be, but it will certainly be much later,' I responded. 'I'm sorry, Philip.'

The detective chief inspector looked askance at me. He obviously thought I was holding something back from him, which I was, of course. In view of David's letter to Lyn, I was not prepared to endanger her life more than it had already been endangered. I kept silent, hoping he'll understand.

'Is there anything I could do to make you change your mind?' Philip asked.

'No, unless you can guarantee, and I do mean guarantee, Lyn's safety and that of her parents and not forgetting me.'

'I am very sorry, Mal. No one can ever give that guarantee,' Carterford replied. 'I cannot guarantee what happens to your friend, or you, once the investigation advances.'

'In that case, at this time, I cannot give you any further help. I, too, am sorry,' I said.

I stood to leave, and Philip stood too. We shook hands but said no more as I left the police station.

I went back to my own house and rang Lyn. I didn't tell her the nature of my conversation with Philip Carterford, and she seemed preoccupied anyway, so it didn't seem to make much difference either way. I told her I would be over at about ten o'clock the following day and that we would make our way to see Mr Haroldsen. She acknowledged, and I left soon after.

When I got home, it was almost five o'clock, so I decided to spend an hour writing up notes on the case, if one could call it that, so far. In the end with all of my thoughts intermingled with facts, it took me until nearly half past six to complete my notes. I certainly could not be bothered to cook and suddenly realised that I was very hungry. Apart from a bourbon biscuit in Philip Carterford's office, I had eaten nothing since breakfast. I dug out the nearest Chinese takeaway menu and telephoned my order through. They accepted my card payment, and delivery was promised in about thirty minutes which suited me fine. It would give me time for a quick shower and a change of clothing.

Twenty-five minutes later, in a pair of lounge trousers and a loose-fitting tee-shirt, I answered the ring of my doorbell. It was Sam from the Chinese takeaway, and I gratefully accepted the food from him, we exchanged our usual pleasantries, and I settled down to eat with my stomach growling.

I slept soundly enough until my mobile buzzed at just after seven. Who the heck was ringing me at this hour? It was Lyn. She seemed to have a habit of ringing early mornings.

'Mal?' she asked. Surely she knew that it was my mobile that she was calling; therefore, who else would be answering the damned thing at seven in the morning?

'Yes, Lyn. What has happened now?' I asked, suddenly afraid that something else had gone wrong.

'Oh! Nothing. I was up, and so I presumed that you would be too. Look, what time shall we go to Sussex?' She wanted to know.

'Not yet. It's too early. I'll ring you later, okay. I'm going back to sleep,' I said and terminated the call.

I cuddled back down under the duvet and immediately fell asleep.

At half past eight, my mobile buzzed again. *Bloody Lyn*, I thought. What part of I'll ring you later didn't she understand?

'Hello,' I said somewhat sleepily.

'Ah! Mal. Sorry to disturb you so early.' I quickly sat up in my bed, hearing Carterford's voice.

'Philip! How can I help?'

'Thought that you would like to know that I have just come off the phone with Avon and Somerset Police.'

'What, all of them!' I said facetiously.

'Mal,' Philip scolded. 'I have just been speaking with the officer dealing with the murder at Wells, and there has been a bit of a breakthrough. The fingertip search eventually turned up the shell case which we believe is the one that killed David. Even better, we, or rather they, have checked it for fingerprints and come up with a match.'

'Great, but how can I help? After all, I do not know any of David's friends or associates.'

'Does the name Dominic Allen mean anything to you?'

'No, it doesn't. Would you like me to ask Lyn or Lyn's mother if the name means anything to them? I am out with Lyn later today, so I could ask her then.'

'Not for the moment, I think. Thank you anyway. Goodbye,' Philip said and ended the call.

I regretted that I had not been entirely open with Detective Chief Inspector Carterford, but I dared not risk it given the threats in David's letter. It was already difficult enough to keep it a secret. I would never forgive myself if anything happened to Lyn or her mother due to my loose tongue.

I got up, showered, dressed, and prepared my breakfast of tea and toast. As a result of my almost lie-in, I did not get to Lyn's until ten thirty.

'Good morning, lovey,' I greeted her.

'Hello, Mal. How long do you think it will take us to get to this address?'

'What was the address again?' I enquired.

Lyn consulted David's letter and read it out loud. The house we were looking for was on the outskirts of the village of Broad Oak, near Heathfield, East Sussex. I checked it on good ol' Google and found an estimated journey time of three hours.

'That doesn't sound too bad, right?'

'Right, we had better get started then, hadn't we?' Lyn said more of a statement than a question, but I took it as a question and said yes, I suppose we should.

We were on our way within a very few minutes. For the first hour, we said nothing.

I pulled into a service area for a toilet break, and as I braked to a stop, Lyn said, 'Mal, what are we going to do?'

'About what?' I wanted to know.

'About the diamonds for a start!'

'Well,' I reasoned, 'David's instructions to you were to see Harry Haraldsen, and he will know what to do about the Swiss account and the stones. So, I suggest that is what we do. I would suggest that we don't mention having gone to the police, though. We don't know how he'd respond to that revelation.'

'But we haven't got the diamonds, have we?' said Lyn.

'No. That is true. We do not have them, but if Harry wants to know where they are, then we tell him where and why we put them there. We need to be honest with him, but not completely honest. Just remember what happened to David,' I cautioned.

'Right, loo break! Let's meet back here in a few minutes.'

Within ten minutes, we were back on the road and arrived at Heathfield just after twelve forty-five. Time for lunch. My stomach was complaining that the two slices of toast I had eaten earlier were insufficient sustenance. Lyn called out that there was a pub just ahead, and we pulled onto the car park of the Heathfield Tavern.

We partook of a delicious, cooked lunch, and I remarked to Lyn that at least we would not have to bother cooking when we got back home. We were already well-fed for the rest of the day.

Back in the car, Lyn put the postcode of Harry Haraldsen's house into her mobile, and the female voice gave us directions which took us to the entrance to a rather grand house on the outskirts of the village, the rather grandly named Broad Oak.

The entrance was guarded by large metal gates, and there was an intercom on one of the supporting pillars, on my side, of course. I pressed the button and stepped back, waiting for a response.

'Yes,' said a rather pleasant female voice.

'Lyn Kendall to see Harry Haraldsen, please,' I said into the intercom.

A few seconds later, there was a click, and the gates swung open. As I drove through, I noticed that they closed just as soon as the rear end of my car cleared them. *Not much chance of intruders getting in through there*, I thought.

The tyres crunched on the beautifully gravelled driveway, and I came to a stop close by an impressive portico entrance. As we alighted from the car, the front door opened, and a very smartly dressed female stepped out to welcome us.

'Good afternoon, Mrs Kendall,' she said, 'will you both come in.'

We went into the large foyer, and she addressed me, 'I know Mrs Kendall, but I do not know you.'

'This is Mal Jones, my friend, and she has been helping me ever since I heard about David's death,' Lyn told her.

'I see,' came the brief reply.

'Please leave your mobiles out here. It is Mr Haraldsen's policy. I am sure that you understand.'

We didn't understand at all but decided against saying so. However, I guessed that it was almost certainly to prevent us from recording anything.

'Mrs Kendall, please come with me,' she asked Lyn, and 'would you please remain here for a few moments, Ms Jones?' she said to me.

Lyn disappeared through a door off the hall, and I stood there feeling like a lemon. I looked around to find something of interest but didn't.

Within a few minutes, the door opened again, and the lady I took to be a secretary reappeared.

194

'Please come this way, Ms Jones,' she said, indicating that I should follow her.

I thanked her and followed her through the door into a grand office.

A man, whom I presumed to be Harry Haraldsen, stood to greet us. I don't know what I envisaged Harry Haraldsen to be. I was perhaps expecting some shady-looking character in equally shady surroundings. Instead, here was the consummate businessman dressed in what was obviously an expensive and immaculate suit, not off the peg, I'll bet. I would place him in his mid-fifties. I could only describe him as dapper and well groomed. His manners were spot on, and he was thoroughly professional.

'Good afternoon, Mrs Kendall; please take a seat. And who is your friend, if I may ask.'

'This is Ms Mal Jones, a longstanding friend supporting me at this time,' Lyn told him.

'Good afternoon, Ms Jones. Now Mrs Kendall. What brought you here today? How can I help you?'

I thought this a strange question because he had obviously been expecting Lyn. I presumed that this was just another check on her. The other thing that struck me almost immediately was that his accent was not English. He spoke very good English, but he did not originate in this country, I thought. Perhaps he was Scandinavian. Didn't they have a habit of adding the word son, often spelt 'sen' to indicate that he was Harald's son? Then I vaguely remembered that the Danes certainly did. I tried my best and it came back to me that since 1856, I think it was, fixed surnames had become law, so the fact that he was named Harald's son did not necessarily refer to him personally. It was probably from a couple of generations back.

'I believe that you know my husband, David.' What Lyn said seemed more like a statement than a question.

Lyn waited for confirmation of this fact and received only the briefest of nods in return.

'Well, he wrote a letter to me, which I discovered secured in his desk, suggesting I come to see you for advice. If you are Harry Haraldsen, then you are the one who can help and advise me, according to David.'

'Yes, I did know your husband, and I am very sorry for your loss.'

How did he know that David was dead, I wondered. He must be connected to this whole affair in some way. The police certainly would not have told him, so how did he find out? I said nothing and just sat and listened. In truth, there was very little conversation to listen to, but I waited.

'Thank you.'

I thought for a moment that Lyn was going to ask Harry Haraldsen how he knew David was dead but if she did believe that, she sensibly kept the thought to herself.

'The thing is, what help can you give me?' Lyn asked.

Harry Haraldsen steepled his fingers in front of his mouth and rested his chin atop them.

'With what in particular?' he asked.

This was becoming slightly comical. If he already knew that David was dead, surely that was the clue as to what Lyn wanted help with. How on earth did he think Lyn had arrived at his doorstep, divine intervention? David had, for whatever reason, put his faith in Harry. It may have been a good reason at the time, but I thought he had made a poor choice. Perhaps, of course, he didn't have any option. I remained silent, waiting to see how the conversation progressed.

I was reminded briefly of the various films about the great train robbery of nineteen sixty-three. In those films, as each robber was arrested, he said to his wife and or partner something like, 'You know who to call.'

One is left to presume that the 'who to call' was, in fact, the Mr Big, as it were, who would look after the robber's dependents after the arrest. If this was why David had told Lyn to contact Harry Haraldsen, to be 'looked after' as it were, then he had not shown much evidence of wanting to do that at all.

'What do you know about a Swiss bank account?' Lyn asked.

'I am aware of a Swiss bank account's existence and that David had some sort of input to it,' Harry said, still not overly helpful, I thought.

'What do I do about it?' Lyn enquired.

'Do? Do? Mrs Kendall. You do nothing; that is what you do. Have you tried to trace the account at all?'

'Absolutely not. I would not even have an idea as to where to start. I didn't think that my own bank would be able to help either,' Lyn told Harry.

'No, they would not be able to help you, but perhaps I can. Do you have the bank account's statements with you?' Harry asked.

How did he know about them? How did he know that David had kept them? If he was 'Mr Big', why didn't he have them? I pondered these questions and kept my own counsel.

'Yes, I do,' Lyn said.

'May I have them please?' Haraldsen asked.

Without waiting to consider the question, she reached into her bag and produced the sheaf of statements. She meekly handed them to Harry.

'Thank you,' he said. He placed the statements in his desk drawer without even looking at them.

'They are all there?' he asked.

'Yes, they were all that were hidden, and I did not find any more in his study.'

I felt myself begin to blush. I just hoped that Harry didn't notice and guess perhaps that I had kept one sheet of bank statement back. I changed my thoughts to something else and felt the blush dissipate.

'Now, Mrs Kendall, do you have anything else for me?'

'Not exactly,' Lyn replied. 'This is all I found… in his office.'

Please don't try and be clever with him, I silently urged her.

'And what do you mean by that?' Harry asked.

Please don't look at me for confirmation to tell Harry about the diamonds; he will certainly notice, I silently begged. I knew this because he was watching Lyn closely. He appeared not to take his eyes off her face, and while he may not have seen my nod or shake of the head, he would certainly have seen Lyn's questioning look.

'Diamonds. I have discovered several bags of uncut diamonds hidden at home.'

'May I have them, please?' he said, extending his hand towards Lyn.

'Well, the diamonds are in safe keeping at the moment,' Lyn replied.

'Where?' Harry wanted to know.

'In a safety deposit box in a bank in Amsterdam,' Lyn told him.

Good girl. Remember, honesty is best. No need to be clever with criminals.

'Why were they put there?' Harry persisted.

I decided that it was time to butt in.

'Mr Haraldsen, as well as being an insurance adjuster, I am also Lyn's oldest friend. Because of that, Lyn asked me about the stones. I thought that I recognised uncut diamonds, but I could not be certain, not being an expert. I, therefore, took a picture of one of the bags of stones and sent the photograph to a diamond dealer in Amsterdam with whom I had had dealings in another case some years back. He gave us all the information we needed about them.'

'And the name of this diamond dealer, Ms Jones,' Haraldsen said, picking up a pen and drawing a notepad towards his right hand.

'I don't see why that is necessary. After all, he has nothing to do with this other than to have valued the diamonds. He has no idea where the stones came from, how they came into my possession, nor why we wanted them valued. He has no idea what happened to the stones after he had valued them.'

'Anyway, he said that while he could not be certain without seeing the diamonds themselves, he thought that they were probably genuine and if I could send them over for him to assess.'

'Please tell me that you did not do that!' Harry interrupted.

'Indeed, I did not, or rather we did not. Instead, to get some value for them, I agreed that Lyn and I go over to Amsterdam and take the stones with us, which we did. The dealer put a provisional value of four million pounds sterling on the stones and was able to confirm that they were diamonds. As soon as we knew this, we arranged for them to be deposited in a safety deposit box in Amsterdam. The only people who know of the existence of the diamonds in the bank safety deposit are Lyn and I and now you, of course. In the interest of openness and frankness, I should tell you that while we were in Amsterdam, our hotel room was broken into and thoroughly searched. Thankfully we had been out at the time depositing the diamonds safely. That is the current position. I presume you were somehow responsible for this burglary as no one else knew we had them.'

Lyn paused long enough for Haraldsen to say, 'No. I was not.' Emphatic!

'What about the burglaries on my home and that of my mother?' Lyn wanted to know.

'I can assure you I know nothing of these incidents either.'

Lyn was on a roll now. Neither of us believed him.

'And my father's kidnapping?'

'The kidnap of…' he began and then stopped as though lost for words. 'I was not aware,' he continued, 'that your father had been kidnapped; therefore, I could not possibly know why he had been treated so.'

Without indicating whether or not she accepted his word, Lyn carried on.

'Going back to this letter which I found. David said that I had to come to see you for advice and that you would know what to do.'

Haraldsen steepled his fingers again.

'Do you have this letter with you?'

'Yes,' Lyn told him.

'May I have it please?' he asked.

'No. That is the last contact I shall ever have with David, and I do not want to part with it.'

'But I need to have it. Those are the instructions I have been given.'

'Instructions?' said Lyn. 'What instructions and by whom?'

'That is not your concern.'

'But it is! It's my husband we're talking about!' Lyn said with genuine astonishment in her voice.

'How,' he wanted to know, 'how can it possibly be of any interest to you?'

'I need to keep that letter. It is very important to me. My husband wrote it to me and therefore remains my property. So, you can stick your instructions where the monkey sticks his nuts for the winter,' Lyn told him.

I did not think this was the best approach for Lyn, although I could fully appreciate why she said it. Lyn was starting to stand up for herself.

'Mrs Kendall,' Harry stood up. 'Please give me the letter.' He was demanding now. 'I do not want you to get into any trouble, so I would advise you to give it to me. After all, that is why your husband sent you to me for advice, was it not?'

The tone of his voice, whether Lyn recognised it or not, I don't know, had more than a hint of menace about it.

'Please, Mrs Kendall. For your own good,' Harry insisted.

I could see the menace and heard it in Haraldsen growing, and I certainly did not want anything bad to happen to Lyn, so I intervened.

'You had just as well give him the letter, Lyn. He is going to take it by force if you do not.'

Harry Haraldsen looked at me now. He was clearly weighing up whether or not I was a threat. He had realised I was certainly there in a capacity that exceeded friendship. He would want to know what that capacity was exactly and what sort of threat I presented to him.

I decided to adopt former England Cricket captain Joe Root's approach to menacing behaviour by the opposition, and I smiled, attempting to appear harmless.

'Listen to your friend Mrs Kendall. Her advice is good. There will be consequences if you do not hand over the letter. I have no desire to see anything happen to you or your family,' Haraldsen said.

'Consequences? For my family? How dare you? What have my family got to do with my husband's death?' Lyn asked with a mixture of anger and fear in her voice. She clearly remembered her father's disappearance and the burglary at her mother's house.

'I would not like you to have to find out, Mrs Kendall.' The more pleasant tone to his voice returned.

Lyn sat back in her chair, watching Harry Haraldsen for probably a minute or two. I then noticed that she eased herself forward in her chair and leaned over Haraldsen's desk.

'Look, Mr Haraldsen. For some reason, my late husband placed a lot of faith in you. He clearly felt that I would be taken care of in the event of anything happening to him. By taken care of, I don't mean finishing up at the foot of a ravine in a gorge in Somerset. I thought, and I hope that I am correct, that I would be taken care of financially and protected from harm. If that is so, can I just say that so far, you have done a bloody awful job! I have been burgled twice, my mother has been burgled, and my father kidnapped. How the hell can that be deemed taking care of me?' By the time Lyn had finished her sentence, her voice was almost at 'shout' level on the vocal scale.

She sat back in the chair again as Heraldsen gazed at her, struggling to respond.

Haraldsen looked at me and said, 'Miss Jones, you do not have too much to say for a best friend.'

'At the moment, Lyn is doing very well all by herself. Trust me, and this is not meant as, nor should it be construed as, a threat, but I will make you a promise here and now that if any harm becomes Lyn or her family again, then I will ensure that the walls come tumbling down around your ears, Mr Harry Haraldsen. Do I make myself clear?'

'Crystal clear, thank you. Although I admit that I do not respond well to threats, empty though they may be.'

I did a Joe Root again and shrugged my shoulders.

Haraldsen took his turn at sitting back in his chair. Then he leaned forward again and yet again steepled his fingers.

After a period of silence that seemed very prolonged but was in fact, no more than two or three minutes lay his hands on the desk.

'Look, Lyn. I do want to help all I can. Let me be clear; the buck does not stop with me. I am a sort of middle man. My instructions are to tell you that we need the diamonds returned to us intact. I don't know how you do it, but you need to. My bosses know exactly how many are there. I also need the bank statements for the Swiss account, which I now have, but I want your assurance that these are all of them. Do I make myself clear?' Again, a hint of menace in the Haraldsen voice.

'Yes. Those are all the statements for the Swiss account I found. There may be others, but I have not located them, and I have checked the house, top to bottom.' I was hopeful that Lyn had her tongue firmly in her cheek when she gave that assurance. I was unaware of this top-to-bottom check, and I had spent virtually all my time with her.

'Very well,' Haraldsen said,' that is all I have been asked to do. However, I am not insensitive to your grief over David. My sincerest wish has been that it could have been dealt with differently. The decision was not mine to make. When I offer my condolences, please believe the sincerity behind them. I truly am sorry for your loss.'

'Thank you, Mr Haraldsen,' Lyn said.

'As far as the diamonds are concerned, how soon before you can get them to me?'

'Well, Mal and I will have to go to Amsterdam to collect them, and barring torpedoes, as it were, we should have them back here by next Tuesday. Does that work for you?'

Lyn looked across at me, and I nodded my agreement. This gesture did not go unnoticed by Haraldsen, but he said nothing to me.

'Right. Today is Thursday, so let us say Wednesday then; that will be a week. Two o'clock. Here.'

'Very well,' said Lyn. 'Wednesday it is then.'

'Is there anything else?' Haraldsen asked.

'Yes. What about David's personal bank account? What will happen to that?'

'We have no interest in his personal bank account. That is up to you what you want to do with it.'

'Right. If there is nothing else,' Lyn said and stood up.

'No, nothing else from us. What about you?' Haraldsen wanted to know.

'Can I have a contact number should it be necessary to contact you without coming all this way?'

He handed Lyn a Post-It note on which he had written a mobile telephone number.

'That will reach me at any time,' Haraldsen said.

Haraldsen switched his gaze to me. It lasted long enough to convince me that he would certainly not require a photograph to know me again. There was also an unspoken menace behind his 'Goodbye, Miss Jones. Until the next time.'

I wished him goodbye but noticed that no handshakes were offered by any of us.

As if by some magic, the office door opened, and the secretary entered with a smile that was clearly forced. There was no warmth behind it; it certainly didn't reach her eyes. We were escorted to the front door by the secretary, and as we reached my car, I looked back in time to see the secretary disappearing inside as she closed the door behind her.

We began the journey back home. I had a sort of feeling that something may be wrong. I nudged Lyn and used the age-old signal for shushing, followed by the drawing across my throat of my forefinger. We were about five miles from Heathfield when I saw a large layby ahead.

'Just pulling in to make a call. Shan't be long,' I told Lyn. She nodded.

I got out of the car and walked to the far end of the layby. Taking my mobile from my pocket, I switched it on and rang a number in Banbury.

Chapter Fifteen

'Darren? It's Mal Jones,' I spoke into the phone.

'Oh, hello, Mal, everything alright with you?' he asked with concern.

'So, so at the moment,' I told him.

'How can I help, Mal? I'm here for you.'

'Darren, what time do you close?' I enquired.

'Six-ish usually. Why?' Darren wanted to know.

'Would you be prepared to hang on until I get to you? Should be shortly after six from here.'

'Yep, that will be okay. I owe you a lot, Mal, so take your time,' Darren said. 'I hope you're not in trouble.'

'Thank you, Darren,' I told him. 'Yes, I will discuss it once I get there.'

'What do you need, Mal? At least tell me what I should prepare for,' Darren asked.

'Could you sweep my car for bugs, do you think?'

'No problem. That's not a big issue. See you later.'

I terminated my call and noticed that Lyn was looking back at me. I beckoned her to join me outside.

'What's up, Mal?' Lyn asked.

'Did you think there was anything strange about them taking our mobiles back there?' I asked Lyn in little more than a whisper.

'Odd certainly.' Lyn lowered her voice to the same volume as mine. 'But I don't want to think too much of it.'

'Yeah! I thought that too, but then again, you can never be too cautious. Look, we are going home via Banbury. I have a friend who will sweep the car for bugs. You know, just in case. I suggest that we keep any conversation between us before then to really mundane things. Okay?'

'Okay,' Lyn replied, and we walked back to the car.

Having put my fear into words, I found myself checking the rear-view mirror every few seconds and making detours at roundabouts to see if any car followed us. No one did.

We pulled up outside Darren's shop-come-workshop at ten minutes to six, and he was waiting for us to arrive.

'Right, drive around the back of the workshop, and I'll do the business,' Darren told me. 'You won't have to worry about a thing, Mal.'

'Thanks, Darren,' I replied.

'Now then, let's see if they put any little perishers in your car, shall we?' said Darren.

Darren brandished what looked a bit like a portable electric fan without a flex. He swept over the whole vehicle, inside and out, very carefully and very thoroughly. I heard a loud beep three times, and Darren checked a dial on his fan-like tool each time. When he had finally ended his check, he smiled and held out his hand. Sitting in the palm of his hand were three tiny black cylinders. There was a look of satisfaction on his face which wore a wide smile.

'Can you neutralise them?' I asked Darren.

'Already done, but I will destroy them to be one hundred per cent certain. Alright?'

'Very alright. Thanks, Darren. How much am I in your debt?' I enquired.

'Don't be bloody silly, Mal. I am very much still in your debt, am I not? This one's on me.'

I thanked Darren again, and Lyn and I climbed back into the car.

'What was all that about, Mal?' Lyn asked once we were underway.

'Lyn. Why do you think anyone would put bugs on to my car?' I asked.

'Bugs! What bugs?' Lyn asked.

'I did not actually know that they were there, silly. But I had a feeling that there were bugs.'

'And who was he?' Lyn asked cocking her thumb towards the rear of the car.

'That was my friend Darren. I did him a favour once, and he has been very helpful ever since. He swept the car with his air fan type gadget and found three of them. They've been neutralised now,' I reassured her.

'Three? How did you know they were there?'

'Something told me that Harry Haraldsen wasn't quite as straightforward as he appeared. I just had a feeling that something wasn't right. It wasn't just the mobile either. Before we got there, what were you expecting exactly?' I asked Lyn.

'Well, in view of David's letter, I secretly thought that Harry Haraldsen was either some sort of Mr Big or some sort of fixer. Again, based on David's letter, I expected him to give me advice and to look after me, as it were. You know, something like a benevolent godfather. He was more like Marlon Brando's version, don't you think?'

'Hm. That is more or less what I expected, but it wasn't what we saw and heard, was it?'

'No, it wasn't,' she said consideringly.

'Did you come away reassured?' I asked Lyn.

'Certainly not,' came the reply.

'Hm. Me neither.'

'Why the bugs, though?' Lyn pondered. 'What was he planning to do?'

'I honestly don't know,' I told her. 'Let's be fair, if it was Haraldsen, what was he expecting to find out? We don't have that much more information than we told him, do we?' I pointed out.

If there was someone else involved other than Haraldsen, then it could have been them. Or was Haraldsen not wholly trusted by his bosses? That could be one answer. It didn't make that much sense, but for the time being, that is all I had. I decided that it was time to be honest with Lyn. I pulled in again at the next layby and switched the engine off.

'Lyn, I have not been completely honest with you. I did not tell you certain things about David's death. I was silent about it for the best possible reason in that I didn't want to distress you any further. Do you want to know? It is not pleasant,' I told her.

There was no response from Lyn, but I hoped that she was considering her reply very carefully. After what I thought was an appropriate pause, I prompted Lyn.

'Lyn!'

'Well?'

'I think that I want to know everything. I have to come to terms with what happened to David, and after all, I did ask you to find out why he died, didn't I?' Lyn asked. 'I can take it.'

'Yes, you did,' I assured.

'Yes, then tell me. What is it?'

'Well, do you remember the meeting I had with Detective Chief Inspector Carterford?' I began.

Lyn nodded.

'At that meeting, Carterford told me that he had been to Wells in Somerset for the post-mortem examination. It had to be done there apparently because David had died in HM Coroner, Wells, area. Well, when the pathologist examined the body, he found that he had sustained injuries that were compatible with a fall from a good height. That, however, did not cause his death. The pathologist found that he had been shot, which was the ultimate cause of his death.'

'So, it was suicide, was it?' Lyn asked.

'If it gives you any more comfort, then please believe that that is what happened. It may be more stressful now to know the truth, but in the longer term, it will help.'

'Tell me then, Mal.'

'Right, prepare yourself. David did not commit suicide. I am certain that David loved you more than to do that. No Lyn, he was shot, but he could not have inflicted that fatal wound on himself. Not to put too fine a point on it, Lyn, he was executed. He was shot in the back of his head in such a way that he could not have done it himself.'

Lyn's mouth fell open, her eyes widened, and tears streamed down her cheek.

After a few minutes, Lyn asked me why.

'I don't know; neither do the police.'

'All they will tell me is that David's death had all the hallmarks of a professional hit execution. They do not know why Ebor Gorge, near Wells, was chosen to do the deed, nor do they know what led up to it. It is a complete mystery to them, and it certainly is to me. I really am sorry, Lyn. To have to tell you about David, I mean. It's just as difficult for me.'

'Thank you for telling me, Mal.'

For the remainder of the journey, I decided to say nothing. If Lyn wanted to talk then, of course, I would do so.'

We arrived at Lyn's house at seven thirty in the evening to the sound of the house phone ringing. Lyn ran into the house and snatched the phone off its cradle.

'Hello!' I heard her say.

Susan's end of the conversation was told to me by Lyn later.

'Why the bloody hell haven't you been answering your mobile?'

'It has not rung all day.'

'Well, I have been ringing you since about three-thirty!'

'Mum! What's happened?'

'It's your father,' Susan said.

'What about him? Is he alright? Tell me, Mum.'

'Can you come straight over?'

'Yes, I'll be there in about fifteen minutes.'

Lyn replaced the receiver and turned to me.

'Mal, have you had any calls on your mobile?'

'No, I haven't. I've made one, though, to Darren from that layby.'

'Did you have to switch your mobile on?'

I thought back. Yes I had. When I wanted to ring Darren, I had to turn the mobile on first. Then it dawned on me, Haraldsen's bloody secretary! She had, for some reason, switched our phones off. Why? I had no idea. Why would she have done that?

'Yes,' I told Lyn.

'Mine was switched off too,' Lyn said as she checked her mobile.

'Bugger!' she exclaimed.

'What's wrong, Lyn?' I asked.

'Something to do with Dad, Mum said.'

'What about your father?'

'Mum wouldn't tell over the phone. Can we go straight over there? She sounded distressed.'

'Of course, come on,' I said, and we almost ran to my car.

Just eleven minutes later, we pulled to a stop outside Susan's house, and as we approached the house itself, the front door was opened, and Susan stood there to greet us and was obviously somewhat distressed.

'Mum, we got here as soon as we could. Is Dad alright?'

Susan smiled briefly before saying that he was alright, but it was something the doctor had told her.

'Well?' Lyn said to her mother.

'I've had a call from the hospital, you know, Doctor Francis. He said that the drug traces they found in your dad's blood were confirmed as Rohypnol. After they had done all of their calculations and so on, it became clear that Dad had been drugged. By this morning, Dad's memory had returned almost to normal and from what he told the doctor, he was kidnapped from here and left to fend for himself in Looe. He is being interviewed by that nice young lady officer now. He should be ready to be discharged at about nine o'clock.'

'That's going to be a bit late to pick him up and get back here,' Lyn told Susan.

'Yes, that's what I thought. I've said that we'll pick him up at about lunchtime tomorrow. Is that alright with you, Lyn?'

'Yes, and you, Mal?'

'Yes. Fine.'

We went in and congregated in the kitchen. Susan had already made a pot of tea. A plate of freshly made sandwiches sat next to a plate with delicious-looking fruit cake sliced up.

Lunch at the Heathfield Tavern seemed an age ago, and the sandwiches and cake disappeared in double quick time. After sating our appetites, we all adjourned to the lounge.

We settled on a comfortable sofa and chairs, and the conversation seemed reluctant to start. The silence was broken by Susan.

'Lyn,' she began, 'what exactly is going on? I do not understand any of this. First there was David's death in Somerset, then the burglaries at your house and mine. Then there was the business with your father. Lyn you must tell me what is going on. I'm beginning to get worried about our safety.'

'Mal knows far more about all this than I do,' Lyn told her mother.

Lyn and Susan both turned their heads towards me and waited for me to start.

'Do you want me to tell your mother everything, Lyn?' I asked.

Although she hesitated, she said yes, she wanted me to tell her everything.

This I did. I went right back to that very first night when I got the call to go to Lyn's house to help comfort her after the news of her husband's death had been imparted to her through our visit to see Harry Haraldsen. The only things I left out were the manner of David's death and finding the bugs in my car. The telling took almost an hour, but at least now it was all out there. The three of us knew everything there was to know, well, almost everything. As I have said, I left out David's death details and the bugs and of course the amounts of money and jewels we had found. There was much which still had to be explained, and I saw no sense in speculating about the unknown.

'Gosh,' Susan sighed a heartfelt sigh. 'What a tale. It's a bit like a drama off the television? You know, the sort where you are kept in suspense until the next episode. Trouble is that it is not fictional. This is real life, and it scares me.'

'Me too,' commented Lyn, 'what about you, Mal?'

'I'm not terribly comfortable with it all; I must admit,' I assured her.

'So, what do we do next, Mal?' Lyn wanted to know.

'I'm not very sure that we should be doing anything. I suppose we ought to get hold of David's bank and see what we need to do with that. Then there is the will. We haven't really looked at that, have we? I am sorry, Lyn, but there are an awful lot of we's which should be I's. I'll tell you what, you make a list of the things you think should be done, and I'll make one too. Then tomorrow, we can compare the two.

I know that I promised to find out why David died and, as yet, I have failed to do that. I had discovered the where and the how but not the why. I could hazard a guess, but there were still doubts. I would see my undertaking through to its conclusion if I possibly could but at the same time, Lyn had to play her part.

We parted company on friendly enough terms, and I drove ponderingly home.

Once I got home, I decided to get my mind off the mystery by putting on the television. After a nightcap of gin and tonic, I retired for a much-deserved early night.

Chapter Sixteen

The following day, I completed my notes file, had breakfast of coffee and toast, and was at Lyn's front door by ten-thirty.

I rang the doorbell, and Lyn admitted me with a smile. She was clearly all ready for the off.

'Come on then, lovey, let's get on the road.'

We called Susan's address, collected her, and started our journey to Plymouth. Four hours later, I brought the car to a standstill in front of the hospital entrance. I left Lyn and Susan to go to the appropriate ward and collect Mr Wright. I guessed that they would be some time by the time the doctor had briefed Susan and all the necessary discharge papers had been signed. I decided to stay back and took the opportunity to ring Detective Chief Inspector Carterford and update him about Lyn's father's kidnapping. I figured it was key information that he needed to know. He listened without interruption and asked the name of the officer dealing with the kidnap or at least the finding of Mr Wright in Looe.

'Thank you, Mal. I'll contact Constable Wyatt, and we can liaise. Can you tell Mrs Kendall that I will contact her later today?'

'Yes, of course. We should be home by seven o'clock, but you can always call her mobile. The drawback to that is that her mother and father will also be in the car and may well be able to hear what you are saying. Lyn may be reluctant to talk to you in front of her parents,' I pointed out. 'I suggest you call her sometime later.'

'Good point, Mal. Tell Mrs Kendall that I will contact her tomorrow morning, would you?' he asked.

'Certainly.'

The call was terminated. And I leaned back in my seat and closed my eyes. Thinking and dozing, I waited.

Half an hour later, Mr and Mrs Wright and Lyn appeared through the entrance. And I got out to hold the car doors open for them. Once ensconced, we left the hospital en route to the Wright's home.

On the way along the M5, Lyn's father told us what had happened.

He had woken at five that morning and gone to the bathroom. Not feeling at all sleepy, Mr Wright made his way downstairs to the kitchen to make some tea. He opened the kitchen door and was immediately seized upon by two men. One attacker held his arms behind him whilst the other put a large piece of cotton wool over his mouth and nose, and the sweet-smelling substance on the cottonwool did its job, and Mr Wright's knees went. The next thing he knew, he woke up in West Looe, outside the hotel. He had absolutely no recollection of anything between his kitchen and Looe. He didn't even realise that he was sitting in his own car. His recollections, such as they were, did not include any of the journeys between home and Looe. His memory only recovered to deliver what happened after he woke up and before he had been knocked out. We all listened to his story intently, shell-shocked that so much had happened that night. Then, he dropped the bombshell.

Reaching into the inside pocket of his jacket, he pulled out a sheet of paper and handed it to Lyn. Written on the paper in black block capitals was the message:

THIS IS JUST TO PROVE THAT WE CAN DO THIS TO YOUR FATHER OR ANYONE ELSE. WATCH YOUR STEP.

The message itself was not actually addressed to anyone in particular, but there was no doubting to whom it was aimed.

'Why on earth didn't you tell us about it before now?' I asked.

'I only found it as I was leaving the hospital. When I had signed the necessary paperwork, I was putting it into my inside jacket pocket, and one sheet crumpled up as I pushed it in. I reached into the pocket, and there this was,' Mr Wright explained.

I said to Lyn, but of necessity, addressed her parents too, 'This does put a slightly different complexion on who we tell and when about everything. My first thought was that this was the work of Harry Haraldsen, but as he had assured us that he had had nothing to do with the burglaries, I do not now consider very likely. Do you remember Haraldsen telling you, Lyn? He said, "I have no desire to see anything happen to you or your family," and "I would not like you to have to find out, Mrs Kendall." Believe me, I am not discounting Haraldsen at this stage, but much as I was not too fond of Haraldsen, strangely, I believed him. It was a threat of what might be done rather than a confirmation of what had been done.'

Lyn thought back to the conversations we had been part of in Harry Haraldsen's office and was clearly weighing them up in her mind.

'I agree, Mal,' Lyn replied, 'on balance, I don't think it was Haraldsen either. It must be someone else. Someone as influential.'

'Hm, but if it wasn't him, then who the hell is it?'

I saw Lyn shrug her shoulders in my rear-view mirror.

'I don't know, Mal. I just do not know.' There was almost a sob in her voice that indicated she was tired of getting caught up in David's mess.

'Let it rest for now, and when we get home, we'll sit down and discuss the whole affair,' I suggested.

'About time too,' interjected Susan.

'I agree, Susan,' I said. 'I shall have to chat with Lyn first, but still, I agree.'

Mr Wright merely nodded his head. I don't think that he had any idea at all about what was going on or indeed had gone on. I am not sure just how much he would take in, even if I told him.

We arrived home almost four and half hours after leaving Plymouth Hospital, thanks to some lengthy road works on the northbound carriageway of the M5.

'I don't feel much like cooking now,' Susan Wright said.

'Nor me, what about you, Mal?' Lyn said.

'No, I do not feel like cooking. I tell you what; I'll get takeaway, shall I?' I offered.

'Make a list of what everyone would like, and I'll pop into town and get the food. Choose whatever you want. There is Chinese, Indian, kebabs, or good old fish and chips, all within easy walking distance. We can sort out the payment afterwards.'

I went to the bathroom, used the toilet, and splashed cold water on my tired eyes. By the time I had come back to the kitchen, Lyn and Susan had prepared a list for me, and all that was left to do was for me to add my own choice.

It took me almost three-quarters of an hour to order, collect and pay for the food and then return to Susan's home.

The food was dished out, and we all sated our appetites in near silence. When plates were cleared as they all had been, we all adjourned to the lounge to rest. Susan and Lyn remained in the kitchen and busied themselves making coffee. Once brewed and cups filled with the brown liquid, we all sat around the lounge.

'Mal. Would you tell the story, please? You are a lot less directly involved,' Lyn asked.

'Everything included?' I asked.

'I think Mum and Dad are entitled to know everything, especially after what happened to Dad, don't you think?' Lyn said.

'It is your decision, Lyn, not mine. If you want me to, I will tell everything.'

'Everything then,' Lyn said decisively.

'Very well. I will begin at the very beginning, as Julie Andrews sang in the Sound of Music,' I said, and I did. I told them absolutely everything. Susan and her husband were stunned into silence almost from the start. I watched Lyn at intervals and could sometimes see tears welling up in her eyes, and whenever the shooting of her husband was mentioned, they flowed down her face. I could tell it was a painful reminder and almost felt guilty about repeating it to her. The story was over an hour in telling, and I left nothing out, absolutely nothing.

Clearly, Susan was appalled by the story and did not believe everything I told her.

'It is just like something out of a television drama, not real life. Things like executions do not happen in England, yes there was talk of executions by the IRA in Northern Ireland, but in England! In sleepy old Somerset! I have been to that area and, in fact, walked the trail at the Ebor Gorge, it could never have happened in the way that you told us. Never. If you are just trying to shock us, Mal, then you have succeeded. I think that you had better leave. How could you be so cruel?' Susan was close to tears herself.

I did not respond and rose to leave.

'No, Mal. Sit down, please. Please, Mal,' Lyn implored.

'Very well,' I said and sat back down. If Lyn had not said that she wanted her parents to know everything and asked me to relate all the happenings, then I would not have been blamed for upsetting everyone.

'Mum? Dad?' Lyn said, and both turned to look at her.

'Mum, Dad, everything Mal has told you is right, at least as far as we know. The one thing that Mal left out is exactly who is responsible for David's death and why, and why and by whom our two houses and our Amsterdam hotel room were all burgled. We have absolutely no idea who is behind it all. That's what we're still trying to figure out.'

There was a prolonged pause while Susan and her husband took in what their daughter had added to the story I had related.

'But from what Mal told us, I thought this Harry Haraldsen chap was behind it all. Isn't he?' Susan wanted to know.

'At first, we thought that he was, at least I suspected it. I don't know what Lyn thought. However, from what this Harry bloke said, it became apparent that he probably wasn't behind the attacks. He was only interested in two things, the diamonds, and the bank statements for the Swiss bank account. He wasn't even interested in David's own bank account. I am definitely not ruling him out, but I don't think he was involved. While I believe that he was not directly responsible for the attacks, nor do I necessarily believe that he was involved in them, I believe that he was aware of the attack, certainly the one on David. I have to be honest and say that I definitely do not rule him out of this affair. I am not a police officer and I do not have access to any intelligence which they may have. So, anything I do say is my own opinion. My own opinion is that there are two different groups of people involved. One group of people, which includes Haraldsen is interested in the diamonds, probably smuggling of them. The other group, probably the larger of the two is involved with something much bigger, possibly money-laundering, something like that. There is, however, something which links the two. Why else would Haraldsen want the Swiss account bank statements? I know it's too much to take in, but this is the story so far.'

'What do you intend to do, then, Mal?' Lyn wanted to know. I noticed her parents' heads turn towards me. It seemed as though all three of them expected far more from me than I was able to give. After all, I knew nothing more than Lyn did, although the conclusions I could draw would be different from hers.

'Right now, I am tired, so I'm off home to bed.'

We exchanged 'goodnights', and I left.

Chapter Seventeen

The following morning, I completed my ablutions. Once I had eaten breakfast and had washed it down with fresh coffee, I felt ready to meet any challenge of the day that might present itself. As an old friend was in the habit of saying, 'You fed, watered, and mucked out?' I smiled at the thought of my friend and his saying, which made me laugh every time he asked this slightly vulgar question in a matter-of-fact and very unvulgar way.

I picked up my mobile and rang Detective Chief Inspector Carterford.

'DCI Carterford', Philip's voice announced.

'Philip, it's Mal. How are you today?'

'I'm good, Mal. What can I do for you?' he asked.

'I am not sure, to be frank. It may be a case of what I can do for you,' I replied.

'Alright, you've got my attention. I'm listening.'

'Not on the telephone. Walls and telephones have ears, you know.'

'What then?' the detective asked.

'Are you free for lunch?' I asked.

'I can be. Where do you need me?'

'What about that pub on the river? What is it, the Trout Tavern?' I suggested.

'Sounds a bit of a dive to me,' he said with a chuckle in his voice.

'Oh, it definitely is not that, Philip.'

'Alright then. Lunch on you?'

'Of course, say one o'clock?'

'Fine, see you then.'

I terminated the call and noted the appointment in my case notes.

The day turned out to be very warm and sunny. Nice to eat out of doors I thought and as I had arrived early I found a table beside the river's edge. I sat down, and in a few moments, a waiter appeared; I ordered Diet Coke. I told him that I was expecting a guest for lunch and if a man asked for a Ms Jones to direct him to my table.

'Of course,' said the waiter, leaving to collect my Coke.

Less than five minutes later, a shadow fell across my table. Philip Carterford bade me a good afternoon and sat down.

'Mal! How are things with you?' he asked.

'So, so. And you?'

'The same. Busy, of course.'

We ordered our lunch and chatted about things until the meals arrived.

Having cleared our plates of what was a delicious lunch, I asked, 'Are you up to date on everything which has happened?'

'I think we are. Why?'

'I need to ensure that you do know everything. That being the case, I would like to tell you everything that I know,' I told him. 'Just to bring you up to speed.'

'Does Mrs Kendall know that you are here?' he wanted to know.

'She does not. The reason that I asked to meet you away from the police station is that I want you to understand that I will deny ever telling you everything. It is too dangerous for Lyn and her parents.'

Carterford just looked me in the eyes and said nothing in response. He seemed taken aback by my statement.

I began my story, repeating it as I had to Lyn's parents. I omitted nothing. When I concluded the saga, which seemed to get longer with each telling, I took a long draught of my Diet Coke.

'Mal. How well can I trust you?' he asked.

This seemed a strange question in the context of our lunch meeting.

'Philip. I give you my word that you can trust me implicitly; with anything,' I assured him.

'Not here then. Let's go somewhere that we cannot be overheard. You'll find out why.'

I followed Philip to the massive car park, which served the whole of the fishing lakes area. With angling being so popular across the country, one estimate for England and Wales put the numbers of freshwater and sea anglers at 1650000, so a large car park was needed.

I followed Philip to one corner, where we were the only vehicles within fifty yards or so. I transferred to Philip's vehicle. This worked well for me, especially since my car had been bugged, and I had no way of knowing it had not been bugged again. When we were settled in the car, we both swivelled in our seats to face each other.

'Before we start, I'm afraid you will have to accept my word that this vehicle is not bugged,' Philip assured me.

Why did he raise the subject of vehicle bugs? I hadn't told him of the bugs I had found in my car. I paused before I responded to study the chief inspector's face and saw no indication that it had been anything but a passing remark.

'I accept that, Philip,' I told him and waited for him to tell me whatever it was that he was going to tell me.

'The thing is, Mal, that we know more about this whole series of incidents than either you or Lyn might think. Why do you think no one has been to see Lyn to speak to her about her husband's death?'

'I do think it is strange; I agree. I just thought that you are still making enquiries, particularly given that the death occurred in a completely different police area, and the cause of death turned out to be murder. I thought that that explained it. That the police are taking their time to gather as much information as possible.'

'That is partly it, I agree. We also know about Haraldsen and some of his activities.'

'I see,' I acknowledged, 'so what I told you didn't help at all!' I said almost with astonishment.

'Mal. I need you to sign this before I tell you anything else.' He reached into an inside pocket of his jacket and came out with a sheet of A4 folded twice. He handed it to me. I unfolded it.

It was headed up Official Secrets Act and referred to as Official Secrets Act dates from 1889 to 1989. I guessed that whatever Philip was about to tell me could not be repeated unless I wanted to risk going to prison. If what he was about to reveal did come under the umbrella of Official Secrets, then I would be bound by the Act. The act of signing an Official Secrets statement underlined that fact and acted as a constant reminder.

Philip passed me a ballpoint pen, and I hesitated before taking the offered pen. I then scrawled my signature at the foot of the page before handing it back to the chief inspector.

I wasn't entirely sure if I had made the right decision, but it was done, and there was no going back.

'Thank you,' Philip said. 'You do understand the implications of breaking the Official Secrets Act terms, don't you?'

'Yes, I do. I have no wish to end up in The Tower of London, like Rudolf Hess!'

Rudolf Hess had parachuted into this country on 10th May 1941 in an alleged attempt to negotiate peace between Nazi Germany and Great Britain through the Duke of Hamilton. The duke was thought by Hess to be an opponent of the Government's war policy. When he landed, he was arrested and taken to The Tower of London on 17th May 1941. He was taken to The King's House where, like Guy Fawkes over three hundred and thirty years before him, he had been interrogated. Hess was likewise interrogated and was removed from The Tower after four days of interrogation.

'Right,' began Philip, 'the most important thing to tell you is that David Kendall was not Lyn's husband's real name.'

'What!' I exclaimed. 'How so?'

'Just let me relate the story as I understand it, and I'll do my best to answer any questions you might have afterwards.'

'Alright, sorry!' I apologised.

'Okay. Well, the reason I know that David Kendall was not his real name is that David was, in fact, a police officer.'

My mouth fell open. That just could not be true. I tried to digest what he had told me. Surely Lyn would have known about this before she married him? How could this possibly be true?

I know that Philip wanted me to wait until he finished, but I could not stop myself from saying something.

'That cannot be true, Philip. Are you sure about this?'

'I can assure you it is Mal, but please let me finish.'

'Tell me, did you find any passports while searching David's office?'

'Yes. We did. Two in fact.'

'In the names of Robert and Gillian Dickson?'

'Yes! That's right!' I said, failing to keep the surprise out of my voice.

'Did you not think it strange that there were two passports, one for a man and one for a woman?' Philip asked.

'Well, yes, we did. For my part, I was convinced that these were getaway passports in case something went wrong with whatever David was involved in. I didn't think this was the background story, though.'

Well,' the chief inspector replied, 'in a way, you are right. Robert Dickson's passport is genuine; Gillian's obviously is not. I suppose, in one sense, you could say that it was legal because Robert Dickson is David's real name. David wanted a passport for Lyn when they married but could not risk obtaining a legal one, so he invented the name Gillian for her. Her surname is, I suppose, legally Dickson. I expect Lyn has one in her real name as she thinks it is, doesn't she?'

'It is all very complicated, isn't it?' I pointed out. 'Yes, Lyn has a passport in the name of Lyn Kendall, which, as far as she is concerned, is her real and married name. So which passport is the false one, I wonder?'

'That is an interesting point,' mused Philip. 'In law, I am not sure that there is no reason why she should not continue to call herself Lyn Kendall. The passport she thinks is in her married name was obtained without fraud. If the worse comes to the worse, the police and the Home Office will ensure that she has the correct passport in the correct name.'

I said, 'I suspect when Lyn finds out what David was and did, especially after the danger he has put her in and the lies he has told, no matter how worthy the cause, I think that she could well revert to her maiden name of Wright. I am only surmising, of course. But my friend has already been through so much.'

Philip Carterford paused a while as if gathering his thoughts.

Then he continued, 'I would rather that Lyn does not find out the truth for the time being. To give him his proper and real name, you must remember that Detective Inspector Dickson spent many months, maybe years, preparing for this deep cover operation. His death does change things. Of course, it does. But the longer we can keep what I have told you under wraps, the more use we can make of what Robert achieved. If we could recover the diamonds, it would be something, and the money, which we believe is salted away in a Swiss bank account, would probably make the operation all worthwhile. What we really want is to arrest those who are running the whole thing. That would be the real icing on the cake, so to speak, but seems a little unlikely now with Robert's death.'

I was trying to take all of this in. It certainly was not what I expected to hear today or any other day for that matter. How can Lyn and her family be protected from whatever organisation this was? I wondered. Lyn had had her house and hotel room burgled, her mother and father's house had been burgled, and her father kidnapped. If it ever got out that she had been talking to the police, well, I had anyway, then the Lord knows what would happen to them. There was no room for doubt that they were ruthless. David, I was still thinking of him as David; it would avoid confusion in my mind; he had crossed them in some way and had been executed for it. There was no other word for it; it was an execution. I presume they would not hesitate to kill Lyn, her parents, and perhaps even me if the occasion arose. I contemplated what to do next after taking it all in.

'Philip,' I said, 'I really wish you hadn't told me all this.'

'Well, I didn't want you putting two and two together and making four or even more, as it were. You are much shrewder than you give yourself credit for and are highly regarded as an insurance adjuster. On balance and with my bosses' permission, I decided it was better and safer for you to know the truth rather than stumbling upon it.'

'Thank you, I think! Thank you for the confidence anyway. I need guidance as what to advise Lyn to do now. We are supposed to hand over the diamonds to Harry Haraldsen on Wednesday at two o'clock. We have to retrieve them from the safety deposit box in Amsterdam first. He has already threatened Lyn and, by implication, me if he doesn't get the diamonds. You see, I thought that Lyn's father being kidnapped was a warning from Haraldsen as to what he could do if she did not play ball. However, having now met with him, I am not so sure. When the burglaries and kidnapping were mentioned, there was absolutely no reaction from Haraldsen. I think two factions are involved here, and both are playing the powerplay game. The problem for me and Lyn, of course, is in deciding which faction is which.'

'That should not be your concern, Mal. Leave it to the police, please,' the Chief Inspector pleaded.

'That is all very well, but Haraldsen clearly knows who Lyn is, and now he knows me. We are the people who have been threatened and attacked. I've already had one fist in the face, which bloody hurt incidentally. I don't particularly relish another one or worse.'

Philip Carterford paused as if considering what I had said.

'I'm sorry that you were involved like that, and, of course, I do not want you involved like that again. I understand it must be exhausting.'

'But,' I pointed out, 'I am Lyn's best friend and have been since we were at school together.'

'I realise that, Mal. I am not asking you to desert her; of course, I'm not.'

'What are you asking of me then, Philip?' I asked.

'I haven't finalised anything yet, but we would like to get you all into a safe house,' he said. 'At least that way, we won't have to worry about your safety while we continue the investigation.'

'How the bloody hell will I be able to help protect Lyn and her parents from a bloody safe house?'

'As I said, just now. Nothing has been finalised, but I would at least like Lyn's parents to go to a safe house for their own protection. Lyn's father being kidnapped should ring very loud warning bells for you. I implore you to think of them. They are not really involved, are they?' Philip asked.

'Not as far as I know. Susan is the sweetest thing, and Lyn's father is lovely too. He had no idea what happened to him when he was kidnapped or why he was kidnapped. I agree they should be protected from whoever or whatever all this stuff is. In lots of ways, I am as much in the dark as they are. I am an insurance adjuster; I investigate insurance claims. I do not mind admitting, Philip, I am completely out of my depth with this stuff. I know precious little about diamonds or money laundering if that is what it is, nor Swiss bank accounts for the matter.'

'Are you prepared to trust me, Mal?' Philip asked.

'Well, in general terms, yes, of course, I am. As far as specifics involving David and Lyn, I am not so sure.'

On the plus side, I did not doubt that Philip and his cronies knew what they were doing, but in the minus column, there was the murder of one of their own. David had trusted his bosses, but could I? I was not too sure that I could, at least not completely.

'What are your plans then?' I enquired.

'Plans?' the chief inspector queried.

'Yes, plans. You haven't forgotten that we have to go to Amsterdam, collect four million pounds worth of diamonds and deliver them to one of the ungodly, the very ungodly!'

'Of course, I had not forgotten! I propose you come to police headquarters, not the local station, and we will wire you up. We will then be able to hear the conversation from a distance. Two undercover officers will also be there and will be similarly wired. They will accompany you on the flight to The Netherlands and then to the bank. Once you have retrieved the diamonds they will escort you back to the UK. You will meet up with Haraldsen as arranged and hand over the diamonds. The second you leave his house, we will raid it and arrest him, his secretary, and anyone else in their company threatening you, Lyn, and her family.'

'Marvellous! Just bloody marvellous! Lyn won't suspect anything, will she? No, not with two hairy-arsed coppers in tow. I mean, I do know that Lyn can be just a little slow on the uptake sometimes, But I think that even she might suspect something when she sees two men get on to the same aircraft and follow us to Schiphol and then to the same bank and wait outside to follow us back to Schiphol and then on to Heathrow. She might even get a bit suspicious when they follow us to Haraldsen's house, don't you think?'

'Calm down, Mal. Of course, she would spot them if they were comic book detectives, but these two are seasoned professionals, and there will be very little chance of Lyn spotting them, so you do not have to worry about that. As far as Haraldsen's house is concerned, we will have a team in place long before you get there. This is the only way we can get to him.'

'That is all very well but don't think that Haraldsen is stupid. He is not; he is very astute. How do you think he has evaded the authorities for so long? Given that premise, don't you think that he will be the tiniest bit suspicious of Lyn and especially me? He doesn't like me very much I can tell. He was clearly suspicious of me from the off and kept a weather-eye on me all the time I was in his house.'

'He can be as suspicious as he likes. We have enough evidence to put him away for twenty years or more, and he will be in custody only after you are well away.'

Philip tried to sound reassuring, but I was far from reassured.

'Look, David died, was executed,' I pointed out, 'for doing something wrong or something the gang didn't like. I don't fancy kneeling side by side with Lyn in some God-forsaken part of the country waiting for a bullet in the back of the head. If my surmise is correct, then there are two factions involved here. One centres around Haraldsen, but even he is not the boss according to him. Even if we get Haraldsen, what will you do about the others?'

'No, he is not the boss. Look, Mal,' Philip said, 'please do not take me for a fool because I am not. I have already lost one officer and am not prepared to risk losing another or anyone else to this mob. Of course, we know there are two factions involved but you are correct in thinking that they are connected. The two big bosses, as it were, are both London-based criminals. They are, not to put too fine a point on it, very clever criminals. They have entered a partnership and make millions of pounds yearly from their joint activities. We know exactly who they are and have them under surveillance even as we speak. However, just to be on the safe side, we will place Lyn's parents in a safe house, under 24-hour surveillance, and with officers on the premises too. That is, of course, if they agree to this course of action.'

'If it is explained properly to them, I think they would agree. When you ask them, I suggest you heavily bias your reasoning with the safety of Lyn. They absolutely adore her and will do almost anything for her. This, mind you, is a very big ask.'

'I realise that, Mal, I really do. I intend to speak to them today and try to persuade them into going to the safe house,' Philip told me.

'Okay, but you haven't forgotten about the diamonds, have you?' I enquired.

'No, I had not forgotten. I'm keeping tabs on everything. Today is Friday. When do you intend to collect them?'

Lyn and I had not discussed when we would be likely to recover the diamonds from the Amsterdam safety deposit, so I felt I had to decide for us.

'Well, Lyn and I haven't actually agreed a day yet. We have to have the stones to Haraldsen by two o'clock on Wednesday. Now I can't speak for Lyn, obviously, but I certainly don't want them in our possession for longer than is absolutely necessary, so I am going to suggest that we go to Amsterdam on Tuesday morning.'

'Okay. Well, could you and Lyn meet me at our headquarters building on Monday at eleven o'clock? You'll probably need to discuss this with Lyn first, but that time would be alright for me.'

I realised then that I had not even mentioned the fitting of a wire, but then, of course, it was better that she didn't know. The fewer people who were privy to the plan the better. It was then that I took the decision not to tell Lyn anything. I knew that I should not be withholding information involving her from her, but in this case I thought it for the best. She does not need more than what she already has on her plate.

'Philip, I think it for the best if Lyn is not only not wired up but is ignorant of the plan to wire me up and to have your two men with us.' The less she knows, the better; it will be less likely for anything to slip out, as it were.'

'Right then,' the chief inspector said, 'I will call around to speak to Lyn's parents either later today or probably tomorrow. I would appreciate it if you didn't tell Lyn until after I have spoken to them.'

'That's fine by me, although I do need to speak to Lyn about Tuesday just to make sure that she is alright with us going on that day,' I pointed out.

The detective chief inspector nodded his agreement, and we made a firm plan to meet at police headquarters on Monday morning.

Philip and I went our separate ways, and I called Lyn to find out where she was. I told her that I wanted to meet up with her. I decided not to say too much over the mobile phone network. After all, you didn't really know who might be listening. She was at her own house, and she said that I could come around at any time.

I met up with Lyn and decided definitely against telling her my plans for Monday and our, hopefully unseen, protection for Tuesday and Wednesday. While I was confident that she would not tell anyone deliberately, she would almost certainly be looking around trying to pick out our escorts, and that could give the game away should anyone be watching. I could not risk us getting in trouble in this covert operation. I had to remind myself that I would have to be very careful that I did not do what I feared Lyn might do. In some ways, it was worse for me because I knew they were there and the temptation to pick out which would be very strong indeed. I just had a couple of days to get into the habit of acting normally in abnormal circumstances.

Chapter Eighteen

We booked ourselves on the nine forty-seven flight to Schiphol the following Tuesday morning and agreed on our meeting time.

'Do we need to contact the bank, do you think? Just to let them know that we are coming,' I asked Lyn. 'It's best to inform them beforehand so they can make the due arrangements.'

'Oh, I don't think so. Nothing was said about that when we deposited the diamonds,' Lyn told me.

I have to say that it did feel the slightest bit weird knowing what I knew and not telling Lyn. I certainly had to take my words out and look at them before speaking. I remember my grandmother telling me once that it was always a good idea, especially if you were in danger of offending someone. I felt that this was one of granny's circumstances where I was at risk of offending someone, in this case, Lyn.

Ah, well, I thought, *it can't be helped.* It was probably for the best; I kept telling myself.

I kept my appointment with Philip at Police Headquarters on Monday morning; the process took over two hours. First of all, over coffee, I was introduced to our two 'shadows'. Names were a no as they had to remain confidential, but we shook hands in a friendly enough manner.

I studied them both as best I could without making it too obvious. Over the course of those two hours, I reckon that I knew enough of their features to enable me to recognise them on Tuesday, should that be necessary. I had to remember that I must not deliberately start scanning people's faces in an effort to identify them while on the flight out and back and to, from, and in the bank. I had to ensure I steer clear of any suspicious behaviour, anything that could give their cover away.

Introductions and coffee completed, I was taken by a female officer down into the basement of the building. The female introduced herself as Lucy and asked me if she could call me Mal. Of course, I agreed.

Lucy took a cardboard box from a shelf and opened the top. She put her hand inside the box and withdrew a long length of very thin cable. This was 'the wire', she told me. *No shit, Sherlock,* I thought, smiling. Hand into the box again, and a tiny black object was being held in the palm of her hand. I had seen something like this before, I thought. Darren had shown me some similarly shaped objects after he had 'swept my car' with his fan-like scanner.

'Where are you going to stick those?' I asked with as much humour in my voice as possible.

'You'll see!' Lucy said with not quite so much humour. She did not seem to appreciate my joke very much.

Several other bits and pieces appeared on the table in front of us, the uses of which I was not made privy to.

I must confess that Lucy's next question threw me off balance a little.

'Do you wear a bra every day?'

That was a strange question, a bit personal, I thought.

'Yes, I do. Why, what has it got to do with you?' I asked, humour beginning to disappear from my voice.

'Well, we've got to put the bugs somewhere, haven't we?' Lucy said with as much humour as had been in my voice, precious little.

'What about a suspender belt?' Lucy wanted to know.

Now, this was getting ridiculous and more than a little personal.

'Sometimes,' I said with a bit of a questioning tone to my voice.

'Bugs again,' was Lucy's brief reply.

'Panties or thong?' was Lucy's next question.

This was a step too far, and I told her so.

'Maybe,' Lucy said, 'but we have to find suitable concealment places for these little darlings.'

'In that case, thong,' I admitted.

'How shy are you, Mal?' Lucy asked right out of the blue.

I was reminded of a poem that an elderly friend of mine used to recite as a party piece where the last line of each verse was 'Just like that, right out loud, bloody rude!'

The last two words of this line immediately sprang to mind, and I was about to give voice to them and say them 'right out loud', too. But I thought better of it. After all, Lucy obviously knew her job. I reminded myself this was just routine and necessary and calmed myself.

'Not especially,' I admitted.

'Right, are you wearing a suspender belt now?' she asked.

'As a matter of fact, I am,' I replied.

She held out her hand towards me, presumably to avoid asking me to take it off.

'Oh, and the bra too, if you don't mind!'

'There is a cupboard there you can use if you are too shy. Oh, and by the way, if you don't like taking your panties off in public, you can take your thong off in there too.'

Lucy was definitely not shy.

'Oh, sod it,' I expostulated and reached up under my skirt to remove my thong and suspender belt, then under my top for the bra.

I noticed that Lucy showed no signs of distaste at the thought of my thong and where it had been.

'It's okay. I only need the top of it, not the intimate bit!'

I handed all three items to her and noticed that while I had been removing them, Lucy had put on a pair of plastic protective gloves.

I was asked to sit down, and Lucy said that she would be a few minutes. There was a copy of the Daily Express on a side table which Lucy gave me permission to read. I picked it up and anxiously rocked in place, waiting for Lucy to return.

About fifteen minutes later, Lucy came over and handed me the thong, bra, and suspender belt for me to put back on.

'Fortunately, I can go without a bra,' I told Lucy, 'So I'll carry that in my bag.'

'No good, I'm afraid. We need you to wear it for testing the signals and so on. I'll go outside while you put the items back on if you'd rather,' Lucy offered.

'No, you're alright, but I'd appreciate you turning your back while I put the bra on.'

Fully attired once more, I went with Lucy back upstairs to the room in which we had gathered earlier. Philip and his two colleagues were chatting, and they stopped when Lucy and I entered the room.

'All done, sir,' Lucy said brightly. 'The signals are good. I tested them while Mal was dressing again. She's good to go.'

'Thanks, Luce.' Philip said, and Lucy smiled across at me as she exited the room.

'Right, Mal. The signals may be good on the bugs, but we need to be able to get the signals from these two.' Philip indicated my two shadows. 'Make sure you don't lose the connection.'

I thought for a moment that he was going to say something like we need to get the signal from your bra and knickers to these two. He didn't, as that would have been most inappropriate! I would probably have laughed, though!

We carried out several tests over various distances and through various wall thicknesses.

Philip asked for the umpteenth time when our flight to Schiphol left Heathrow, and for the umpteenth time, I told him that it was nine-forty-seven. I went over the plan for the day yet again for his assurance.

Lyn and I leave Heathrow on the nine-forty-seven flight.

Allow two hours for check-in.

From Schiphol Airport in Amsterdam, taxi to the bank.

Ask to retrieve the diamonds from the safety deposit box.

Receive diamonds and sign receipts.

Taxi from the bank back to Schiphol Airport.

Allow two hours for check-in.

Catch four thirty flight from Schiphol back to Heathrow.

Arrive at Heathrow at about five-thirty.

Taxi to Lyn's house.

Lyn and I stay at Lyn's house overnight.

Twelve thirty on Wednesday, leave home for Harry Haraldsen's house.

Lunch at Heathfield at about two o'clock.

Arrive at Harry Haraldsen's house at three o'clock.

Deliver the diamonds and leave as soon as possible.

Keep going until we arrive back at Lyn's house.

'Mal, lastly, we need an abort,' Philip told me.

'Abort?' I asked, completely mystified.

'The word you can use if you want us to come in and get you out of whatever situation you find yourself in that you do not like. Understand?' Philip said.

'Yes, I understand,' I replied, 'but how to decide on the word?'

'Well, it has to be something which you would not normally use in conversation. Let me see, what about a singer you like a lot?' he prompted.

'Well, I like to listen to Jessica Andrews, if that helps,' I suggested.

'Never heard of her!' Philip said.

'Let's hope that the ungodly are in the same position then,' I said.

'Well, who is she?' Philip asked.

'Jessica Andrews is an American country singer. I first heard her singing the theme song to *Sue Thomas' FB Eye*. You've heard of that surely!' I exclaimed.

'Nope. No idea what that is, sorry.'

'Ah well, that will be our abort code then. I am sure you could introduce her into a conversation without arousing suspicion.'

'I am sure that I can,' I replied.

'That's it then.'

Once everyone involved with the collection of the diamonds was as satisfied as they could be, we wished each other good luck and went our separate ways.

Philip Carterford indicated that he would like an extra word out of earshot of his two colleagues.

'Don't worry, Mal. We will look after you,' he assured me. 'These two will not let you out of sight.'

I stood very close to him, looked deep into his eyes, and simply said, 'Thank you, Philip'

Our faces were quite close together and the smile on his lips definitely reached his eyes. I felt a stirring deep inside my being and realised that Philip Carterford had been responsible. His eyes spoke volumes, and I knew with absolute certainty that he had felt it too. I reached up and kissed him on the lips.

It was a promise of things to come rather than any sort of commitment on either of our parts. I lingered in his arms before taking a step backwards, smiled, and turned to leave the room.

''Bye,' I whispered, and Philip smiled at me in return.

Chapter Nineteen

I rang Lyn to confirm our departure time. I was to go to her house and then we would taxi to Heathrow. It would have to be a very early start as we had to be at Heathrow to check in two hours before flight time. I spent the remainder of the day completing my case notes and generally relaxing at home. Although I had been on my own for a long time, there were times when I felt lonely, and this was one of them.

I sat on the sofa and rested my head on the back of it. Just staring at the ceiling. I was lost in my thoughts.

When I was just twenty years old, I fell head over heels in love with a very handsome young chap named Roger, who worked in the same office as me. We went on a run-of-the-mill date, had dinner in a very nice restaurant, and returned to his flat. Two bottles of wine later and lots of passionate kissing, we ended up in his bed. He had taken my virginity with love and great care, ensuring that the experience was enjoyable for both of us, and it was.

After that first time, we were rarely out of each other's company. We spent all of our working days in each other's company at the office and every evening and every weekend together, making love whenever and wherever we could. It was a blissful time in my life. I was so in love and could not imagine having it any other way.

After only a few months, we moved in together and later bought a house in joint names. We were both very happy indeed, or so I thought.

I had returned from visiting a girlfriend one Friday evening and found the house empty. Roger was nowhere to be seen. He hadn't mentioned that he was going out, so I checked our bedroom. Perhaps he had gone to bed early. No, he had not done so. I have no idea what made me do it, but I opened the wardrobe door. My boyfriend's side was devoid of any of his clothing. His chest of drawers had been emptied of his underclothes, socks, and the other bits and pieces he had stored there. He had disappeared without a trace. It was as though he had never existed.

I rang his mobile but found that the number was unobtainable! How could that be? I rang his sister's mobile but could get no reply. He was an orphan, he told me, so there were no parents to ring. It was as if he had never been in my life.

I had been devastated, bursting into tears whenever anyone mentioned Roger or whenever I thought about him. I was bereft. I went to the office the next day only to find that my now ex-boyfriend had resigned and left the firm with immediate effect on Friday night. I never saw nor heard from him again.

I had placed the house on the market, and of the proceeds of the sale, I had placed half on deposit for him should he ever turn up to claim it. The other half I had used as a deposit so that I could buy my present home. I had not so much as dated a man since. I was too heartbroken to think of trusting someone again.

I hadn't really missed men at all. I suppose I missed the amazing sex we had experienced, but now my work was my everything. It gave me a good standard of living, and I did enjoy doing it.

I let out a huge sigh. I began to wonder if my life was as fulfilled as I thought that it was. Apart from my work, the only distraction I had experienced recently was this business with Lyn. Was it a distraction, though? Yes, of course, it was. Surely with the workload I usually worked under, was I not entitled to something else to distract me? Surely I deserved it. Anyway, wasn't what I was doing with Lyn allied to the sort of work I did day in and day out?

I let out another huge sigh and pulled myself from my thoughts.

What the hell had triggered all of these thoughts? Initially, I had no idea. I had not experienced such thought since Roger had left. Maybe, just maybe, it had been the episode with Philip Carterford earlier. Surely one little kiss couldn't disturb me this much. Or could it? Of course, it could be wishful thinking with the wistfulness being sparked by the kiss.

I dismissed all of these thoughts and, with another glass of wine drunk to clear my mind, went to bed. It took me a while to drop off, but when I did, I dreamed of Philip Carterford and what we did together!

The next morning the alarm brought me to full consciousness, and I climbed out of bed feeling more refreshed than I had felt in a long time. I remember someone telling me that if you can remember your dreams, then they weren't dreams at all; they were what you wished to be true. Well, I couldn't remember all the details of my dreams from last night, but I could remember some, and I smiled at the recollection. It had been a while since I had a dream like that for a man. Another thing someone told me was to make your dreams come true; you have to reverse them! How does that work then, I mused? If I had to reverse the parts of my dreams I could remember, why was I feeling so refreshed and with my happiness at a slightly higher level than yesterday? I can't remember who had told me these things, but how many old wives did I know?

I completed my ablutions, and the fresh coffee had been percolating while I was doing so. I sat down for coffee and toast and found that my memories of last night's dreams were fading already. Perhaps those old wives, whoever they might be, were right after all!

The doorbell brought me back to the present from my reverie. It was my taxi. It was time to get to business.

The driver wished me good morning and asked, 'Where to, love?'

I gave him Lyn's address; we picked her up within ten minutes and were on our way to Heathrow Airport.

Conversation was stunted between Lyn and me. I had deliberately kept it this way as we didn't want the taxi driver overhearing anything we didn't want him to hear and possibly have us exposed. I found myself wanting to check out of the rear window of the taxi to check that my shadows were already in attendance. I thought better of it. I did, once only, on the journey, use the mirror in my handbag to surreptitiously have a look behind us. I could only have a brief look so as not to arouse any suspicions in either Lyn or the taxi driver. I could see nothing. My shadows, thus far anyway, had lived up to their reputation. I just hoped that they were watching us somehow, somewhere.

The taxi dropped us outside the airport departure entrance and took the cost of the fare in twenty-pound notes. It was an extravagance, I knew that, but it was the one way that we could complete the journey to the airport in one go, as it were. If we had gone undetected by the ungodly, it had been worth every penny.

We went through check-in without incident, and despite checking occasionally, I still couldn't see our shadows. It was a good thing in one way, of course, but at the same time not very reassuring. What if they weren't following us at all?

We landed at Schiphol just ten minutes late, due to a headwind probably, I thought.

There was a rank of taxis waiting outside the arrivals lounge. We waited outside while some of our fellow passengers got into taxis on the rank. It was probably the fifth or sixth in line that we eventually took and began our journey into Amsterdam. So far, our little operation had been smooth as ever.

The taxi dropped us outside the bank's entrance. I paid the driver, and we waited until the taxi was well out of sight before making our way into the banking hall. We went to the safety deposit desk and, when asked, handed our paperwork to the clerk.

The clerk smiled and, immediately picking up on the fact that we were English began speaking to us in our own language. I had often marvelled at the fact that residents of mainland Europe routinely learned more than one language, and one of them always seemed to include English. Be that as it may, it was working in our favour today.

We were escorted to the strongroom, which held the safety deposit boxes, and the clerk opened the strengthened metalled barred gate across the strongroom to one bank of safety deposit boxes. He inserted his key and turned it and turned to leave, allowing us privacy to examine our deposit.

'I will be just outside when you're ready. Just press that button on the table there,' he said, pointing to a gleaming white button contained within an equally gleaming brass surround.

'Thank you,' Lyn said and waited until he had left us alone.

'Right, here goes,' said Lyn, inserting her key into the box front and turning it.

The key turned easily, and the door opened.

Lyn reached in and pulled out the bags of diamonds. They were all there, and Lyn and I looked at each other and breathed a sigh of relief. Lyn stowed the diamonds in a zipped compartment of her capacious bag, and within a few minutes, we had relocked the safety deposit box.

I pressed the button on the desk, and almost simultaneously, the door opened, and the clerk re-entered.

'Is everything in order?' he asked us politely.

'Yes, thank you,' Lyn replied and handed her key to the clerk.

Once more, at the desk in the banking hall, Lyn paid her fee for using the safety deposit box, and we left. I tried, believe me, I did try, to ignore the other people in the banking hall, but I could not stop looking around for my two shadows. I did not spot them, and neither did anyone stand out to me as being with the ungodly. I turned to Lyn to ensure she hadn't grown suspicious. She had not.

We emerged onto the street, and a taxi saw us and pulled alongside us. Caution being ever to the fore, we ignored it and walked away. The taxi followed us for only a very short distance before taking the hint and drove off down the street. Out of habit, I mentally noted the taxi's ID number. We walked a short distance until we spotted a police officer standing in a corner.

'Where is the nearest taxi rank, please?' I asked.

'Down this street here towards that church you can see in the distance and take the third left. There is a taxi rank. It should not be too busy at this time of the day.'

We thanked the police officer and walked off in the direction he had indicated. Again, a taxi pulled alongside, and the driver asked if he could take us anywhere.

I tried, as politely as possible, to tell him that we did not require the services of a taxi. The driver obviously took the hint and drove off. As he drove away, I noted that the ID number was the same as the one we had seen a few moments earlier. Coincidence? Nah! I do not believe in coincidences. I could feel my heart had begun to race.

'Did you see that, Lyn?' I asked her.

'Yes, I did. Was it the same taxi and the same man?'

'It was certainly the same taxi, and I'll lay odds that it was the same driver. Let's turn around and go back to the main street. We should be able to catch a tram there.'

We did exactly that and jumped onto the first tram which came along. Neither of us had any idea where the tram was making for.

The conductor came along for our fares.

'The nearest stop to the railway station, please,' I said, taking a chance that the tram would go somewhere close by.

'We have to go in the opposite direction to the rail station,' the conductor told us. 'We then wait for ten minutes and turn around to come back.'

'That will be good,' I told him. He, in turn, told me the cost of the two tickets, and I handed over the necessary euros.

I kept a weather eye out for the taxi, and although I saw plenty, I did not catch sight of the taxi I had twice seen.

We eventually arrived at the Amsterdam Centraal Station and alighted.

We went into the rail station and enquired as to availability of trains to Schiphol Airport. We were looking for the earliest train out of the city.

'The 1430 train will take you there, and the journey takes about twenty minutes,' the ticket collector said helpfully.

We purchased two tickets to Schiphol and waited on the appropriate platform. There seemed to be plenty of people waiting with us but still no sign of my shadows. Good thing or bad thing? Equally, there was no one obviously ungodly. Good thing or bad thing? Definitely a good thing, that is, if I was accurate in my assessment.

The train arrived on time, and we waited until almost everyone had boarded before us. The only people waiting to board were a family of two adults, three young children, and three middle-aged ladies all chattering with each other. None appeared to be a danger to us.

We jumped on the train and were fortunate to find seats with good solid and high backs to protect us. The journey passed without incident, and we alighted near the airport entrance.

We grabbed a quick lunch in a small eatery on the airport complex and were able to check in for our flight, albeit a little later than we should have.

The flight was uneventful, which was a relief for both of us. I didn't disguise my check of the people around me this time. My shadows were obviously very good at their job as I still could not see them. I sighed with relief the closer we got to home.

Whether it was just this fact or the fact that the operation was drawing towards its close which affected my judgement, I do not know. The row of taxis moved forward slowly, and we both climbed into the first vehicle in the queue. It was a bad choice, certainly a wrong one anyway.

'Where to, lady?' The taxi driver said rather brusquely and with more than a hint of a New York cabbie.

I gave him my home address, and he just said, 'Okay.'

Lyn and I leaned back in our seats and relaxed. We both began to doze with the steady rhythm of the taxi tyres on the motorway surface.

There was a loud blast from our taxi's horn.

'Bloody drivers!' said our driver.

This minor incident brought me to full consciousness, and I realised that we were not, in fact, going the correct way to my address. I suddenly had a feeling of dread. Had the ungodly managed to take us after all? Not knowing was not helpful and if we had been taken, then doing nothing was not an option.

I nudged Lyn, who was instantly alert beside me. She immediately saw the alarm in my eyes and said nothing. An eyebrow raised towards me was the only communication between us. Where the bloody hell were my shadows? Surely they were still there?

I had forgotten the wire I was wearing. I had not needed the damn thing, but it was still there, and I hoped it was still in working order.

'Excuse me, driver!' I called our driver.

'Yes, love,' came the reply.

'This isn't the way to the address I gave you.'

'You were asleep, so you didn't see the diversion signs did you?' he wanted to know.

'No, I didn't. Where are we exactly?' I asked.

'About twenty miles from Heathrow,' the driver called back.

'Yes, but where?' I persisted.

'Don't know exactly where, love; I'm just following the diversion signs.'

'Oh. Okay,' I acknowledged trying to sound as laid back as I could.

I watched the road ahead for another five miles or so, and despite passing several major junctions, I saw no diversion signs. Now the highway department may not always be the best in this country and seem to be able to create chaos at the drop of a hat, but the one thing that they do excel at is signing diversions; they often employ overkill in that way. The feeling of dread was growing stronger in me, and I began to evaluate my next step. Was it time to call for help? I wondered.

I looked at Lyn and gave her an almost imperceptible wink, more the merest movement of an eyelid. I began rubbing the eye just in case the driver had picked up on it.

'What are you doing tonight, lovey?' I asked Lyn, who looked at me in total puzzlement. I had never asked her anything of such nature since I had known her. Regardless, she played along.

'Oh, I don't know; I suppose I shall watch some TV,' Lyn said. She repaid my faith in her intelligence by swiftly picking up on what I was meaning. Well, sort of, because she was totally ignorant of the code word I had arranged with Philip Carterford the day before. I hoped that my summation of the driver's intelligence was correct and that he wouldn't pick up on anything I might be saying. I did not doubt that he would listen intently to everything we said in the hope that he would pick up on the fact that we had not caught on to what was happening. What I hoped was that he would hear only idle chatter about tonight's television.

'Me too,' I told Lyn. 'I think the Alibi Channel is repeating that programme about the deaf FBI agent and Levi, her dog. I shall definitely be watching that. I love that dog, and I like the singer who plays the theme song. You know Jessica Andrews?'

'Oh yes. I remember. I like that programme too. Yannick Bisson is in that, isn't he?' Lyn said.

'Yes. He is.'

'I love him. He stars in the Murdoch Mysteries, too, doesn't he?'

'Yes, he does.'

We talked about various television programmes we liked and the reasons for liking them. I hoped my shadows had picked up on the code word and were on their way to the rescue.

It was all I could do not to look behind us, but I was able to restrain myself from doing so. We had gone no more than five miles when a marked police patrol car overtook us. I suppose there was nothing unusual in that, and I had no way of knowing if its presence had anything to do with my use of the code word. More importantly, there was nothing unusual enough about the police vehicle's presence to cause any concern to our driver. The police car had two uniformed officers and two plain clothes officers, or so they turned out to be. The police patrol car slowed very slightly as it slotted in between our taxi and the lorry in front of us.

'Shit!' exclaimed our driver.

'What's the matter?' I enquired nonchalantly.

'Bloody police!' was all that he said without qualifying his outburst.

'Looks as though they are on their way somewhere with four of them in there,' I commented, trying to be as offhand as I could.

'Maybe,' he said.

Our driver slowed a little, apparently in an attempt to put some distance between his taxi and the police car. I presumed that this was preparatory to an overtaking attempt, but I could, of course, have been wrong.

'Bloody hell!' was the next exclamation from our driver.

'What is it now?' I asked, trying again to be only interested out of politeness.

The taxi driver said nothing more at that stage but was definitely acting in a more agitated way. By then, it was certain we had taken the wrong taxi. He seemed to spend his time looking anxiously between the police vehicle in front of us and his rear-view mirror. I thought that taking a quick look behind me now would not be untoward. After all, the taxi driver was quite overtly concerned about the following vehicle, so it seemed only natural for me to follow suit.

I recognised the front seat passenger as one of my shadows and immediately cut short my inspection of the following vehicle.

'Why the fucking hell don't he pass me? There's enough room in front of me or in front of that cop car.'

I said nothing but thought that I ought to show some sort of concern.

'What's going on, driver?' I asked.

'No fucking idea, love,' came the reply.

I noted the use of foul language and agitation and was quite sure that indicated our taxi driver was not what he purported to be. I couldn't imagine any taxi driver in this country using that sort of foul language in front of two relatively young women. At least I had never heard it!

We continued this way for another mile or two when our driver said, 'Right, there is a long straight piece of the road coming up, so I should be able to overtake the police car and still keep within the limit.'

His comment was not lost on me. If, as he had earlier said, he had no idea where he was, how did he know that a long straight piece of road was coming up? Yet another indicator that our driver was one of the ungodly. I stole another very quick glance behind me and saw the passenger give an almost imperceptible shake of his head.

Do nothing; he was clearly saying. I turned around and stayed put.

The taxi driver began to drop back a little more, increasing the distance between us and the police car.

Unfortunately for our driver, the police car decreased speed slightly too!

'Sod it!' another exclamation from our driver.

Not to be deterred, he pulled out onto the offside lane to check the road ahead. From my seat, just behind him, I could equally see the road ahead. There was nothing coming for as far as the eye could see, which was somewhere in the region of a mile ahead. Our driver then changed to a lower gear, began pulling out, and then accelerating sharply. The plan, from his viewpoint anyway, was put into operation. He kept his foot to the floor, but his attempt to pass was thwarted when the police car pulled out before he could even begin to pass the police car and the following vehicle, which was a Range Rover, closed up tight behind our taxi.

'Oh, bloody hell!' yet another exclamation.

At this point, it was obvious he had lost control of the situation. I looked over my shoulder only to see another Range Rover overtaking the one directly behind us. This second Range Rover pulled alongside our taxi and slowed to match our speed.

'What's going on, driver?' I asked.

'No fucking idea, love,' he said.

I tried watching all three vehicles, which were now boxing us in, but it was a fruitless task. All I was going to do was to put my neck out! Lyn and I inched closer to each other in the back of the taxi for moral support as much as anything.

We passed a turning on our nearside, but access to that was blocked by another marked police car.

'Shit! Shit! Shit!' our driver said and banged his hands on his steering wheel.

I saw him reach the front passenger seat, and his hand reappeared, holding a mobile. I reckoned that he was going to call for backup. That was the last thing I wanted.

While the driver glanced down at his mobile to dial the number he required, I held up my hand briefly in the worldwide sign for 'phone me', hoping that my shadows would understand. I swiftly changed my signal to a pointing finger towards our driver. The whole thing took me no more than two seconds.

I surreptitiously took Lyn's hand in mine and looked across. This was my effort at reassurance and trying, without saying anything, to get Lyn to brace herself. I felt her body tense, and in turn, I tensed mine.

Sure enough, a second or two later, there was a tremendous jerk as the Range Rover behind us bumped into the taxi's rear.

Our driver dropped his mobile into the footwell beneath his feet. He reached down with one hand while trying to watch the road ahead, behind, and to the side. Not an easy task!

The continued foul outburst told us that he could not find it. In the process of trying to find his mobile, the taxi had slowed to quite a considerable extent. I took the opportunity to look at the front seat passenger in the following Range Rover, who gave me the hand signal for forwards. I took this to mean that they were going to stop the taxi.

The police car in front of us, the range rover at the side of us, and the one following us all closed in tightly, leaving our taxi no way out.

When our driver looked up, then straightened up, he was presented with the sight of three police vehicles closing in at a smart rate. There were slight bumps at three sides of the taxi as the police vehicles closed in and began decelerating. There was absolutely nowhere for the taxi driver to go. He accepted his fate and stopped, not that he had any other choice.

He reached inside his jacket but withdrew it again when he saw the two plain clothes officers from the police patrol car pointing their weapons at him. Discretion became the better part of valour for him, or rather better part of stupidity might be more appropriate.

Our taxi driver turned briefly to look at me. He would certainly know me again if our paths ever crossed, but I was quite certain they would not. I tried my Joe Root impression on the taxi driver and got a scowl in return. I just sat back and sighed in relief.

The front passenger door was pulled open by a police officer.

'Right you, out!' he shouted, keeping his handgun carefully trained on the driver.

'Keep your hands where I can see them. We are armed,' a somewhat superfluous statement, I thought.

The driver shuffled himself over to the front passenger seat. He didn't achieve this action easily. The handbrake and gear lever impeded his progress, and the taxi meter didn't help too much either. The armed officers were patient and did not try to hurry the taxi driver in his endeavours. The taxi driver was trying to look at the police officers brandishing their guns and where he was putting his hands, legs, and feet all simultaneously.

All that the driver said to anyone was in the form of four-letter words and their derivatives. Whoever sent him sure trained him not to open his mouth.

As he finally climbed out of the taxi with hands held high, a uniformed officer searched him for weapons and came out with two handguns. Once they were satisfied that he was concealing nothing else, Detective Chief Inspector

Carterford appeared from the rear seat of the Range Rover, which had been immediately behind us.

'You are under arrest on suspicion of kidnap. You do not have to say anything. But it may harm your defence if you do not mention something you later rely on in court when questioned. Anything you do say may be given in evidence. Do you understand?' Philip said.

Nothing from the taxi driver. He just stared at him straight-faced.

'Do you understand what I have told you?' Carterford asked again.

'Yes,' came the softly spoken reply. It was a voice of defeat.

The driver clearly would only be a very small cog in the greater wheel, and I doubted that he would be of any real help to the police in finding the other members of the gang. The intelligence they might gain from his mobile, his record, and a search of his home will provide some useful leads, though.

I personally doubted that the taxi driver would be prepared to help the police.

The taxi driver was led away, handcuffed by two officers. He was put into the rear seat of the marked car, which sped away to the nearest police station, I presumed.

'You two alright?' Philip asked us.

Neither of us answered. Clearly, we were in shock. I had never been kidnapped before, and I presumed that Lyn hadn't either. Then there was the boxing-in of the taxi by the three police cars, the fact that the driver, Lyn and I, were held at gunpoint.

'Lyn, Mal?' Philip said a little louder, 'you okay?'

His voice shook me out of my thoughts, and I found my voice before Lyn could find hers, and yes, I was alright. My voice, however, was only just above a whisper. Once I had spoken, Lyn found her voice and said that she was alright too.

'Come on, you two. Let's get you back to the police station,' Philip Carterford's voice was reassuring to both of us, and we allowed ourselves to be helped out of the taxi and into the rear seat of the large black Range Rover, which was parked behind the taxi. As I passed the front of the Range Rover, I could not help but look down to see what damage had been caused when it had knocked into the rear of the taxi. The taxi, I noticed with some satisfaction, had far more damage than the slight dents and scratches of the Range Rover. He surely deserved it too.

Philip noticed my looking and merely remarked by way of explanation, 'Reinforced!'

Chapter Twenty

We arrived at the police station and were ushered into the interview room normally used for interviewing sex crime victims and children. The room had a pleasant smell, and Lyn and I instantly felt relaxed upon walking in. The chairs were of the armchair variety, all in matching colours. It was designed to set the victims at ease, and children could be interviewed while playing with the plethora of toys stacked in the corner. Philip Carterford joined us, and the door was closed behind us all.

'Well, ladies, that was fun, wasn't it?'

'Fun! Fun!' screeched Lyn. 'If that was your idea of fun, then I pity you. I can tell you that it scared the shit out of me. I thought we almost died.'

'Alright, alright, Lyn, wrong choice of words. Perhaps exciting would be better,' Philip said with a slight smile playing around his mouth.

I sat there in silence.

'Mal?' Lyn prompted.

'What?' I replied.

'Don't you have anything to say about this incident?' Lyn asked.

'No,' I replied curtly.

Lyn looked at me with a very puzzled expression for several seconds.

'You knew, didn't you?' Lyn said, her voice slightly raised.

I said nothing.

'You did, Mal, you bloody knew! I can't believe you didn't utter a word to me.'

I merely smiled as I didn't know how much Philip wanted me to tell Lyn. I looked over at him and raised an eyebrow.

'Lyn. Mal did know, but she was under the strictest of instructions from me not to tell anyone. If you want to hold someone accountable, it should be me. Mal was only following orders.'

'Why. Don't you trust me, for Christ's sake?' Lyn asked.

'It wasn't a question of trust at all. You must understand that what we did, we did to protect both of you. We had to be in a position to know where you were at all times. Let's face it, surely that is what you would have wanted?' Philip reasoned.

But Lyn was not for turning.

'It's not that; it is the fact that you didn't trust me enough to tell me. Could I have not kept it a secret?'

'How can I convince you it was never a matter of trust? It was all done on a need-to-know basis, and to be quite honest with you, you did not need to know!' Philip countered.

'Of course, I needed to know. I was involved! It is my husband's case, after all!' Lyn retorted.

'I am afraid then, Lyn, that we are going to have to agree to disagree. But, if I could have found a way of putting a wire on Mal without her knowing, then I would not have told her either!'

'Don't be ridiculous! I know that's not true.'

'Calm down, Lyn,' I said as calmly as possible. Then added, 'why don't you wear the wire tomorrow then?'

I looked at Philip. I could tell he wasn't keen on the idea, but he said, 'Yes. I'll get Lucy to wire you up, shall I?'

'What's involved? Lyn wanted to know.

Philip nodded towards me.

'Lucy will want your bra and panties to fix the wires to.' I said helpfully.

'Not bloody likely. I don't want anyone else messing about with my underwear!' she said loudly.

'There you are then, Lyn. Another reason we wired Mal up. She was willing to let Lucy mess about with her undies!' Philip said with just a little too much triumph in his voice for my liking.

'Are you sure you don't want to wear the wire tomorrow, Lyn?' Philip asked.

'I do not want a) anyone messing with my intimate apparel and b) anyone listening to my intimate apparel. I do not like the idea, even if they cannot hear anything. That is that. No arguments,' Lyn said adamantly.

'Very well. Then, Mal, I would expect that you would want to wear clean underclothes tomorrow, so we are faced with a bit of a dilemma. How can we, sorry you, wash your panties and keep the bug dry? And what about the bra?'

'The bra, I can cope with wearing a second day but not my panties. However, like every good woman and indeed everyone who was ever a Boy Scout, I am always prepared!' I said and produced a clean thong from my bag.'

'Tah, dah!' I said as I waved them in the air.

'Don't tell, I know that song, *Leap Up and Down (Wave Your Knickers In The Air)*. If memory serves me, the band was something like St Cecelia,' said Philip Carterford triumphantly.

'Who the hell were they?' I enquired.

'One of the so-called bubble gum bands of the 1970s. I only know that because I take part in quizzes whenever I get the opportunity. It is surprising the facts that you pick up,' was Philip's reply.

I saw Lyn's eyes turn upwards as if in disgust, and I swear that I heard the beginnings of a tut or something like that. She did not complete the sound. Clearly, she could not hide her disappointment.

'Can I get Lucy up here then?' Philip directed his question towards me.

I nodded my consent, and this time I heard a sound from Lyn that sounded a bit like tsk!

Philip lifted the handset of the telephone on the side table and dialled.

'Lucy? It's Philip Carterford. Can you come down, please? We need another wire.'

He replaced the handset and informed us that Lucy would be a few minutes.

I surprised both Lyn and Philip by reaching up my back and beneath my top, unclipping my bra and producing it a few seconds later with a smile on my face.

'And no one saw a thing!' I said triumphantly.

Lyn jerked her head and made the tsk sound again. I just smiled at her.

We sat and waited for Lucy without further conversation.

There was a tap on the door, and it immediately opened.

'Ah! Lucy!' Philip greeted her.

'Were the wires successful?' She wanted to know.

'Oh yes,' said Philip Carterford.

I nodded and said,' They may well have saved our lives, Lucy.'

'I'm glad,' she said with more than a hint of satisfaction at a job well done.

'Same again?' She directed her question towards Philip.

'Yes, please. Will the bug in the bra be okay for another thirty hours, do you think, Luce?'

Yes, probably. I am not happy with probably, though, so I will replace them both,' Lucy replied. 'It's better if we're cautious.'

'Where are they then?' Lucy asked.

I pointed at my crotch and my breasts and laughed out loud. I noted that Lyn managed to raise a smile, but Philip blushed slightly.

'Ah. Shall we go somewhere more private then, Mal?' Lucy asked.

'No need, Lucy!' I said with a chuckle.

'If you are sure.'

'I'm sure,' I said and produced my bra and spare panties from behind my back with something of a flourish. I held them out towards Lucy, who regarded the panties with something like disguised distaste.

'The panties are clean!' I assured Lucy.

Lucy took the garments with her gloves on and went off to do her work on them.

'Philip, when did you or your men first pick us up?' I asked.

'Well, your two shadows were with you all the way to Amsterdam and back. My Range Rover had you under observation from the moment you emerged from the terminal building.'

'I didn't see you,' I told him.

'Nor should you have. That means we were doing our job properly then,' Philip said with some satisfaction. Once on the road, we were only two or three vehicles behind you; the other Range Rover was a few vehicles farther back. Clearly, your taxi driver had no idea that we were there. At one stage, I was concerned that the bugs had failed somehow because we couldn't hear anything,' Philip pointed out.

'Neither Lyn nor I suspected anything throughout the whole journey, and I didn't really think about precautions. I had become lax, and that is probably why we got into the first taxi in the rank. If I had been on my toes, I would have selected the third or fourth taxi. That would have pissed the ungodly right off!'

'Never mind, it all worked out in the end. Well done for not giving the game away, especially when you realised you were on the wrong road. Incidentally, I liked how you got

Jessica Andrews into the conversation!' Philip was embarrassing me now. 'That was a smart tactic. I'm sure the driver had no clue.'

There was a perfunctory tap on the door before it opened again.

'All done,' Lucy said, handing the bra and panties to me.

'I'll dress properly again when I get home, if you don't mind!' Lucy and Philip laughed loudly, and even Lyn raised a chuckle.

'Right now, you two,' Philip began.

'Including me today then, are you?' Lyn sarcastically wanted to know.

'Indeed, we are. Ideally, I would like your bra and panties to be bugged as you will be the main player. We will have to rely on Harry Haraldsen to have both of you present for the diamonds' handover. Do either of you think he will object to you being there, Mal?' Philip wanted to know.

'I shouldn't think so unless he was involved in any way in today's fiasco,' I replied. 'He was okay with me being present the last time.'

'We do not think so. Certainly, that driver was not one of his employees. He drives for a completely separate group of criminals, so, unless Haraldsen is sub-contracting, he has nothing to do with it,' Philip tried to reassure us.

'We will change the abort again tomorrow. Any suggestions?' Philip asked.

'What about Vera?' Lyn suggested, 'she's my favourite television detective.'

'Okay, Vera it is then,' Philip said, indicating that his input to the conversation was at an end, and he left the room.

Lyn and I looked at each other and said nothing.

A few seconds later, there was another perfunctory knock on the door, and immediately it opened.

What I took to be a plain clothes police officer came in.

'If you are ready, I am here to take you home. By the way, I am Detective Constable Brewster.'

'Pleased to meet you,' I replied. 'Yes, we are ready, thank you.'

DC Brewster held the door open for us to leave the interview room, and then we followed him to a car park which was completely surrounded by buildings on all four sides.

'Security,' DC Brewster enlightened us if one can call it enlightenment.

We got into his car, and Brewster motioned the driver to drive off.

Thirty minutes later, we were dropped off at Lyn's house. DC Brewster went about his duties with a cheery 'Goodbye!'

Chapter Twenty-One

The next day dawned with bright sunshine in the sky. I had slept the night in Lyn's spare room, and it had been a totally untroubled night. The wine we had drunk over a takeaway dinner had probably helped, but whatever the reason, I went downstairs refreshed.

Lyn already had fresh coffee brewing, and there were scrambled eggs, bacon, and toast already on the kitchen table. While it all looked tempting, I wasn't sure whether or not I fancied such food, but it would be impolite indeed not to, so I tucked in. Surprisingly, once I began eating, I felt hungry, and the food was as welcome as it was plentiful.

'What time do you think we should leave,' Lyn asked.

'Well,' I replied, 'it took us about three hours the last time, so I think we should allow the same today. After a breakfast like this, I don't think we shall need a lunch stop but perhaps a break at the same pub as last time. What was it called?'

'The Heathfield Tavern,' Lyn replied without even thinking about it. She was very good at pub names. Not that I would suggest for one second that Lyn was a boozer, it was just that she remembered the names of pubs she visited. She had a good memory.

'In that case, we need to be away from here no later than eleven o'clock,' I advised.

'Right then. What time is it now?' she enquired.

I realised that it was a rhetorical question. The sort of question people ask themselves just as they check a watch or a clock.

As this thought sped through my mind, Lyn checked her watch!

'So, about an hour's time then,' Lyn said, as a statement almost to herself. I could not make up my mind what was wrong with her. She seemed very jittery. I have to admit it did concern me a bit.

'What's wrong,' I asked.

'Nothing is actually wrong, but for some reason, I am very nervous about seeing Haraldsen again. I don't know why exactly, but I just cannot help thinking that I am doing the wrong thing.'

'Why so?' I asked.

'Well, it was that kidnap attempt on us at Heathrow. First my dad and then us. Coincidence?'

'Maybe,' I agreed.

As I have mentioned before, I don't believe in coincidences, and Lyn was quite right. That had been one hell of a coincidence. When she mentioned her father's kidnap, Harry Haraldsen did seem genuinely puzzled and, oh, I don't know, but I think that on balance, I believed Haraldsen. After all, if we were going to deliver the diamonds directly to him today without coercion, what need did he have to kidnap us? He was getting the diamonds without taking any real risks. Perhaps Lyn was right to be nervous about things.

'Lyn?' I said to get her attention.

'Yes,' she replied.

'This might seem a bit random, but do you know anyone called Dominic Allen?'

'Why?'

'Oh, no real reason. It was just a name that DCI Carterford asked me a few days ago, that's all. Of course, I had no idea who that was.'

'Dominic Allen?' Lyn repeated the name in the form of a question addressed to herself as much as me.

'Yes. Do you know the name?' I repeated.

'I know David had a friend called Dominic, but I don't know his other name. I suppose it could be him. Why do you ask?'

'As I said, DCI Carterford asked me, and I didn't know the name. Look, we've got an hour before we need to be on our way. Let's quickly check David's desk again,' I suggested.

'Yes. Okay. Do you think this Dominic Allen had anything to do with Dad's kidnap, the burglaries, or our kidnap?'

'I don't know. It is always possible, I suppose. Whoever he might be.'

We spent the best part of forty-five minutes going through David's desk before I spotted something in David's diary. *Meet DA,* the entry said. The most significant factor which absolutely leapt off the page and hit me fairly and squarely between the eyes was the date. Two days before his death! Suddenly, all the alarms in my head went off.

I read it out to Lyn, who immediately realised the significance too.

'Bloody hell, Mal! Could DA be Dominic Allen? I mean, it could just as easily be Doug Arnold or any combination of names, really.'

'Yes, it could,' I agreed, 'but it is another coincidence, isn't it?'

'Yes, it is, and I know how you feel about them!' Lyn replied.

'Hm.'

'Look, Lyn. I reckon we ought to ring Chief Inspector Carterford now and tell him, don't you think?' I asked.

'Yes, I do.'

I picked up my mobile and tried Carterford's office number. There was no reply. I dialled the number again to ensure I had dialled correctly, and a female voice answered.

'Chief Inspector Carterford's office, Lucy speaking. Can I help you?'

'Lucy. Hello, it's Mal Jones. Is Philip there, please?'

'No. I'm afraid not. He has just left to go on an operation. Is there anything I can help you with?' she asked.

'Yes. I need to speak with him urgently. It may have an impact on this operation. Do you have his mobile number?' I enquired.

'His personal mobile is on his desk, but his work mobile is with him.'

'Can I have that number then, please?' I asked.

'No, I'm afraid we have very strict instructions not to give that out to anyone. However, if you think it is that urgent, I'll ask him to ring you. How about that?' Lucy offered.

'That would be fine. Thank you, Lucy.'

Less than two minutes later, my mobile warbled its ringtone. I pressed the green telephone icon and was immediately greeted by Philip Carterford's voice.

'Philip. Do you have a few moments? It is important,' I asked.

'Yes, certainly. What is it, Mal?'

'Do you remember a while ago when we spoke just after you went to Avon and Somerset area about David's death, you asked me if I knew a Dominic Allen?' I asked him.

'Yes, of course, I remember, and you said that you didn't know him,' he said.

'Neither did I, but Lyn and I were talking while we were getting ready to leave, and she said she felt nervous. She couldn't put her finger on the cause but thought it might have been a combination of her father's kidnap, the burglaries, and our kidnap yesterday. She felt they were all coincidental, and I am inclined to agree. I don't know whether or not you are aware, but I do not believe in coincidences. Anyway, right out of the blue, I asked if she knew anyone called Dominic Allen. She didn't know that name per se, but she told me that David had a friend called Dom, which is probably a Dominic but that she did not know his other name. I suggested we spend some time reviewing David's papers on his desk again but this time specifically looking for any reference to Dominic Allen. I believe that we may have hit the jackpot. I found an entry in his diary two days before his death. It just read *Meet DA!* They have the same initials. It's too much of a coincidence.'

'Well done, Mal. That could just be a piece of the jigsaw that will complete the picture or nearly anyway. Can you bring the diary with you?' Philip wanted to know.

'Yes. I don't see why not.'

I pointed to the diary, and Lyn nodded.

'Yes, I can bring it with me, but I do not fancy the idea of carrying it into the Haraldsen house. What if he tries to get a hold of it?'

'No, you are probably right. Any suggestions?'

'We've got to be there at two o'clock. If you could meet us at The Heathfield Tavern at half past one. We intended to stop there for a quick coffee and a loo break before going to Haraldsen's.'

'Okay. Fine. See you then.'

The call was terminated.

'We had better go now, Lyn,' I said, picking up David's diary.

We set out for Broad Oak and arrived at the Heathfield Tavern without incident. We hurried inside, and I ordered two coffees while Lyn paid a visit to the loo. As she disappeared through the toilet door, the lounge door opened, and Detective Chief Inspector Carterford appeared, and right on time.

'Hello Mal,' he said.

'Hello, Philip. Here you are,' I said, handing him David's diary.

He took it, turned, and said over his shoulder, 'Thank you. Sorry, I got to go. Something important came up on my way here. See you later.'

With that, he had gone before Lyn had returned from the toilet.

'Right,' I said, 'a quick coffee, and we are away.'

'What about Chief Inspector Carterford?' Lyn wanted to know.

'He's been and gone. He could not stay to say hello but said he would see us later,' I told her.

She picked up her coffee and muttered, 'Oh.'

A few moments later, we were on our way once more.

At just three minutes to two o'clock, I pulled up outside the metal gates and pushed the intercom button.

'Can I help you?' came the female voice, unmistakeably the voice of Haraldsen's secretary.

'Lyn Kendall to see Mr Haraldsen,' I said on Lyn's behalf.

There was a few seconds delay before the intercom buzzed, and the metal gates slowly opened to admit us.

I drove to the front of the house and parked, as I had on the occasion of our previous visit. As we alighted from the car, the front door opened, and the same female secretary stood to welcome us, although welcome was overstating things considerably.

Without either of us looking around and appearing suspicious, considering we didn't want to give anything away, we entered and stood in the foyer.

'Mobiles, please,' the secretary said in a not unpleasant tone and pointed to a 2-inch-deep plastic tray. We obliged.

The secretary bade us follow her, which we did, through the solid-looking wooden door to the same office we had met Harry Haraldsen in before.

'Well, do you have them?' demanded Haraldsen.

'Whoa, back,' Lyn said. 'Before I hand anything over, I want to know what yesterday's fiasco was all about. We know it was you.'

'Fiasco? What fiasco?' he responded.

'Don't deny the fact that you tried to kidnap us,' Lyn said quite fiercely.

'I am trying to deny nothing, Mrs Kendall. I have absolutely no idea what you are talking about, and I am being truthful in saying that,' Haraldsen replied.

'Well, someone did and almost succeeded. If it wasn't you, then who the hell was it?' Lyn persisted.

'I can assure you, Mrs Kendall, that I have no knowledge of such an incident.'

He paused and then said, 'However if it makes you feel any better, I will contact my superiors and ask them to find out who it was.'

'Yes, I think you should,' Lyn insisted.

'Very well,' Haraldsen said, lifting the telephone handset on his desk. He obviously had it on speed-dial because he only pressed two keys.

'Harry here,' he said into the mouthpiece, 'I have Mrs Kendall and her friend here now, and Mrs Kendall is insisting that she and her friend were kidnapped yesterday and that I, by association, you, have some knowledge of such an event. I am putting the telephone on speaker now so they can hear your reply.'

'Mrs Kendall,' said a rather refined voice, 'my organisation has no reason to attempt to kidnap you. After all, we are only interested in the diamonds and the Swiss Bank account statements. We have the statements, and I trust that you have the diamonds as you promised. Therefore, it must be apparent to you that we have or indeed had nothing to gain by kidnapping you. I trust that neither of you were injured or harmed in any way.'

The refined voice was convincing in his argument. I had no doubt in my mind that he was telling the truth and neither, did it appear, had Lyn.

'No, we were not harmed. The question still exists, though, what do they want? Are they after the same thing that you are?' Lyn asked in a calmer voice.

'It may be the case. I cannot say as I have no knowledge of another group's interest in these commodities,' the refined voice said. 'I am unable, therefore, to help you further. I apologise that you had to go through a traumatic event as such.'

Haraldsen switched off the speaker and turned to Lyn, ignoring me completely.

'I trust that we have now answered all of your questions, Mrs Kendall,' Haraldsen said.

'I suppose so,' Lyn replied, almost mumbling.

I noticed a smirk on Haraldsen's face but was able to keep a straight one myself. You just wait, I thought; that smirk will be wiped off your face soon enough.

'The diamonds, please.' Haraldsen demanded.

Lyn removed three bags from her bag, and I removed three from my own. We both placed the bags on Haraldsen's desk.

Haraldsen selected a bag, apparently at random, for we could see no markings of any kind on the bags. He poured the dirty-looking pieces of stones onto his blotter and counted them. Obviously satisfied with what he now had in his possession, his smirk turned to a smile.

Again, ignoring me, Haraldsen said to Lyn, 'Are you catered for financially, Mrs Kendall? Did David leave you sufficient funds for your needs, or do you require assistance?'

This was the first time since we had met Harry Haraldsen that he had shown any concern for Lyn's welfare.

'Yes, I am,' was Lyn's clipped reply.

I heard the office door open behind us and turned to see the secretary enter and wait at the door, presumably to escort us safely off the premises. I could only assume that Haraldsen had summonsed her by secretly pressing a button beneath his desk, either with his foot or his knee. Our interview, or whatever else the meeting could be termed, was clearly at an end.

We rose slowly, and Haraldsen said, 'Goodbye, Mrs Kendall' but again completely ignored me.

We were again escorted to the front door, where the secretary held out the tray once more, and we were allowed to take our mobiles.

We walked slowly towards my car and, without turning around, and got in. Lyn and I maintained our silence throughout.

'Don't say a word,' I whispered without moving my lips or at least moving them to enable my words to be lip-read.

I slapped my forearm as if swatting a fly, and Lyn understood the meaning, bugs, and said nothing.

We were almost five miles from Haraldsen's house when we saw the first sign of police activity. There was a roadblock up ahead. I was now in a dilemma. Did I stop as the police officer was clearly going to signal me to do, or did I drive on through, causing uproar and possibly find ourselves being chased by high-powered police cars for failing to stop? If I stopped, I did not want to risk any conversation being picked up on any possible bugs in the car. I had to think fast and on my feet, well backside, but you know what I mean.

I came to a halt at the uniformed officer's request and as I wound down the window I put my fingers to my lips in the age-old signal for silence.

'Hello there, sorry to bother you, but which way do I go for Oxford, please?'

I immediately stepped out of the car, threw my mobile phone onto Lyn's lap, and walked a few steps away from the car.

'Officer, my name is Mal Jones,' I politely introduced myself.

Before I could say anything further, he held up his hand.

Pressing a button on his collar-mounted radio, he said into it, 'Checkpoint number five, sir.'

'Roger,' came the curt reply.

We walked even farther away from the car, and then the officer said, 'That was Detective Chief Inspector Carterford, Ms Jones. He wanted to know when you had arrived at a checkpoint; you are both okay, aren't you?'

'Yes, we are both fine, thank you. What does he want from us now?' I enquired.

'You go home, and Mr Carterford will contact you later,' we were told.

We did as requested, and it was later when Philip Carterford came to see us at Lyn's home, that we learned what had happened.

Chapter Twenty-Two

As soon as we had left Harry Haraldsen's house, the noose had begun to tighten, as it were. No one showed themselves, however, until it was confirmed that we were at a safe distance from the house. The house itself had been under covert surveillance for several days before, we learned, which made us both feel just that little bit better about the whole chain of events.

Once the officer had received confirmation at the checkpoint that we were at a safe distance, the whole house was surrounded. Even a mouse would have found it difficult to extricate itself from the cordon. On the word from Detective Chief Inspector Carterford, upwards of fifty police officers, some armed, some with dogs, raided the house. Every exit was covered, and even a secret getaway passage, discovered on the house plans when planning the operation had begun, was blocked. Armed police covered that one. The police went in fully prepared to bring Harry in for investigation.

Once inside the premises, the secretary demanded to know what was happening and why. The search warrant was waved in her face and the, what must have seemed like a swarm of officers, entered the foyer. The secretary was immediately taken into custody, handcuffed, and taken outside to a waiting prison van.

Detective Chief Inspector Carterford did not knock on the office door; he merely opened it and walked in.

'Mr Harry Haraldsen?' the chief inspector had asked.

'Yes, I am he. What is the meaning of this?' he had demanded.

'I have a warrant to search these premises,' Philip Carterford said, again brandishing the official paper in his hand.

'For what purpose? I didn't do anything wrong.' A perfectly normal question from Haraldsen.

'If you read the warrant, it will tell you that we have authority to search the whole of the house,' Chief Inspector Carterford informed him.

'Yes, but what for,' he persisted.

He was ignored by the chief inspector, who immediately went to the desk at which Haraldsen had been sitting.

'Unlock the drawers, please, Mr Haraldsen,' Philip Carterford demanded.

'And if I refuse? What will you do?'

'Then I will get them opened for you, which seems such a shame to ruin such a beautiful piece of furniture, don't you think?'

Haraldsen had, very reluctantly apparently, handed over the bunch of keys he had taken from his pocket. He did not help the police officer by pointing out the correct key for the desk, but the officer quickly found it, had the drawers unlocked, and opened it quickly.

No bags of diamonds were found. Everyone had a confused look on their face. Where could they go?

A slight smirk of satisfaction, which I had seen before, had spread across Haraldsen's mouth. This swiftly disappeared when the officer engaged in opening the drawers suddenly let out a 'gotcha!'

'Sorry, sir, did I say that out loud?' the officer asked his senior officer.

'You did,' the chief inspector replied, 'but I would have done the same.'

The smirk was wiped off Haraldsen's face as quickly as the light goes out when switched off.

Chief Inspector Carterford went to the side of the desk where all the drawers were now open and had been pulled out, including a hidden drawer, which had been located up under the top of the desk's kneehole. In that concealed drawer, the chief inspector produced six small leather bags like rabbits from a conjuror's hat. These he opened in turn and poured the contents into a waiting tray.

'Tsk, tsk, Mr Haraldsen. And these are?' Philip asked.

'Some rough diamonds I am holding for a client. I am having them appraised by a professional diamond dealer. He is a site holder in Amsterdam and is coming over later today to appraise and value them.'

'Good answer, Harry,' Philip Carterford said, 'good but no cigar.'

'Meaning?' Haraldsen asked.

'All in good time. I must tell you that you are under arrest on suspicion of handling stolen property. You do not have to say anything but it may harm your defence if you do not mention something which you later rely on in court when questioned. Anything you do say may be given in evidence. Do you understand?' Philip said.

'I understand the words but not why you are saying them to me. After all, I am a legitimate businessman. I have lawful possession of the diamonds. I don't understand any of this.'

'All in good time, Mr Haraldsen, all in good time,' the chief inspector gave nothing more away.

The search continued apace. Even though the prime objective, the diamonds, had been achieved, every document, every item in every room had to be checked and searched. The small army of searchers, or so we learned, had taken two whole days to complete the search.

The bank statements from the numbered Swiss Bank account had been seized together with several passports in various names, which had contained the photographs and descriptions of Haraldsen and his secretary. All had been in false names and were from various countries. The Chief Inspector was particularly interested to see that two passports, one for Haraldsen and one for his secretary, were purportedly Brazilian.

Two days later, Philip Carterford rang and asked if anything untoward had occurred. I was able to reassure him on that point and neither Lyn nor Susan, her mother, had been in contact about anything at all.

'Will it be possible for me to come and see Lyn, yourself, and Lyn's parents tomorrow, please? Preferably all at the same place?' He wanted to know.

'I'll arrange it,' I told him, 'What time would suit you?'

'Can we say eleven o'clock? In the meantime, can you warn Lyn and her parents that our engineers will be around this afternoon to fit alarms to all three houses and panic buttons as well? This is an interim measure until we decide whether or not a removal to a safe house is necessary?'

'I'll ring Lyn now,' I assured Philip.

'Thank you. See you tomorrow then,' the call was terminated.

Later that day, the engineers that Philip had promised did indeed call, and an alarm was fitted with pressure pads, window alarms, and panic buttons. While I did not consider them necessary, I was pleased that the police took our safety seriously. I spoke to Lyn in the afternoon and passed on

Philip's request. She was going to spend the day with her parents anyway, and I was more than welcome to join them.

That night I had a Chinese takeaway and a bottle of wine, and after my meal, I settled down to think.

What had it all really been about? I wondered. The killing of David, apparently by execution, the kidnap of Lyn's father, the burglaries at our houses, and the assault on me, these in some ways seemed not to be related, and yet clearly they were. If Harry Haraldsen and his mob were after the diamonds and the bank statements, what were the burglaries about, not to mention the kidnap of Lyn's father and our own kidnap attempt just a few days ago? Clearly, they had to be connected in some way, but how? If Haraldsen was to be believed, and on the whole I did believe him, then he and his organisation had nothing to do with the burglaries or the kidnaps. Assuming that to be the case, then who was responsible for them?

Then a name came into my mind that Philip Carterford had asked me about some time ago, *Dominic Allen!* Who the heck was he? I hadn't heard the name before or since. I thought some more about what the chief inspector had said about him. His fingerprint had been found on the shell casing, presumed and most likely to be the bullet that killed David at Ebor Gorge. Whatever else this Dominic Allen might have done, he had certainly been involved in David's murder. The question remained, who the hell was he? Lyn remembered that David had a friend called Dom, who may or may not be that Dominic, but it was all a bit tenuous. Whoever this DA might have been, David clearly trusted him and was quite open, well fairly open, about him putting a possible, probable even, reference to him in his diary. He had to be the key to whoever else was involved other than Harry Haraldsen and his gang, and he certainly had some involvement in David's murder.

On the off-chance, I checked the internet and found tens of thousands of Dominic Allens. It was, as I had heard it referred to in a television detective drama, like looking for a needle, not in a haystack but in a pile of needles! I tried Dominic Allen Somerset, but that found hundreds of people. The only difference between this and the first search was the size of the pile of needles! I was at a loss to find any further avenues for inquiry and decided to speak to Philip Carterford tomorrow if I could get him alone.

As I relaxed and stopped thinking about David's possible murderer, I began to think about Philip Carterford, the man. That strange feeling in the pit of my stomach made itself manifest again. Surely, Philip couldn't be the cause of that, could he? After all, I barely knew him. The more I thought of Philip and that brief kiss, the stronger that feeling became until it began to spread below my stomach. Oh, Christ! I thought. I know that feeling! It's happening again. I crossed my legs to stop it from spreading but failed miserably. If Philip was the cause, what the bloody hell should I do about it? The last time I remember this feeling was when I met Roger for the first time, and I remember only too well how that had turned out. *What if the same happens with Philip?* I wondered. Somehow I didn't see Philip seducing me on our first date! Hell! That bloody feeling became more intense.

I went to bed and almost straight to sleep, where I dreamed loving dreams of Philip Carterford.

Chapter Twenty-Three

The next morning, I awoke refreshed, having slept soundly. After the usual morning routine, I sat down to scrambled eggs and toast. I found that my appetite was sharp this morning!

I arrived at Lyn's parents' house with about thirty minutes to spare. Parked outside, I spotted Philip Carterford sitting in his unmarked police car. He instantly recognised my car and waved for me to stop. We were parked just out of sight of Susan's house. We sat in his car, and we looked at each other. His eyes were very talkative! That bloody feeling in my stomach started crawling about again, and my heart began to race. I think Philip could hear my racing heartbeat too. Damnation!

'I wanted a quick word before we go in Mal,' Philip began.

I smiled and shuffled about ever so slightly. Philip Carterford was unsettling me, and I could not make up my mind exactly how I felt about it.

'Are you sure you are alright after all of what has happened?' Philip asked.

'Yes. I was scared when I realised that we had been kidnapped, and I was very nervous at Haraldsen's house,' I admitted. 'If things had gone south, we probably wouldn't even be here.'

'Mal…' Philip began again. 'Mal, when this is all over, would you let me take you for a drink or a meal, perhaps?' He had gone all shy, bless him. It certainly did not suit him and was not like him at all.

I smiled and cast my eyes downward.

'You don't have to say yes if you'd rather not go,' Philip said, again shyly.

I couldn't bring myself to tease him, so I said I would love to go out with him. He brightened considerably, and the shyness almost disappeared from his face, only to be replaced by a blush! How sweet.

I smiled at him fondly, and we got out of his car.

I rang the doorbell, and Lyn answered it.

'Come in, please,' she invited.

We went in, and Susan greeted me with a hug, and both Susan and her husband shook hands with the plainclothes police officer.

'Mrs Wright, I hope that the engineers installing the alarms yesterday did not cause too much disturbance for you.'

'Oh, good gracious, no. They were very nice people, polite and keen not to interrupt us.'

'Good,' said Philip, 'now I have to tell you what we know so far, that is, if Lyn hasn't told you already.' He paused and looked at Lyn.

Philip didn't receive any response from Lyn, so he updated Lyn's parents on everything that had happened since that fateful day Lyn had been informed of the demise of her husband. I was surprised to hear him tell everyone that David Kendall was not really David Kendall. He told them that he was an undercover police officer called Robert Dickson. There was an audible gasp from Susan Wright, and her husband made a sound in his throat, which could have meant almost anything. Their faces went pale in shock. Lyn buckled at the knees and almost fell onto the settee. She didn't pass out, but she was very close to it. Tears were flowing freely down her cheeks. Her mother rushed to her side and held her by the shoulders, giving as much comfort as possible.

'I'll fetch a glass of water for her,' I said to Susan.

'No, brandy,' she said, pointing towards a side table.

I partially filled a glass and handed it to Lyn. The colour gradually began to return to her face. Philip had stopped talking immediately after he had dropped his bombshell. He stood looking from one to another and waiting for a sign that it was alright to continue.

I crossed the room to Philip's side and brushed a reassuring hand against his. No one seemed to notice the gesture, or if they did, they did not mention it.

After about ten minutes, Lyn had clearly regained her composure. I noticed that Susan, too, had been upset, the redness of her eyes giving away the fact that she had been crying.

Philip continued his tale, outlining Robert Dickson's glittering career and his long time undercover. It had been a long and involved process and had entailed him trying to gain the villains' trust while building his undercover image. Certainly, Philip told us, five years was quite common.

Robert, I was trying to learn to call him by his proper name, had clearly been a very brave man. He might have been brave, but ultimately his bravery had cost him his life, but then history is littered with brave people who were treated similarly. These are the ones the criminals love going after. Nurse Edith Cavell was one that always stuck in my mind. She had assisted in the escape of more than two hundred British troops and was executed by firing squad for her troubles, despite having saved the lives of soldiers from both sides of the conflict. I didn't put Robert into that category exactly, but nevertheless, he had been executed for doing his job.

'Robert knew the risks that he was running on a daily basis, but it didn't stop him from being a police officer.'

Philip was watching Lyn closely and doing his best not to upset her more than he had to as he continued. We knew the diamonds involved Harry Haraldsen but didn't know about the numbered Swiss Bank account. We guessed it mind you, but we did not know. Thanks to your daughter, Mrs and Mr Wright, and Mal here, for their bravery, we could discover which bank the massive amount of money had disappeared into. That is a line of enquiry which we are already working on. All that said, I have to tell you that we do not believe that Haraldsen and his cohorts were responsible for your husband's death. We believe that there is another organisation involved somewhere along the line, an organisation possibly more threatening. We believe, and this affects all of you, that the burglaries, the assault on Mal, the kidnap of yourself, Mr Wright, and the kidnap of your daughter and Mal are all connected. We hope the bogus taxi driver can be persuaded to give us some leads.

This was all new to Mrs and Mr Wright, although only some of it was also new to Lyn.

I looked across at Lyn's parents just to see their reactions. Susan was obviously shocked at the revelations, but Mr Wright was harder to fathom. I just got the sense that he already knew! Then I admonished myself that that just was not possible. Surely, I was wrong.

'The massive thing about this other organisation is that we believe them to be responsible for your husband's death, Lyn. I can assure you that we will pursue this mob until we can get our hands on the bastard that killed Robert. I'm sorry for the language; that is how it makes me feel. Robert was one of our own.'

'You do not need to apologise for anything,' Lyn said, 'I feel exactly the same way.'

'Well, we would like you all to move into a safe house, at least for the time being. We are not under any illusions that they are a well-organised gang; witness your kidnap Mr Wright. We believe that there may still be a risk. Our problem is that we have no idea what they are after. It may be the diamonds, the Swiss bank account, or both. Of course, the diamonds are in our possession, but I don't think we can do anything without the bank statements.'

'Didn't you find them when you searched Haraldsen's house?' I enquired.

'No, we did not. Didn't you, Lyn, hand them over to Haraldsen the first time you went there?'

'Yes, of course, I did! Where could they go?' Lyn replied as if surprised by her own action.

'Can you remember anything about the bank?' asked the chief inspector.

'No, not really,' Lyn said.

'When you say not really, what can you remember? Absolutely anything might be a help.'

'It just had a number, no account holder's name,' Lyn was clearly still thinking about the account.

Suddenly I remembered that as Corporal Jones in *Dad's Army* said, 'I have come prepared for such an eventual' I had indeed prepared for an eventuality such as this. I opened my handbag and produced a single sheet of bank statement. On the top of the statement, it clearly said NUMAC and the account number. I handed it to him, and the mind-boggling balance at the foot of the sheet did not even send Chief Inspector Carterford's eyebrow one millimetre higher, which I have to say did surprise me somewhat.

'Thank you, Mal. That will be very helpful. Having said that, the chances of us ever being able to access the account are extremely thin but one never knows. The Wiesenthal Organisation had been given a list of some 12000 Swiss Bank accounts discovered in a building in Buenos Aires or so it was reported. The organisation believes that at least a proportion of it was illegally taken from Jewish victims in Germany. The Wiesenthal organisation is reported to be in contact with Credit Suisse in an attempt to settle things with the surviving holocaust victims. That being the case, there is always hope. We all need that, don't we?' Philip Carterford said.

'We do indeed,' said Mr Wright. 'Susan and I do not believe that we are in too much danger. After all, they could have finished me off when they had me, but they didn't. So, if you don't mind, we will stay put.'

'Obviously, I cannot make you go, but perhaps a prolonged holiday somewhere might help protect you,' Philip suggested. 'It will also help get your mind off the recent fiasco.'

'Holiday? Where?' Susan exclaimed.

'Anywhere you would like to be.' This came from Lyn.

'May I suggest we arrange a month's holiday in North Wales or The Lake District perhaps,' Philip Carterford suggested.

'Both sound very nice. How about it, Alex?' Susan asked her husband.

'I have never been to The Lake District, so okay, let's go! It will be nice for us,' Alex Wright said with a wide smile on his face.

'That is settled then; I will make the arrangements. You must only communicate through me. Do not ever contact Lyn or even Mal directly, always through me. I will supply a dedicated number that will be staffed twenty-four hours daily. Any letters or other mail you wish Lyn to receive must be sent through the police; again, I will give you an address that will ensure as speedy a delivery as possible. Please keep this in mind until such times as I contact you to tell you that you can come home. We will arrange a special code word so that you know that it is me calling you and not someone impersonating me. Any suggestions?'

'I just can't think of one,' Susan said.

'Is there a singer that you particularly like to listen to?' I asked.

'Well, Don Williams. I love his songs, and you can always hear all the words.' Susan said.

'Do you have a favourite song?' I prompted.

'I do like the words to Amanda; that is a lovely song,' Susan said.

'Right then, Amanda it is. I will work it into our conversation nice and early so that you will know that it is me. If you do not hear Amanda in the first two sentences, then ring off and contact me on that number.'

'Sounds awfully complicated and not a little cloak and daggerish!' Susan said to Alex.

'For the best, my dear, for the best. When do you want us to leave, chief inspector?' Alex asked.

'As soon as possible. Give me twenty-four hours to make the necessary arrangements. As an afterthought, how do you fancy a guest for the holiday?'

'Male or female?' Susan wanted to know.

'Female, actually. Let us say that she is your niece and staying with you while you are away.'

Lucy, I thought.

The arrangements were discussed in detail, and by the time Philip Carterford had finished, Susan and Alex were looking forward to their long break.

Philip Carterford then turned his attention to Lyn and me.

'Right, what are we going to do with you two?' he said with a smile.

'You, Lyn, are the link between Robert or David and the missing millions, as it were. I know they are not missing, but you know what I mean.'

'Only too well, inspector,' Lyn said.

'What about me, then?' I asked.

'Harry Haraldsen doesn't like you very much!' Philip said.

'At least the feelings are bloody mutual. I didn't like him from the moment I laid eyes upon him. That said, why should he or his organisation come after Lyn or me?'

'I'm not saying that Haraldsen's organisation will come after either of you. Let us be fair, you, Lyn, gave him everything he asked for, didn't you?' Philip pointed out. 'Is there anything else you kept in your possession?'

'Well, almost. I don't think he realised that Mal had taken one bank statement sheet. I didn't know myself until just now!'

'Well, I would like you two to go into a safe house for a couple of weeks at least. We've got one that we use now and again in North Wales. It purports to be a guest house and occasionally takes in ordinary everyday common or garden tourists, at least when we aren't using it. The proprietor and his wife are former police officers, he was a superintendent, and she was an inspector. They can be trusted implicitly. If you need to contact Lyn's parents or me, do it through the guest house proprietor, who will know what to do. How does that sound?'

'Fine by me,' Lyn said.

'Well, my problem is that if I don't work, then I don't earn, and my money is beginning to run out!' I told him.

'I am told that there will be a reward for the recovery of the diamonds, and even at five percent, which is a low finder's fee, it will be quite a lot of money, even between two of you,' Philip pointed out. 'It will be enough for years to come.'

'Okay, then. I'll go too.'

Chapter Twenty-Four

The following morning Lyn and I set off in a hired car for North Wales. The police hired the car to ensure we were travelling in a secured vehicle. We avoided the motorways wherever possible; we decided that the smaller roads were safer for us as it was easier to see if we were being followed. As far as I could tell, no one was following us.

The safe house was discreetly situated in an area surrounded by woods. The property was built in what could easily be mistaken for a forest clearing, which it was not. The trees had been planted by a previous owner when he sought privacy from his neighbours. It suited its purpose of a safehouse admirably.

We were greeted by the proprietors and were immediately made to feel very welcome.

'Lyn, Mal, welcome to the Pen y Coed Guest House. My name is Paul, and my wife is Christine. Please feel free to roam the house and grounds as you wish and feel at home. We have to share one or two ground rules before I show you to your rooms. First, please give Christine your mobile phones and tablets, if you have them. She will return them when you leave. If you wish to contact Detective Chief Inspector Carterford, you may do so at any time. Christine or I will make the call on your behalf. We have been briefed and know his number. If you need anything that requires going shopping, then tell Christine or me, and we will shop for you. You already know how to contact your parents, Lyn, should the need arise.'

'Now, while this may seem idyllic, which it is. It is also isolated, and boredom may become a problem. There is an ample supply of books and so on, which you are very welcome to use. We have a recreation area at the rear of the premises. There is a heated swimming pool and a tennis court. You can use these with impunity as you cannot be seen from the sides or above. It is extremely well camouflaged. Should you see anyone you think is lurking, then let Christine or I know via this little box of tricks. Just press the button, and we'll come a-running. Similarly, if we have doubts about anyone, we will signal you, and you should immediately go to your rooms and remain there until we call you. Is there anything which you want to ask us?'

Lyn and I shook our heads and followed Christine up the grand staircase to the first floor. We were shown to adjoining rooms.

I sat on the bed and immediately thought to myself, *what the bloody hell am I doing here?* I flopped back onto the bed and stared at the ceiling. I let my mind wander back over the past few weeks. It had all started with a telephone call asking me to go to my best friend's house to offer some comfort following the sudden death of her husband. An innocent enough task and one which I was more than happy to carry out. Little did I realise that as a result of that Samaritan act, I would get into so much trouble. Oh, I know that good samaritan usually refers to doctors and other health professionals who come forward to help when they are not on duty, but surely it refers to any act of kindness when one is not duty-bound to carry it out. I suppose I was morally bound to support Lyn as her friend, but not duty-bound per se.

I am sure that people sometimes wonder if these acts of kindness are worthwhile. Of course, mine had been, if one could refer to it as an act of kindness, but what happened afterwards made me wonder several times whether or not I should have helped and supported. I guess to every action, there is a consequence. The actual quote from Richard Eyre was, in fact, that, 'Every action has a consequence, so always try to be good.' He was, of course, referring to actors on the stage, but the general principle surely applies. Certainly, there were some consequences to my simple, friendly action. And what consequences! I had been burgled and assaulted, and I had been kidnapped. Not bad for a simple action, one might say, but far more than I would have wanted. I couldn't help but chuckle at the thought.

I tried to get everything that had happened clear in my head. It had started with how Lyn had been informed of her husband's unexpected death and almost complete lack of any follow-up by the police or anyone else for that matter, with the possible exception of the ungodly, of course. Then there was the discovery of the diamonds and their subsequent valuation in Amsterdam, which resulted in a burglary of our hotel room. At least Lyn and I weren't harmed there. Then Lyn's father's kidnapping and subsequent safe return, albeit after he had spent time in hospital recovering from the drugs he had been unlawfully given. Susan's house was robbed, Lyn's house had been burgled, and I had been assaulted, presumably having disturbed the culprits. The search for a will in David's belongings and the subsequent discovery of the bank statements and the false passports, one of which turned out not to be false at all but David's genuine one. The discovery of the last letter from David to Lyn and the advice to go to Harry Haraldsen. Lyn, certainly and I suppose myself, had been expecting a Mr Big type individual looking after his followers even in death. A sort of godfather figure, if you will. Instead, it had been a tense and not very pleasant experience at all.

Then when we got back from retrieving the diamonds in Amsterdam, Lyn and I were kidnapped. Alright, we had been rescued by the cavalry in the form of Chief Inspector Philip Carterford and his merry men, but nonetheless, we had been kidnapped. The police car chase was quite an experience, I must say. Then there had been the second visit to Haraldsen and the handing over of the diamonds. The 'help' Lyn had been anticipating did not materialise from him. It subsequently transpired that Lyn and I had played significant roles in the arrest of Haraldsen and the taxi driver involved in the kidnap. These two actions alone would have consequences that neither Lyn nor myself would have classified as good, so our trying to be good, or in our case doing the right thing, had far from good consequences. So why the hell did we try to be good in the first place? What good did it bring us?

I thought over, again and again, the sequence of incidents that had led us to North Wales and Lyn's parents to the Lake District. I just could not shake off the feeling that someone was forcing a guiding hand upon us. We were all his chess pieces, and he was moving us around his board to suit his needs and completely disregard ours. Was there someone we had overlooked? Someone whom we all knew but would never suspect. There was a tiny niggle in the back of my head that refused to go away, it did not seem to get any stronger, but it was there, nevertheless.

I remember a friend saying, when he was trying to work out who the murderer was in a television drama, it was usually someone who was often there, usually in the background, and very often had been seen at some stage in the episode riding a bicycle. My friend was correct more often than not; especially it seemed in both his favourite British television detective drama and mine, as it happened,

Midsomer Murders, he had a success rate up in the high nineties in his guess as to who had 'dunnit'. Oh, if he were here now to talk through his logic with. Alas, even if he had been available, the circumstances were such that no one outside of a chosen few were to know where Lyn and I were.

I fell asleep with all these facts churning around in my mind, like butter it was, round and round and round. Under normal circumstances at home, with this going on in my mind, I would have lied awake for hours, totally unable to sleep. Life is strange sometimes.

A knocking at my door brought me out of my slumber. It was Paul, bearing a tray with two mugs of what turned out to be tea on it.

'Thank you, Paul. How long have I been asleep?' I enquired.

'Oh, I shouldn't think any more than half an hour,' Paul informed me. 'You should've gotten more rest.'

'Is Lyn about?' I wanted to know.

'She too is in her room, and I have brought her a cup of tea. You know, the old British panacea for all ills. Works wonders, well it does sometimes.'

I remember seeing newsreels of the war years in London and the bombed-out residents of houses being offered comforting tea by neighbours who had been luckier than they. Anyway, as Private Potter said to his senior officer, played by Sean Connery, in the film *A Bridge Too Far*, when he offered his CO a cup of tea, *'it can't do no harm, sir.'*

I took the tea and gratefully began to sip the sweet brown liquid. It certainly couldn't do any harm! It was, in fact, relaxing, with my mind going in circles.

I washed and stood draining the remains of my tea while I stared out of the window at the beautiful North Wales countryside. I wasn't specifically thinking about anything, and almost inevitably, my mind went back to my thoughts before falling asleep.

I remained, just staring ahead when, for some unknown reason, Lyn's father came into my head. If he was the Mr Big, then I immediately rejected the thought. Of course, he wasn't. He was Lyn's father, after all. There is no way on this earth that he would cause her distress let alone hurt her or put her in danger. I not only rejected Alex Wright as a likely candidate for Mr Big, but I also shoved it as far back in my mind as I possibly could.

Dinner that evening was one of the finest lasagnes I had ever experienced. The garlic bread was cooked to perfection, and the French fries were crisp and light brown, just as the captured submarine captain requested of Captain Mainwaring in Dad's army.

We sat around in the lounge after dinner while the automatic dishwasher did all the hard work in the kitchen.

We each held a glass of brandy in our hands and just sat staring into the log fire which blazed away in the hearth. It was a lovely evening. The meal had been perfect; the brandy was of high quality, and the company superb. Paul and Christine certainly knew how to entertain. Lyn and I had a relaxing evening for the first time in weeks.

Just after eleven o'clock, Lyn expressed that she was tired and was off to bed. Christine followed suit, sensing perhaps that Paul wanted to talk to me alone. I presumed this was apparent after countless years of working together, married to each other, and absolutely comfortable with each other in what they were doing in retirement.

When we were alone, I asked Paul, 'How many real guests do you get in a year?' This was by of being an icebreaker.

'Not very many at all,' came the reply.

'Then how on earth do you manage to make ends meet? Surely it is not all down to the value of your combined police pensions,' I enquired.

'Goodness, no. We get paid an extremely generous annual retainer by the home office to offer our guest house as a sort of safe house. We bought the place initially to run it purely as a guest house, and then right out of the blue, I got a letter from a home office minister asking if he could come to see Christine and me. Well, the upshot was that the home office funded all the necessary refurbishments to make this as secure as possible; they fund all the gadgetry. The rest, as they say, is history. We've been running this place as a cross between a safe house and a guest house for nearly fifteen years now, without incident,' Paul was clearly proud of what he and Christine had achieved. Theirs was a valuable service indeed. 'It's nice to have guests over at times, especially when they're good company.' Paul gave me a warm smile.

'What did you really want to talk to me about?' asked Paul.

'How much can I tell you?'

'Whatever you like. Christine and I signed the Official Secrets Act and have very high-security clearance. It is not only the police who use our facilities, you know.'

'Really!' I exclaimed with genuine surprise.

Paul didn't elaborate but sat there watching me and waiting for me to ask the question I had really wanted to ask.

'Paul, how much do you know about this case?' I began.

'Enough.'

'Well, are you aware of all the characters, as it were, who have shown up in this real-life drama?'

Paul steepled his fingers and rested his chin on them, an action that Harry Haraldsen had used at least twice during our visits. Fleetingly I wondered whether Paul could be involved somehow but immediately dismissed the idea. He couldn't possibly have anything to do with it. After all, it was a common enough gesture and one I had seen used hundreds of times by bosses of businesses where I was making enquiries about my job.

'Yes, I am. Philip Carterford has fully briefed myself and Christine; we could not do our jobs properly unless that were the case.'

I was reassured.

'Just before I dropped off to sleep this afternoon, I was trying to put all of the last few weeks' events into some sort of order. I got the impression, no more than that, mind you, but I got the impression that there was a guiding hand involved somewhere.'

'A sort of Mr Big, you mean?' Paul asked by way of a prompt.

'Yes, sort of,' I replied.

'And have you come to any conclusions?'

'I have had this one thought, which I have to tell you I dismissed almost immediately as being too bizarre.'

'Tell me,' encouraged Paul.

'Well, quite simply, there is one thing that doesn't fit into the general pattern of what has happened, and I can see not how or why it should disturb me, but it does.'

'What is it?' Paul, encouraging again.

'This is going to sound really stupid and off the wall, but it is Lyn's dad,' I said, immediately regretting giving voice to my thoughts.

'Lyn's father!' Even Paul couldn't believe it.

'Yes. Specifically, his kidnap. It is the one part that doesn't have any rhyme or reason to it. It just doesn't make any sense. Doesn't fit the pattern, you know?'

'I know what you mean in general terms, but I am not sure that I understand the specific meaning of what you are saying. Why would he be involved in this?'

'Let me try to explain further, Paul. Alex Wright was kidnapped right out of the blue and allegedly abandoned in Looe, in Cornwall. He was found to have been drugged with Rohypnol. There is no doubt about that; the hospital has confirmed that he was drugged. If one assumes that he was genuinely kidnapped, then why? The note that was found said it was 'because we can'. Why would they, whoever they might be, do that and write that? Obviously, they are kidnapping him because they can. I am now beginning to think it wasn't a warning to Lyn, her mother, or himself. I think that was done to make us believe we were all in danger. It doesn't make any sense otherwise.'

'What you say makes sense, Mal. Why would he do it?' Paul asked.

'Let us suppose, just suppose, mind you, that Alex Wright is heavily involved in this whole thing. He would want to throw us off the scent, wouldn't he? He knows that Haraldsen was involved because he was involved too. By making us think that there were two groups of villains, he would divide the troops as it were. If there was only one group, then he would have only half of the police and so on to deal with. Don't you see?' I asked.

'Indeed, I do see. Have you told Philip Carterford any of this?' Paul wanted to know.

'No, I haven't. It was only this afternoon that I began putting two and two together and making four instead of five or six. Is it too late to tell him now?' I asked.

'No. He said that I could ring him any time of the day or night. Let me do it now,' Paul said, suddenly galvanised into action. He went to the landline telephone on a side table and dialled.

'Philip? Paul here. Can you speak?'

'Yes. Give me a moment to go outside.'

Then a few minutes later, 'Okay, Paul, go ahead.'

'Philip. I have been talking to Mal this evening, and she has had a wild idea that I believe could have some mileage in it. I don't want to say anything over the telephone. Is there any chance we could meet up, you know, the three of us? We have something you might want to hear.'

'I don't see why not if you think it will be worthwhile.'

'Yes, I do. It will be your decision, of course, but as I said, I think she may be onto something.'

'Where do you suggest?'

'What do you think about Lancaster Services, suit you?'

'That will be fine, Paul. I'll be there by, say, eleven o'clock?'

'Yes, that'll suit, Philip. All I've got to do now is to find a reason to leave Lyn behind.'

'I'll leave that to you; I'm not doing your job for you!' Philip chuckled.

'Thanks, see you tomorrow then.'

'Bye.'

Paul hung up and smiled across at me.

'What are we going to tell Lyn? She'd want to know why I'm leaving the property,' I asked.

'Any suggestions?' Paul was at a loss too.

'Tell her I have an appointment at the dentist's because I have an awful toothache. How about that?' I proffered.

'Well, it will pass muster, I should think,' Paul said with a slight smile of satisfaction.

We returned to the safe house, and I played the part of the aching tooth sufferer. It was not something I suffered from, and I thought I played my part rather well. At any rate, Lyn believed me, so that was the main thing.

The next day, Paul drove me to Lancaster Services, still holding my jaw convincingly. We met up with Philip Carterford in the car park far from the restaurant and shops. Philip's smile on seeing me alight from Paul's car was a delight that truly warmed my heart, and I felt that familiar stirring when I returned the smile.

'Good morning, Paul. Hello Mal. Toothache?' Philip asked.

It was then that I realised that I was still nursing my non-existent toothache!

'No,' I replied, 'subterfuge.'

'Ah!' The reality struck Philip, and he smiled again.

When we were seated in Philip's car, I began to relate my theory concerning Lyn's dad. I told him that I felt that Alex Wright had been kidnapped right out of the blue. There was no reason for that to happen because Haraldsen already knew that he would be getting the diamonds and the numbered Swiss bank account statements, so Haraldsen could, in my view, be discounted. His car and subsequently he himself were found in Looe, Cornwall. It was apparent to the officer who located him that he was under the influence of some sort of drug. Subsequently, this was found to have been Rohypnol. There is no doubt about that; by the way, the hospital has confirmed that he was drugged. The tests couldn't go wrong.

The one thing no one, including allegedly Mr Wright, can say is by whom the Rohypnol was administered. If one assumes that he was genuinely kidnapped, then why? The note that was found said it was 'because we can'. Why would they, whoever they might be, do that and write that? I am now beginning to think that it was intended to act as a distraction, you know, away from the fact that no ransom demand was made. There was no urgency from the kidnappers to get in touch and demand money in return. It could also have been an attempt to put the authorities off the scent to discount the fact that he was involved. I think he also intended the note to make us believe that we were all in danger. Maybe to scare us enough so we back off the case. It doesn't make any sense otherwise.'

There was a period of silence. Clearly, both Paul and Philip were attempting to take in my theory and test its viability silently. It was quite an uncomfortable silence for me, though, until, at last, there was the nodding of heads and a smile for me from both.

'What you are saying, Mal makes perfect sense to me too,' Philip said. He continued, 'the problem for me, though is how to test the theory.'

He was clearly waiting for a response from either Paul or myself. I, for one, did not feel qualified to make suggestions, but with all his experience, Paul was in a far better position to do so.

I said nothing, and Paul was deep in thought.

After ten minutes or so of silence, Philip said, 'Look, I'll think some more on the drive home, and then I'll discuss it with my team, and I'll let Paul know what we decide. He will know how to tell you and possibly Lyn. That suit you two?'

'Suits me,' we both said almost in unison.

On our way back to Paul's safe house, my 'toothache' miraculously disappeared. I noted that Paul took several detours and doubled back several times on our way back. I had seen nothing untoward and realised that this was Paul's instincts that made him take these precautions.

We arrived at the safe house without incident, and Lyn immediately asked me how my tooth was. I was able to say truthfully that it did not hurt at all at the moment. *Always include an element of truth in your lies*, I thought.

It was mid-morning on the next day that the landline rang, and Paul picked up the receiver and introduced himself.

'Good morning Philip,' he said, 'I did not expect such an early call from you. Have you come up with a way to deal with this theory?'

I am not sure that I liked my idea being referred to as 'this theory thing', but I suppose that is all it was for the time being. I moved closer, intending to listen to their conversation.

'Yes. I have. The thing is, I believe that the best way of breaking this to Lyn is to appear to be breaking it to all of you at the same time. So, any chance that I could come up this afternoon?' 'Philip enquired.

'Yes, sure, I'll get Christine to make up a bed. Long day for you?' Paul asked.

Obviously, Philip said it had been a long day and told him that he would see us all later, probably between six and half past.

'That will be fine,' Paul told Philip, 'will dinner at eight suit you?'

It appeared to suit Philip Carterford, and the call was terminated.

I felt awful that I had had to keep Lyn in the dark, but I hoped that when it all came out, she would understand why I had done it. I couldn't possibly tell her about my speculation until I had proof.

Just after six o'clock, the doorbell rang, and Paul went to answer it. He returned to the lounge, where Lyn and I were sitting, accompanied by Philip Carterford.

Philip saw me, and his face lit up with a smile. It was a smile that, if Lyn and Paul had noticed, they could not mistake for anything other than true affection.

Paul offered drinks to us all, and Philip said that, as it had been a long drive, he would love a glass of beer. Paul had whisky and soda, and Lyn and I had gin and tonics. We settled comfortably, and I felt sure Philip was about to begin to reveal his planned method of proving my theory.

'First of all, I have to tell you that a theory has been put forward. The theory is that this whole situation came about because of viable threats made against you Lyn and you Mal.' He bowed his head slightly in our direction.

'The saddest and hardest part of what I am about to tell you is that this theory supposes that your father, Lyn, could, at this stage only could, mind you, but he could be involved.'

'That is absurd!' Lyn exclaimed as we all expected that she would. 'How on earth can my own father be involved in this affair? I mean, he was kidnapped, for Christ's sake! You people have lost it.'

I said nothing but recalled what Alex Wright had said when the suggestion of a safe house had been made. He said, 'Susan and I do not believe we are in too much danger. After all, they could have finished me off when they had me, but they didn't.' Of course, they didn't, I thought, especially if they did not exist in the first place.

'Lyn,' said Philip, 'let us just suppose for the moment that your father is involved in some way…'

Before he could continue, Lyn interrupted him.

'I'm not going to listen to this for a second longer. It makes no sense.'

Lyn stood up and made as if to leave the room.

'Sit down!' the Detective Chief Inspector said, almost but not quite shouting and in a very commanding voice. 'Sit down, please, Lyn, please.' His voice getting quieter with the last, please.

Reluctantly, Lyn sat back down again.

'Alright,' she said, 'go on slagging my father off but don't expect me to be any part of it. It is a ridiculous notion you are suggesting.'

'Very well, Lyn, that is your prerogative, but I would like to continue to expound this theory, if I may?'

Lyn waved a hand which could have been interpreted as a yes, you carry-on gesture.

'Right, to continue,' said Philip Carterford in his normal voice. 'Let us suppose just for a moment that your father has a part to play in all of this. What does that leave us with?'

He paused slightly, but I realised that the question was rhetorical.

'Well, firstly, it suggests that only one group of villains is involved in this affair. Harry Haraldsen is not Mister Big. From what he said to Mal and yourself, Lyn, we know that with certainty. However, he is fairly high up in the chain of command, if I may call it such. He was the face for people to see and the one through whom everything was designed to go. Witness the letter which your husband left for you, Lyn, that advised you to go to Harry Haraldsen, did it not? I believe, and so do my colleagues, senior and junior, that there is a Mr Big, who is now and always has been, close to what has occurred. He has been watching the case unfold a bit too closely. I believe that this Mister Big was directly or indirectly responsible for your husband's death, Lyn. The theory which has been put forward is that your father is, in fact Mr Big. He's always been a part of this behind the scenes.'

Philip Carterford paused for effect and to let what he said sink in. In fact, it was solely for Lyn's benefit because I had put the theory forward in the first place.

The look on Lyn's face was one of bewilderment and disbelief all rolled into one.

'How can you even suggest such a thing?' Lyn asked Philip.

'Because, Lyn, I believe it to be true,' the chief Inspector replied. 'I understand this might be hard for you to accept, but with the look of things, it had to be someone close… close to you.'

'Absolute rubbish. What evidence for such a thing is there? None! You are clutching at straws!'

'Lyn?' Philip Carterford said. The question was really not a question at all, but her name was said in this form to get her attention.

'Lyn,' Carterford tried again. 'When your father was kidnapped, did your mother hear anyone in the house?'

'No, not as far as I know. She certainly didn't say anything,' Lyn said.

'Don't you think that this could have been done in complete silence if at least one kidnapper and possibly two of them came into your parents' bedroom and hauled your father out of bed? Would he have gone quietly? Even if he had been knocked out with chloroform, wouldn't he have made some noise?'

Lyn let this sink in. I stole a glance at her and reckoned that she was weighing everything up in her mind. Surely the silence of the kidnapping was compelling!

'I can see why you should think this is so, but I know my father and he would never let anything bad happen to me! Neither would he ever harm my mother,' she added almost as an afterthought.

'How long have they been married?' Carterford asked.

'Well, I'm twenty-six, so at least twenty-seven. In all of that time, there has never been a suggestion of anything untoward. He has nothing to do with any of this.'

'Lyn, this is not unusual. After all is said and done, I arrested a paedophile a few years ago who had a family of three and a wife who not only had no idea what her husband was up to but told us theirs was a very happy marriage in every way.'

Nothing in response from Lyn.

Philip said, 'I have a team working, as we speak, on your father and mother's backgrounds. We do not suspect your mother in any way, but we are thoroughly checking both of their backgrounds.'

'My mother too. For God's sake, what is wrong with you people?' Lyn almost shouted.

'As I said,' Philip replied very calmly, 'we do not suspect her at this time, but we are including her in our in-depth background check on your father.'

'I want to ring my mother, now!' Lyn exclaimed and rose as if to cross to the telephone.

'Please, Lyn, do not do that. If you try to contact your mother or father, then I shall arrest you too,' Philip Carterford told her. I gasped, and Lyn glared back at him.

'Oh, for God's sake. Now you suspect me! What about Mal? What about Paul and Christine? Are they under suspicion as well?'

'Now it is you who is being a little ridiculous, if I may say so. Of course, I do not suspect you of anything. If I had, I most certainly would have excluded you from this get-together. It is just that if you question your mother, our suspicions will almost certainly reach your father's ears. Until we can clear him or otherwise, that would prejudice our enquiries.'

'Rubbish!' Lyn said but stayed where she was.

I glanced at the mantle clock and saw it was almost eight o'clock.

There was a brief tap on the door, and it opened to reveal Christine pushing a hostess trolley towards a table. We sat and ate our meal in almost complete silence. The only interruption was Philip's mobile warbling its ringtone.

'Excuse me. I've got to take this. I'll take Paul outside if that's alright.'

Paul waved an agreeing hand, and we continued with our meal.

As I learned later, the call was from Philip's Deputy Detective Inspector Norman Cox. The conversation went along these lines.

'Guv? Norman here. Can you speak without being overheard?'

Philip Carterford had reassured him that he could not be overheard and could speak freely.

'Right then, Guv, the background checks into Alex Wright. This has turned up some strange anomalies. The main one is that there was no such person before twenty years ago, none at all.'

'But he must have existed, Norman. You'll have to dig deeper.'

'We will keep digging, of course, but here's another strange thing, you remember Dominic Allen?'

'Of course!'

'Well, he ceased to exist twenty years ago. A coincidence, don't you think?'

'I do not like coincidences Norman, neither do I believe in them. What about his fingerprints? There must be something?'

'They were taken when he was arrested for armed robbery thirty years ago. I have checked our records, the Police National Computer, and a contact at the local prison. Dominic Allen was indeed convicted of armed robbery but got a very light sentence. He was released at about the same time as Alex Wright first surfaced when he married his present wife, Susan. He apparently changed his name to make a fresh start, as they say. You know the sort of thing wipe the slate clean and start again.'

'Just to be clear then, Norman, what you are saying is that Dominic Allen and Alex Wright are the same person.'

'As far as I can tell without fingerprints. We have Dominic Allen's prints from the armed robbery conviction, which were also found on the shell case at the scene of Robert Dickson's murder. What we do not have is the fingerprints of Alex Wright. How are we going to get those without giving anything away? Any suggestions?'

'Leave that with me, will you? I'll get it done,' Philip said.

They wished each other goodnight, and Philip returned to the lounge.

'Any news?' I ventured.

'Well, yes and no,' Philip replied rather cagily.

After we had finished our meal, Philip asked me if I would care for a stroll with him and, of course, I said yes, I would, very much. Again, that now becoming familiar flutter in my stomach.

We walked in the woodlands at the rear of the house, and after a while, Philip's hand reached down and took mine. I did not hesitate in any way. In fact, not only did it feel pleasant, but it felt natural. Philip gave me a sideways glance, and I smiled up at him, in reassurance as much as anything.

When we were as far away from the house as we could safely get, Philip stopped and removed his hand from mine.

'Mal, ever since I first met you, I have been longing to do something,' he said.

'And what might that be?' I replied as coyly as I could, although, in truth, I could easily have guessed what he meant.

'This!' Philip said and immediately took me in his arms and kissed me deeply.

I had to come up for air, and I leant back in Philip's arms and looked deeply into his eyes. He was smiling, and there was a look that bordered on satisfaction.

'Wow!' I exclaimed and meant it.

'Wow as well,' Philip whispered back to me.

We repeated the kiss several times more, and I think it was this evening when I realised that this was something more than an acquaintance or a friendship. If I had to label it, perhaps the beginning of love was the most appropriate.

We stood there just staring into each other's eyes and smiling warmly at each other. We did not need to fill the silence with words, as just standing next to each other, holding each other's arms, was more than enough in that moment.

Philip told me of his dilemma regarding the fingerprints of Dominic Allen and Alex Wright. He told me that he did not want to approach Alex personally as this would be too upsetting for Lyn and her mother. He didn't want to employ subterfuge either, as this could compromise any case that might emerge at some stage down the line.

We kissed again, and he held me so close to him that I could feel his body heat and the stirrings of his manhood. He broke away as soon as he realised, but I pulled him back again and whispered to him, 'It is alright, and I am very flattered.'

Eventually, we turned back towards the house and strolled very slowly along the path, still hand in hand—content at that moment in companionable silence.

'Philip,' I said. 'What about Looe?'

'What about it? I know it is a very pretty little town; I have holidayed there several times over the years.'

'No, I do not mean the town itself, although I am sure it is very nice. I was thinking more of Alex Wright and Looe,' I offered.

'Go on,' Philip encouraged. 'What about it?'

'Well, when Amelia Wyatt found him, she was not a hundred percent certain as to his identity, was she?'

'No.'

'What would be the obvious thing to do to try and establish it?' I prompted.

'A Police National Computer check, and if that was negative, then the next obvious step would be his fingerprints. They must have his data! Mal, you are marvellous and wonderful,' Philip said with obvious sincerity.

'What time is it?' Philip looked at his watch. It is still reasonably early; let's ring Plymouth, and they should be able to tell us when Amelia Wyatt is on duty again.'

Philip took his mobile from his pocket and dialled the number he had already stored there.

'Good evening. This is Detective Chief Inspector Carterford of Thames Valley CID. Is it possible that Constable Amelia Wyatt is on duty?'

There was a pause, and then Philip said, 'She is? Is she available, do you know?'

'Yes, she is at Looe Police Station at this time report writing. Would you like me to put you through?'

'Yes, please,' Philip replied with a nod of his head towards me which I took to be the equivalent of a thumbs up.

'Amelia! Detective Chief Inspector Carterford, Thames Valley CID, good evening. The reason for my call concerns that chap Alex Wright you found in Looe. I have a few questions. Well, to begin with, were you able to identify him straightaway?'

The answer was negative.

'Did you by any chance take any fingerprints of him?' Philip wanted to know.

'Yes, I did. In fact, talk about coincidence, but I have them in front of me. I am just preparing the paperwork to have them destroyed. Well, they aren't relevant now, are they? So they have to be destroyed.'

'Look, Amelia, are you on duty tomorrow?' Philip enquired.

'Good. Look, can I come down and speak to you and collect at least a copy of the prints?'

'Yes, I am on duty tomorrow, so that is eight in the morning until six in the evening. Barring jobs and torpedoes, can I meet you at Looe Police Station at eight?'

Philip did a quick mental calculation and told Amelia he would be there, barring holdups in traffic.

They wished each other good night, and Philip dialled another number.

'Norman, Philip Carterford again. Could you get the fingerprints out of the file and meet me at Strensham motorway services southbound at say ten o'clock tomorrow morning?'

'Yes, Guv. Can do. Where are we going?' Norman wondered.

'We are not going anywhere, but I am going to Cornwall!' Philip replied almost triumphantly.

'Alright for some! Goodnight, Guv.'

Philip returned his mobile to his pocket and, taking my hand again, he looked me in the eyes and said, 'Fancy a trip to the seaside with me?'

I chuckled and jumped at the chance, and we went back inside, careful not to show the feelings which were beginning to emerge between us.

'Problems?' Paul wanted to know.

'Problems, no. But I have to return to Thames Valley tomorrow, so if you can accommodate me for the night, Paul, I'd be grateful.'

'Yes. Can do.' Christine immediately left to check that the bed was ready.

'I shall be taking Mal with me as I want her to cast her insurance adjuster's eyes over some documents which have turned up from Haraldsen's. Is that okay with you, Lyn? Would you mind if I borrow your friend for a while?'

'Doesn't bother me one way or the other,' Lyn's mood was obviously sullen, still not having forgiven Philip for suggesting that her father may have been involved.

Chapter Twenty-Five

The next morning, we set off at seven-thirty. Doctor Google told us that the journey time would be about two hours fifteen minutes, so we should be at Strensham Services by nine forty-five. We decided that breakfast could be eaten at the services, giving Philip time to catch up with his deputy.

As things turned out, we were held up and pulled into the services just after ten o'clock. Norman Cox was patiently waiting near the main entrance. He greeted his boss warmly, who, in turn, introduced me. We shook hands, and he raised a questioning eyebrow towards Philip. Philip merely smiled and made no comment about me, to keep the meeting strictly professional, I assume.

We ate a typical motorway services breakfast which was not at all bad. Philip took the fingerprints contained in a large brown envelope, and we left Norman Cox still drinking his second coffee. The journey to Looe, again, according to Doctor Google, would take us just under four hours, so if we were to meet Amelia Wyatt on time, we couldn't hang about.

There were long tailbacks which we found were caused by a serious collision on the M5 just south of the Avon Bridge. It was clear that we would not make our appointment with Amelia Wyatt, so Philip rang her on his hands-free mobile to prompt her about the delay. As things turned out, almost inevitably, she would be late for the appointment, too having been called to deal with a sudden death and not knowing how long she would be involved there.

Philip looked at me with a raised eyebrow. I could hear both sides of the conversation as Philip's phone was on speaker.

I nodded my consent, although to what I wasn't too sure at this stage, and we arranged to meet Amelia at eight o'clock the next morning at Looe Police Station when she was due to begin her shift for that day.

Philip estimated that it would be close to five o'clock before we got to Looe, and that too would depend on the traffic and road works, of which there seemed to be a plethora.

We crossed the River Tamar via the Tamar Bridge, completed in October 1961 and opened in April 1962. The view was breath-taking, and one could never fail to be impressed by The Royal Albert Bridge, designed by Isambard Kingdom Brunel and opened in May 1859, which runs alongside.

As we entered the County of Cornwall, my thoughts changed from bridges already built and in use to bridges yet to be built between Philip and myself. What exactly were his intentions? Where were we going with this? I felt sure that his intentions were honourable, but how honourable? We were probably going to stay the night in Looe, but what would the sleeping arrangements be? What did I want them to be? Did I want them to be the same as Philip would like? Oh, God! Questions, always questions.

As we approached the turning to Looe, Philip found a layby, pulled in, and stopped.

Turning towards me, he asked, 'Are you hungry?'

Alright, it wasn't the question I was expecting, but as we had not eaten since the breakfast stop at Strensham, I felt more than a little peckish. I didn't really think that this was the question that Philip wanted to ask either.

I smiled at him and said, 'Why don't you just ask what you really want to know?'

'What do you mean?'

'Oh! come off it, Philip; neither of us is naïve enough to think that you are contemplating separate bedrooms surely.'

'Well, no, not really.'

'Please don't expect me to ask the question,' I told him.

'Alright then, shall I book one room or two?'

'One, then, and with a double bed.'

'Are you sure you want this as much as I do?' Philip wanted to know, although why did he want to know? Heaven alone knows.

'Just book the bloody room, Philip. Time for questions later, much later.'

Philip leaned over and kissed me with more than a little passion which I returned in spades.

'Right! Food! Have you been to Looe before?'

'No,' I replied truthfully. 'This is the first time I've been here.'

Philip took his mobile out and searched Doctor Google for a contact number for, I presumed, a hotel. I presumed wrong.

'The Old Bridge House,' said a charming voice.

'Good evening. Do you, by any chance, have a double room for one or possibly two nights? One night for certain anyway?' Philip asked.

He sounded nervous, and I felt a little relieved that he was not used to taking females for dirty weekends away.

'Certainly, sir. When for?'

'Tonight, please.'

'That's fine. When will you be arriving?' The charming voice once more.

'About five, if that's alright.'

The obliging charming voice told Philip there would be no problem with that.

As things transpired, we pulled into their free parking area at twenty past four.

We booked in, and the charming telephone voice was genuinely so when we booked in. We went to our room, and Philip had obviously come prepared as he was carrying a two-handled bag. I looked at it with a questioning raising of my eyebrow.

'What's all this then? Had you planned this all along?' I asked suspiciously.

'Actually, no, but in some ways, I wish I had.'

'If you had planned it all along, then we would now be in separate rooms!' I replied.

'No, I always carry a small bag with a change or two of underwear, socks and shirt, a washbag, and sleeping attire. You know, in case something crops up in an enquiry involving an overnight stay somewhere.'

I just used my best knowing Joe Root smile at him, but I did not believe him. He definitely had it planned.

'Did you not come similarly prepared, Mal?' Philip asked with a smug grin.

I opened the capacious bag, which I carried everywhere, and produced a clean bra, knickers, and a clean top with a flourish.

'Ta-dah!'

Philip smiled, came to me, and wrapped his arms around me. We kissed again, this time with a passion that hinted at what would come later.

'Right! We've been cooped up in that car all day; let's stretch our legs as far as the seafront and back. By the way, do you like fish and chips?'

'Yes, I do if they are well prepared and cooked. Who doesn't?'

'Then I will introduce you to the best fish and chips in Cornwall and in my view, anywhere else. Come on.'

We left The Old Bridge House and walked along the quay at the side of the East Looe River. The tide was in, and it was a joy strolling along, hand in hand, with a man whom I liked very much. We watched the boats riding at anchor or arriving back in port after a day at sea. It truly was marvellous. All my cares and fears for the safety of myself and others were virtually forgotten, at least for tonight.

Having taken our fill of sea air, we wandered back towards the Old Bridge House, taking in the town. For a late afternoon, there were still plenty of people about, but to both of us, they were just background and nothing else.

As we got to the bridge over the East Looe River, Philip pointed out the police station situated on the river bank. He told me he had been tempted to join the Devon and Cornwall

Constabulary when he was younger, hoping he could get stationed there.

We paused on the bridge and made a dinner appointment at some place called the Coddy Shack. It sounded a bit dubious to me, but Philip advised that I postpone judgement until we had eaten. I obliged, thinking he probably knew better.

We wandered past the Old Bridge House and found a pub called The Globe Inn. Over a glass or two of beer, we talked about everything except the coming night, but I could sense the tension in the air between us. Neither of us was exactly shy, but we were not experienced enough in life to be blasé about spending the night with someone for the first time. But that was for later.

The taxi took us to a wooden construction stuck in the corner of a car park. Not a good start, I thought. When we walked towards the entrance, it became abundantly clear that this was a popular eatery. The queue at the takeaway window had probably twenty people in it, always a good sign.

We were met just inside the restaurant entrance by a very personable young maître d and shown to a corner table for two.

Our waitress was Betty, and she asked if we were ready to order drinks. We ordered two glasses of wine, and she handed us a menu each. My stomach roared as I browsed the menu, indicating it needed a big meal.

'Choose the regular cod and chips,' Philip advised. 'There will be more than enough for you on the plate, I assure you.'

'You seem to know Looe very well. Do you bring all of your fancy women here?' I said with more than a little laughter in my voice.

Philip did not smile back. Oops!

'Firstly, I do not consider you to be a fancy woman, mine, or anyone else's for that matter. Secondly, you are the first person I have even considered having some sort of relationship with since, well, you know…And thirdly, I believe that you are becoming special to me. But to give you the brief and truthful answer, no, I do not.'

'That's alright then,' I replied, eyes down, smiling and apparently completely engrossed in the menu.

Betty returned and took our order, and we both ordered the regular cod and chips. When it arrived, it was absolutely delicious. Certainly, the best that I had ever tasted, and Philip was absolutely right, it was certainly enough for me, but I did manage to clear my plate; it would be rude not to! I read that Trip Advisor had rated The Coddy Shack as the best fish and chips in Cornwall, and I am sure they were. I could not get them off my mind long after I had finished my meal.

Later, I discovered that the top twenty fish and chip shops did not include Rick Stein's at Padstow. So much for celebrity chefs! We kept any conversation to generalities and did our best to avoid what was to come later so as to not make things awkward.

The taxi took us back into Looe itself and dropped us at the river bridge. It was dark, but lights were twinkling almost everywhere one looked. It was certainly a different place at night.

Inevitably it was time for us to turn in, and we strolled back to the guest house and went straight upstairs.

It was an almost embarrassing interlude, that first casting off our clothes. Philip was watching me, and I was watching him. We alternated with garments and took far too much care with the discarded items, almost as if we were trying to delay the inevitable for as long as possible. At last, we stood facing each other, completely naked.

'I don't usually wear nightclothes, so I do not have any,' I whispered.

'Then don't wear them!' Philip chuckled. 'I love the way you look without them. The twitching of his manhood evidenced his appreciation of what he was seeing. It seemed to embarrass him a little, but I felt flattered. I went to the side of the bed where he was standing and threw my arms around him. I ignored the hardening of his penis, and he appeared to ignore the hardening of my nipples, although I was quite certain that neither ignored anything!

Our first lovemaking was one of exploring each other, our likes and our dislikes, and what pleased us and what didn't. When we finally climaxed together, it was the most wonderful feeling I had ever experienced. It was far more satisfying than anything I had experienced with David, which had been great. It felt as if we were perfectly in sync.

We virtually flopped back onto the bed and lay there staring at the ceiling while we waited for our breathing to return to something approaching normal. Once that had happened, I turned my head to look at Philip, fully expecting him to be asleep after his exertions but was surprised and very pleased that he was looking at me!

'Well?' I said, 'how was that for you?' I was laughing as I spoke.

'Bloody marvellous, but I do not need to ask how it was for you. I could easily tell,' Philip said, also chuckling.

After twenty minutes of light kissing and touching, I could feel that Philip had grown hard again, and I pulled him on top of me. This time, it was a pure animal need but just as satisfying for us both. Philip slid off me onto his side of the bed and almost immediately fell asleep. I followed suit within minutes.

At just after six o'clock, a beeping sound awoke me. I forced my eyes open and for a second, only a second mind you, wondered who this man was in my bed. I blinked my eyes to wake myself up and found Philip switching the alarm off on his mobile phone.

'What time is it, for pity's sake?' I asked.

'Just gone six. Breakfast will be at seven-thirty, and our meeting with Amelia Wyatt is at eight, I would remind you,' Philip explained. 'We need to get ready.'

'Yes, but why so bloody early?' I persisted.

'For this!' Philip said and began kissing and caressing me until I returned the actions, and we made love again, this time completely at ease with each other; all the pent-up need expended last night, which was wonderful.

Afterwards, I watched Philip as he readied himself for the shower and thought that I could easily fall in love with Philip Carterford. Without thinking, I began humming the tune of the Cliff Richard hit; *I Could Easily Fall in Love with You*. Philip came out of the shower with a towel wrapped around him; whether by coincidence or design, he was humming the same tune. I did hope that it was by design.

We ate a light breakfast of toast and coffee supplemented by fruit juice. It would have been difficult to eat a full English breakfast while holding hands. This time neither of us made any attempt to hide our relationship.

At exactly eight o'clock, we rang the bell at Looe Police Station and Amelia Wyatt, who had clearly been on duty for a while already, opened the door to admit us.

We went to an office where Amelia had already arranged three chairs, and three steaming mugs of black coffee were on the table waiting for us. Milk and sugar, if required, we were told.

We had only just sat down when the office door opened. I had not heard a bell anywhere, so I presumed this was a police officer or a police support person. It turned out to be the latter.

'Chief Inspector Carterford,' Amelia began.

'Philip, please. I much prefer first names,' Philip said.

'Philip and Mal, this is Scenes of Crime Officer Alistair Burden. I asked him to come here so we can have an expert to compare the prints we have and believe me, Ali is the best we have in Devon and Cornwall,' Amelia effused.

Philip opened his document case, produced the set of fingerprints Norman Cox had given him at Strensham and passed them across the table to Ali Burden for further inspection. Amelia did likewise with the prints she had taken of Alex Wright in hospital following his so-called kidnap.

Ali Burden removed a magnifying glass from his pocket and carefully cleaned it with a soft cloth he had also been carrying. He leaned over the sheets which sat side by side on the table, and we all awaited his verdict.

After almost a quarter of an hour, Ali Burden looked up with a grin on his face.

'I'm no expert,' he began.

'Oh yes, you are,' interrupted Amelia, 'and you know you are.'

'Alright. Just my little joke. Philip, I would say that you are looking at the same person here. I believe that there is very little room for doubt. However, to be absolutely certain, I would need to take them back to Plymouth and compare them electronically. If you don't mind my asking, are you contemplating an arrest based on these prints?' Ali wanted to know.

'Yes. I am indeed,' Philip replied.

'Then I would suggest that you need to be absolutely certain of the ident. I'm not trying to teach granny, you understand,' Ali said.

'I fully understand, and I agree. When could you do them for me?' Philip wanted to know.

'Well, I'm on my way to Crown Court at the moment. I just called in here for this,' Ali told us. 'However, I can do them as a priority later today. Could you collect them from Plymouth Police Station later?'

'Of course, we could, but that would mean a long drive through rush hour traffic at the end of the day. Tell you what, we'll collect them from Plymouth tomorrow morning. How would that suit?' Philip wanted to know.

'That suits me fine. It takes some of the pressure off me too,' Ali replied. 'I'll definitely do them before I go home tonight, Philip. Thanks for that.'

Thanking both Alistair and Amelia, we left the tiny police station.

'Well?' I asked, without qualifying my question.

'Well, let's have a look around the area, shall we? We have plenty of time for ourselves,' Philip suggested.

'I do not know this area, so I am in your hands,' I said, smiling.

'That comes later!' Philip retorted, and his smile was as wide as mine.

'Right, let's go back to The Old Bridge then.'

'Whoa, back there! I know we both enjoyed the lovemaking, but you're not considering a repeat, are you? I mean, during the day and probably before housekeeping have been to the room! Tut! Tut!' I exclaimed.

'No, to extend our stay till tomorrow!' Philip exclaimed.

We spoke to the proprietors of The Old Bridge and went off searching for somewhere pretty. Well, pretty would be nice, but to be absolutely truthful, as long as I was with Philip Carterford, I didn't really care one way or the other.

We made our way to Polperro, only a few miles from Looe. The car park on the outskirts of the village was busy but only about half full. We strolled together hand-in-hand down the sloping main street towards the harbour. There was a mixture of tiny shops, quaint houses, coffee shops, and other refreshment premises.

We passed one restaurant, which was, a sign told us, closed for a holiday. The menu board, however, had been left on display. It was difficult to try and work out what the various items were. Several of them prompted giggles from us both. The battered seagull and chips was one, cactus curry – hot and spikey- and my personal favourite was the squirrel casserole – may contain nuts! We continued our way down to the tiny harbour and passed a narrow lane leading off to who knows where named Little Laney. This street name prompted repeated laughter from us both.

The tide was out, and small boats stood on the estuary bed with owners working on their charges, sloshing about in the wet seaweed. We followed the path until the vista of the outer harbour opened up before us. With the tide out, there were plenty of rocks to sit on and admire the view. The sun shone warmly upon us, and Philip and I cuddled together, enjoying it all. Everything seemed to be falling into place at the moment.

Tummy rumblings suggested that the toast had stopped doing its job of satisfying our appetites. We saw what appeared to be a quaint-looking pub, The Blue Peter Inn. We took a table and ordered a seafood platter each. It lived up to its advertising of one of the quaintest pubs you may ever come across. The food from the award-winning menu made it obvious how they had won such an award as Taste of the West Gold in 2016.

After lunch, we wandered back up to the car park and took the six-mile journey to the village of Polruan. From here, we took the Mevagissey Ferries boat over the river to Fowey. We wandered around the village, hand-in-hand again and oblivious of everyone except each other.

We caught the last ferry back to Polruan and thence drove to Looe again. We parked up and made our way along the road to The Globe Inn. We sat at a window seat watching the world go by and again lost in each other and our own thoughts. After the fine pub lunch, we decided on sandwiches rather than another meal, and by ten o'clock, we were ready for bed. The day had been wonderful and would linger in my memory forever. I knew as we walked back to the Old Bridge that I was very definitely falling in love with Philip Carterford… and maybe he was too.

Chapter Twenty-Six

The next morning Philip and I confirmed our feelings having expressed them twice the night before and made our way down to breakfast. Today we decided that, as there was no rush, we would each partake of the full Cornish breakfast on offer and delicious it was too.

We thanked The Old Bridge House proprietors for their hospitality, and they accepted with knowing looks. Clearly, nothing escaped their notice, but neither Philip nor I cared what anyone else thought. At least not down here.

We collected the fingerprints and statement of evidence from the front office of Plymouth Police Station and began our three hundred and twenty-odd miles drive back to Pen-y-Coed. The happiness and companionability which we felt when we began dissipated with every passing mile. Philip and I both knew what was to follow, and neither of us liked it very much.

The return journey time of five hours and twenty-five minutes proved to be optimistic. With roadworks and then two separate collisions on the motorway, our journey lasted almost an hour and a half longer. We had finally left Plymouth Police Station by ten o'clock, and as we drove into Paul and Christine's safe house, the time was pretty much five o'clock.

We wearily made our way inside the safe house, and Lyn immediately jumped up and came over to us.

'Where the bloody hell have you been? I have been worried to death about you, Mal. Well, not literally, of course.'

'I have been assisting Philip with his enquiries, actually,' I said, trying my best to keep the smile off my face.

'Oh! And?'

I looked at Philip, who asked Lyn to sit down.

'Lyn, I am extremely sorry to tell you what I am about to relate, but I have to do it,' Philip began.

'Well?' Lyn asked, clearly irritated.

'Lyn, you remember that I told you about a theory which had been put forward?'

'Yes, I remember; what of it?' Lyn wanted to know.

Philip looked at me and hesitated. I nodded at him, a gesture which did not escape Lyn.

'What have you two been cooking up? More lies?'

'Lyn,' I began, but Philip touched my arm to stop me. This was his job, and he knew it.

'Lyn,' Philip began, 'we have not been to Thames Valley at all. Mal and I have been to Looe.'

He paused, not for effect, but purely to get his words right. Lyn took it as an opportunity to have another go at Philip and me.

'Been stirring it up down there now, have you? And I thought that you were my friend.'

'I am Lyn. I am. Please believe me. I'm just trying to help,' I said before Philip again touched my arm, and I said no more.

'Lyn, anything I tell you is down to me, no one else, do you understand?'

From Lyn, nothing.

'Lyn, do you understand?' Philip said, having raised his voice a little.

'Yes, I suppose so,' Lyn said without any sincerity at all.

'Right. Well, the purpose of our visit to Looe was to meet up with Amelia Wyatt, the constable who had traced your father. 'I took copies of the fingerprint found on the bullet casing, which almost certainly killed your husband,' Amelia told me when I spoke to her before we left here that she had taken your father's fingerprints in an attempt to identify him. As things turned out, he remembered his name and address, so the fingerprints were not required for that purpose. As I am sure you already know, these fingerprints cannot be retained on police files and, by pure chance, when I spoke to Amelia Wyatt she was completing her report to accompany the destruction of the prints. That is why Mal and I went to Looe at such short notice. To retrieve them before they're wiped from the official records. We had a fingerprint expert examine both sets of prints manually and electronically, and he is prepared to swear in court that the two sets are identical.'

This was the bombshell that both Philip and I had been dreading, but it had to be dropped, and that was that.

I looked across at Lyn, who sat with her eyes glued on Philip and her mouth wide open in disbelief.

'Mal?' she said, 'Is this right?'

'I am very sorry to say that it is correct, lovey. Your father was involved in David's death somehow. Whether he pulled the trigger, we do not know because the weapon was never recovered, but he was there. And he definitely had something to do with it.'

'No! He couldn't be involved in killing David. He really liked him. He always said that David was the son he never had. That is why I just cannot get my head around this,' Lyn said, and you could hear the sob in the back of her throat.

'I know it is a cliché, but fine words butter no parsnips, Lyn. What I mean is…'

Lyn interrupted me and said, 'Don't you dare quote your old adages at me, Mal. This is my father we are talking about, and he may have killed my husband. Bloody parsnips and buttering them just do not help.'

Philip, who had been silent for the past few minutes while the exchange between Lyn and I went on, spoke.

'Lyn, how well do you know your father?'

'He's my dad; of course, I know him well. Didn't you know your dad well?' Lyn asked.

'Actually, no, I did not. He was killed in a road collision when I was just a toddler,' Philip said. I hoped for effect, but if it was true, I made a mental note to try to comfort him when we were alone next time.

'I'm sorry, Philip, I didn't know,' Lyn apologised.

'Apology accepted if one were required,' Philip said. 'Your father, Lyn, led a strange life. It appears that he used to go under the name of Dominic Allen and then got himself arrested for armed robbery. He was a young man, and of hitherto good behaviour, so the judge gave him a light sentence. When he was released from prison on parole, he changed his name to Alex Wright. We have no idea what prompted that, but one reason could be that his fingerprints would have been on record as Dominic Allen, so unless anyone really checked, he would have a clear field of play.

'But he gave his fingerprints quite willingly at Plymouth hospital when Amelia Wyatt found him! Why would he do that if he were guilty?' Lyn pointed out.

'Indeed, he did,' said Philip, 'but he remembered who he was quite unexpectedly, and it was not necessary to check his fingerprints any longer, and they were about to be destroyed. It was his bad luck and the police's good luck, if you like that, we remembered that Amelia had taken the prints from your father. Synchronicity took care of the rest, and we identified Dominic Allen as Alex Wright. I really am sorry, Lyn, but fingerprints do not lie.'

'No, I suppose they don't,' Lyn said, 'but it doesn't make acceptance of the fact that one's father may well have killed one's husband, does it?'

Philip paused and then said, 'Lyn, I cannot imagine in my wildest dreams what you are going through at the moment, but there is a chance, just a very, very slim chance, that we have got it wrong. I do not think we have got it wrong, but it is a vague possibility. But there is more grief, I'm afraid. We have to tell your mother. I am certain she knows nothing of this affair, but she has to be told. The plan will be, I'm sure, that when we arrest your father, and we will, an in-depth search of his home will be made, and deep background checks will follow. Your mother has got to be told. The question is, do you want to be there when we do that? It will not be a pleasant experience, I can assure you.'

'You've done this sort of thing before then?' Lyn wanted to know.

'Not exactly like this, but I once had to search a house with the wife and children present after I had arrested a paedophile. It literally blew that family to pieces. I had no option; the wife had to know. It was heartbreaking, but it's part of the job.'

Philip paused again to let the enormity of it all sink in.

'And your mother has to know too, Lyn,' Philip said as comfortingly as possible.

'Yes. I realise that. When though?' Lyn asked.

'Not for at least a few days. I would very much like you to be there when we carry out the arrest as your mother will need it, and I am sure she will appreciate all the support she can get. I must also add one other thing. Please do not blame Mal for what has happened already and what is inevitably going to happen. All the decisions are mine and mine alone to make, do you understand? She was only trying to help us.'

Philip paused again to let this sink in. It was an awful lot of bad news for Lyn to absorb all at the same time, and I knew she was hurting. Despite what Philip had just said, I also knew that she would heap some blame on me at some level. All in all, I couldn't really blame her, I suppose. After all, I had suggested Lyn's father as a suspect to Philip.

'Lyn,' Philip spoke again, 'I need you to give me your word that you will not contact either of your parents before I can complete my enquiries and make the arrest. I won't do anything so childish as asking you to swear that you won't or ask to swear that you won't make contact, but I do need your word. Do I have it?'

Lyn was clearly in two minds about whether to ring her mother. I could almost hear the cogs going around in her head. Eventually, she said, 'You have it. I will not make any contact until you give the go-ahead. You can trust me on this. Is that good enough for you?'

'Yes. Thank you,' said Philip.

Philip turned to Paul and asked if he could have a bed for one more night, and the offer was made and accepted.

'I want to make an early start tomorrow; I have a lot of work to do back at Thames Valley.'

Philip apparently said this to no one in particular, but I knew he was telling me not to creep into his room that night!

Christine came into the room pushing a hostess trolley.

'You need to have a good meal then, Philip, so here we are. Dig in everyone,' she said.

Philip and I went for a walk after our meal and made our way straight into the woods at the rear of the house, away from prying eyes. Once we were out of sight, Philip took me in his arms and kissed me passionately. Then we stood there and stared into each other's eyes for as long as I could remember before he broke the silence.

'Gosh! I needed that,' he said, smiling almost lovingly.

'Philip, do you remember that first morning in Looe?' I asked.

'You mean after we had, you know…'

'Yes, I know! Can you remember the song I was humming while you were in the shower?' I asked.

'Indeed, I can! Cliff Ricard's *I Could Easily Fall in Love with You.*'

'Well, I think that it has started,' I said softly.

'Don't tell me that you know already!' Philip said.

'Unless I am wildly wrong, I do.'

'I dare not even think along those lines for the time being, but I will tell you. If I ever do fall in love again, it will certainly be with you. Will that do for now?' Philip squeezed me to him.

'I'll settle for that for now. What time are you going tomorrow?'

'I want to be on the road by seven-thirty.'

'I'll try and manage tonight on my own then,' I said and touched his manhood with the back of my hand.

'Think of Looe, then!' Philip said.

Chapter Twenty-Seven

The next day, when I came down to breakfast, Philip had already left for Thames Valley, and Lyn was standing looking out of the window. As I entered the room, she turned around and smiled at me. Well, that was a step in the right direction, I thought. I walked up to her, hoping she had forgiven me.

'How are you feeling this morning, lovey?' I asked her.

'I have accepted the worse now, Mal. It won't sink in fully for a while yet, but I do see why Philip did what he did and has to do what he has to do. Mal, I do not blame you, and I am very sorry if I have tried to. What do you think my mum will do when Dad gets arrested?'

'I don't know, lovey, but I suspect she will cope. She's a strong woman, after all. Do you think that she suspects anything?'

'I shouldn't think so for one minute. Dad has never been anything to me other than a loving father, and as far as I am aware, he has never been anything other than a loving husband. I suppose it is always possible, I suppose, that she did know or at least suspect.'

We ate our breakfast in companionable silence and then decided to take a walk on the grounds, if only to get some air. We were on the fringes of the woods chatting as we wandered when suddenly Lyn clutched at her shoulder, cried out, and fell to the ground.

'Christ, Lyn! What the hell was that?' I shouted.

'I think I have been shot,' Lyn said in a strangled voice.

'Bloody hell!' I said and emptied my bag onto the ground to find Paul's box of tricks, as he called it. I located it and pressed the button, hoping that someone would come running.

I stayed as low as I could and tried to protect Lyn at the same time by throwing my body on top of hers.

'You are hurting me, Mal. Get off!'

I had worked out the direction from which the shot had come and lay on the ground next to Lyn to protect her as much as possible.

I knelt up, and immediately the sound of another shot rang out, and a piece of tree bark flew off above my head. Back down flat, I went. Whoever the sniper was, they were not terribly good at their job. That gave me a little comfort. I turned my attention back to Lyn and could see the blood spreading as it soaked into Lyn's top, so I struggled to get my own top off. Having succeeded, I rolled it up as best I could and told Lyn to hold it as tightly as she could over the wound.

'Where's Paul?' she asked. She sounded much weaker to me now. That'll be the blood loss, I thought.

'I don't know. I pressed the panic button,' I whispered.

'Look, Lyn, I'm going for help.'

'No, no, please don't go,' Lyn called to me, her voice just a soft whisper. 'Stay with me, Mal.'

'I have to. If we don't get help soon, you'll bleed out. You are losing a lot of the stuff. I will be as quick as I can,' I said and crawled on elbows and knees, trying my best to keep under any cover the trees might provide.'

Once well away from Lyn, I got to my feet and, crouching as low as I could, hurried as fast as I could towards the house. When the driveway came into sight, I saw Paul's car pulling up. Apparently, he had been to the village and was carrying his box of tricks in his hand. It transpired that he had driven back as fast as he could when the box of tricks activated.

Breathlessly, I told Paul what had happened, and he called for an ambulance. 'Get inside, Mal. I'll see to Lyn.' He opened the boot of his car and produced a bullet-proof jacket which he put on as he ran towards Lyn.

'Lyn! Lyn!' I heard Paul calling, but I could not hear Lyn's response, if there was one.

It seemed an age before I heard the whirring of helicopter rotors and saw the outline of a helicopter coming across the sky towards the house. It had only been about ten minutes, but it seemed much longer. Although I did not believe in such things, I silently prayed to God that Lyn would be alright. I wouldn't be able to cope if something happened to her.

Suddenly it was as though all hell had broken loose. Ropes suddenly appeared below the helicopter, and figures began sliding down them. I saw another helicopter hovering on the other side of the woods; similar ropes were dangling, and figures were sliding down at speed.

There was the sound of shouting coming from the direction of the woods, and it was difficult to understand exactly what was happening and who these people were. No one came towards me, and I was therefore left to presume that they were not the ungodly.

Behind me, I heard the sound of a siren drawing closer, and within moments an ambulance came into view and drew to a halt beside me. The doors were flung open, and three figures disappeared towards the wood, clearly without thought for their own safety.

A shot rang out, and the ambulance personnel stopped in their tracks. Paul then appeared on the edge of the wood waving his arm, and the ambulance personnel began running again.

Only later, when we were sitting in Paul's lounge, the whole chain of events began to unfold.

There was a pre-planned operation, or so it turned out, triggered by Paul's bag of tricks. Unbeknownst to me, besides alerting Paul, the alarm sounded in the local police control room, and the operation was put into effect. This entailed the helicopters and ground personnel surrounding the woods. It seems that this was something Philip had anticipated might happen, and all of this action was catered for. There had been ground personnel already in place when we first went to Pen-y-coed hence the very swift response.

Lyn had been taken to the hospital, and it was found that she had lost a lot of blood, but transfusions took care of that. Although she was detained there, the hospital said that she would make a full recovery. I sighed in relief upon finding out she was out of danger. The mental scars would take so much more time to heal, though.

The last and single shot which rang out was the sniper being shot dead by the police after failing to lay down and surrender his firearm. He was taken away by the coroner's officer, and the cause of death was confirmed as a gunshot. The saddest part of this whole saga was that the so-called sniper had, in fact, been Lyn's own father. We couldn't believe it! It transpired, when they found a note left by him, he was determined to kill me but that by awful irony, the first bullet he had fired had hit his daughter and not me. The second, thankfully, had hit the tree and missed a human target.

When the police went to Alex Wright's home to relay the tragic news, they found the house locked up. One of the officers tracked around the outside of the premises, looking in as many windows as were accessible and saw a pair of legs poking out from behind a cabinet in the kitchen. A forced entry was made, and Lyn's mother, Susan Wright, was identified as the victim. The house was searched, and a letter was found from Alex Wright, also known as Dominic Allen, confessing all he had done since he married Susan. The letter went on to say that he did not want Susan to suffer the shame he had caused and that he was saving her this trauma by killing her. A twisted logic, if ever there was one. It was clear, too, that he intended to end his own life once he had killed me, and at least the police had saved him from carrying out that act. How I became the villain of the piece was unclear to me then, and even now, looking back on all that occurred, it is still as unclear.

Lyn was informed of her parents' deaths while she was still in hospital, and there is little doubt that her physical recovery was prolonged because of it. I personally doubt whether she will ever make a full recovery from the severe blow to her mental health. I vowed to make myself available whenever she felt she was ready to see me. After all, she was only left with me to turn to for support.

As far as I was concerned, I wanted no more to do with crime in any form and made it known that I was no longer acting as an insurance adjuster. My relationship with Philip Carterford was put on hold for a few weeks as he ploughed through the mass of paperwork that two murders, an attempted murder, and a police shooting would inevitably generate.

Six weeks later, I received a call from Lyn. She was back at her own home, still recuperating from her trauma. She said that she dearly wanted to see me, and I dropped everything to go to her support. Together over the coming months, we gradually put her together again. I took care of the sale of her parents' house for her, and I knew what I wanted to do to replace my insurance adjusting service, real estate sales. I supported her throughout the trauma of the coroner's inquests into her parents' deaths. They were held separately as they were in two coroners' areas, and Lyn sobbed her way through both. As far as her deceased husband was concerned, Lyn was called to the coroner's inquest in Wells, Somerset, only to give evidence of identification.

When the trauma of the inquests was over and her parents' funerals done with, there was only the burial of her husband to worry about. In reality, she didn't worry about it; she just did not attend. There were whispers about this, but Lyn ignored these and felt that her conscience was clear. She wanted to move on from the past. She would now perhaps be better placed to start rebuilding her life. The one regret I had was that I was not fully able to answer her original question: why? Between us, we had resolved the when, the where, the who, the how but only a speculative why. I knew that would not be good enough for Lyn, but I hoped she would accept it.

After all the trauma of the past few weeks, Lyn decided that she wanted to get away from everything for a while and focus on her recovery.

I received a telephone call from her asking me to see her as there was something that she wished to discuss. David or Robert, depending on who was referring to him, but her late husband, anyway, had left her very well off. She would have no money worries.

I arrived, and when I heard her call for me to come in, I went to her lounge. Bright, colourful catalogues surrounded her, or so I thought. I realised as I sat beside her that they were holiday brochures.

'Care to come on holiday with me, Mal?' she said quite cheerfully. 'Just the two of us.'

'Well, I didn't expect this sort of cheerfulness,' I said to her.

'I look at things this way. David was not a thief or a criminal, according to Philip Carterford, but he lied to me throughout our courtship and marriage. I do not like liars. My father was a coward and probably a murderer of my husband and definitely the murderer of my mother. Even if he had survived the police shooting, I would never have forgiven or spoken to him. Not under any circumstances. I have a massive amount of money which my solicitor tells me is mine and mine alone. I intend to have a complete break from everything and get the whole of the last few months out of my memory.'

'I am very glad to hear that,' I said. 'Where are you going?' I added pointing to the holiday brochures.

'Not I, we!' Lyn said almost triumphantly.

'What do you mean?'

'Like I said, just the two of us! What about a cruise?' she asked.

'I have never been on one,' I replied.

'Then check your passport because you're about to! We sail from Southampton in two weeks' time.'

'Where are we going?' I enquired.

'There and back to see how far it is!' she replied laughingly. Shades of my own mother, I thought. That is exactly what she would have said whenever I asked her where she was going.

I laughed out loud, shaking my head.

'No, Mal. Exactly that. There and back. We are booked onto a world cruise. Ninety-nine nights. That should be enough to clear my mind and help erase some of my memory, don't you think?'

'I could never afford that. It will cost thousands!' I exclaimed.

'Just under eleven each, actually. You don't have to be able to afford it. The fares have already been paid, and that is that.'

'I just do not know what to say,' I was genuinely lost for words.

'All you have you say is one word, and that word is yes.'

The happiness on Lyn's face was there plain as the nose on your face. Did I say no to her offer and cast aside a valuable olive branch? I couldn't do that. Not to my dearest and long-lasting friend. Yes, we had had our ups and downs in recent weeks, but, given the circumstances, that was only to be expected. And I did not take anything she said to me to heart.

'Oh! Come on, Mal, please, please say yes. Say you'll come,' Lyn was almost pleading.

'Alright then, thank you so, so much. I would absolutely love to come with you,' I told her.

She jumped up, came to me, and threw her arms around my neck. All thoughts of her recent troubles were temporarily cast aside. I could see she was happy, and if Lyn was happy, then I was happy too.

I met up with Philip the following weekend and imparted the news to him. It would mean a very long three months apart, but he understood and wished me happy holidays.

Epilogue

The cruise was absolutely wonderful; unforgettable would also describe it. It was everything that I had imagined that it would be and more. We had visited places that I had only heard or read about. From the beauty of Bermuda and the grandeur of the Panama Canal to the exotic-sounding Honolulu and Hawaii to the cultural differences of the countries of the Far East. The hundred- and one-mile transit along the busiest shipping lanes that comprise the Suez Canal was so beautiful. As we passed along it, I remember wondering whether or not the canal designer and builders could ever have imagined just how busy it would become and the size of the ships that would use it. I doubted it somehow. After all, 1869 was a very different time to today. I must have taken thousands of photographs and knew that I would happily spend time remembering the places Lyn and I had visited and the sights we had seen. The cruise proved to be a great opportunity for us to rekindle our friendship.

Lyn and I came home fully recovered from our various ordeals, ready to face the world again. There was not even a trace of regret in either of us as we watched the cruise ship dock at Southampton once more. It was a strange feeling; on the one hand we were glad to be home once more and on the other we knew that the adventure was over, but there was no trace of any regret.

We collected our luggage from a huge warehouse-like building, presumably just what it was in days gone by, a warehouse. As we stepped into the light, pushing our trollies of luggage, the first person I saw was Philip. It was an absolute joy to see him again; he had been the last person I expected to see if I was really honest. Granted, Lyn had said that she had arranged transport for us on our return to Southampton, but this! There was no doubt that I was overjoyed at seeing him again. I had not realised just how much I had missed him. That old and well-used adage that absence makes the heart grow fonder was a truth of monumental proportions for me at that moment. Our relationship had barely gotten off the ground before I had sailed away, but the foundations of it had been firm enough to survive the absence. To say that he was a sight for sore eyes was understating things in the extreme. His car was parked at the kerbside with the boot lid wide open. He stowed my luggage in the car without comment on the amount of it and was just able to close the boot.

I stood before him, and we linked arms to gaze into each other's eyes. We smiled widely at each other, and by mutual, unspoken agreement, we did not kiss. We stood there, just happy to be together once more. I was just glad to be able to see him again.

'What about Lyn?' I asked.

'She'll be making her own arrangements to get home.'

'Really!' I exclaimed.

'Yes. Lyn arranged all of this!' Philip said.

I returned to where Lyn was standing and threw my arms around her this time. 'Thank you for this,' I said, indicating Philip.

'You were there for me when anyone else would have walked away. I do not forget friendship like that. Now go!' Lyn replied.

I went, and Philip took me straight home and straight to bed. Yes, I was tired, but even more so after our lovemaking.

We lay side by side, hands intertwined, looking at the ceiling. I gradually dozed into a deep sleep and dreamed of a worldwide paradise.

The next morning when I eventually managed to get my eyes open, I saw a mug of coffee on my bedside table. Leaning against it was a note. It simply read, *'Will You Marry Me?'*

I sipped my coffee which was still fairly hot and scribbled the word *'Yes'* underneath.

I finished my coffee, pulled on a dressing gown, and padded my way downstairs to the kitchen. There stood Philip Carterford, detective chief inspector of police, smiling at me.

'This will wipe that smile off your face,' I said and handed him my reply.

He read it, but it didn't, and he kissed me passionately.